EXPORTING ENTERTAINMENT

Frontispiece: from 'Moving Picture World News Reel for February', *Moving Picture World* 31, no. 10 (10 March 1917), p. 1551.

KRISTIN THOMPSON

EXPORTING
ENTERTAINMENT

America in the World Film Market
1907-34

BFI Publishing

First published in 1985 by the British Film Institute
127 Charing Cross Road
London WC2H 0EA

British Library Cataloguing in Publication Data

Thompson, Kristin
    Exporting entertainment:
    America in the world film market 1907–34.
    1. Moving-pictures – United States – History
    I. Title
    791.43'0973   PN1993.5.U6

ISBN 0 85170 156 6

Cover: John Gibbs
Printed in Great Britain by The Whitefriars Press, Tonbridge

For Janet Staiger, whose work as student, collaborator and colleague on the Hollywood mode of production has greatly influenced my own studies.

Contents

Preface

'Louis XIV is said to have exclaimed, "L'état? – c'est moi!" The American film-makers can then say, "The motion picture business? We are it!"'

('Business', *Motography*, 19 Sept. 1914, p. 408)

Aside from the invention of the cinema itself there are probably two sets of events which, more than any others, have decisively shaped cinema history. One was the Hollywood cinema's rise to a strongly dominant position on world markets during World War I, the other the dissemination of television. The first has meant that for an astonishingly long period – from the mid-teens to the present, with no end in sight – a large number of films screened in most countries have been of one type: the classical Hollywood narrative film in continuity style. As a result, most other styles – whether on a national commercial level (for example, German Expressionism), on the level of the personal commercial (for example, Yasujiro Ozu) or on an experimental independent level (for example, Surrealism, New American Cinema, Michael Snow) – have generally been seen as *alternatives* to this style. The other key set of events, the use of television as a new means of distributing mass entertainment and information, has also had a tremendous effect on how films are seen in many areas of the world; we are still in the midst of the struggle of the cinema industry to adjust to a shrinking theatrical market in the face of expanding costs. (Even here, the effects of Hollywood's long hegemony on world markets carries over into television, with some American programmes receiving similarly wide distribution.)

The American takeover of world markets touches many basic subjects that film scholars are now exploring. Most national cinemas we might study consist not only of domestic tendencies, but also of the influences film-makers and audiences picked up from the presence of American films. Many foreign auteurs have acknowledged their debts, positive, negative or ambivalent, to Hollywood. The most familiar genres tended to originate there. Some foreign industries copied Hollywood's methods, hoping also to imitate its success.

In spite of all this, we know remarkably little about the American rise to hegemony, except that it happened during World War I and resulted from the decline of foreign industries. Most older survey histories (or newer histories based entirely on the standard works) say little more than this. Yet now we are at a stage in film studies where scholars are re-exploring the most basic questions of film history, altering older views or at least finding adequate evidence to confirm them; they are also trying not simply to document 'the facts', but to construct arguments to account for series of events. There is a need for monographs on many topics before we can proceed to rewrite the synoptic histories of the cinema on a sounder basis.

In this study, I shall present extensive documentation which has not previously been used in exploring the question of American distribution abroad. Government publications and contemporary trade papers provide a mass of data. Most of these data were, I think, as accurate as the sources could make them, since they were intended as aids to the industry itself in exporting; the general public would not be intended to see these publications and hence distortion for publicity purposes should not be a particular problem. I shall be drawing upon detailed customs statistics which recorded all footage leaving the USA by destination, as well as American consuls' reports from the individual countries; these help establish a sense of when individual countries began using American films extensively. Material in the Edison archives also reveals much about the role of the Edison–Pathé struggle in the formation of the Motion Picture Patents Company.

But a collection of facts does not add up to a straightforward story of the period. Rather, I shall try to show *how* the American takeover occurred by examining the data in the light of the film industry's practices. For example, I shall be arguing that the long-term American dominance came about not only because American firms were able to export more film during the war itself, but because they instituted new distribution procedures abroad; rather than selling primarily through agents in London, they opened their own offices in a variety of countries. In relation to this, I shall also suggest that the key markets in the wartime takeover were Australia and South America rather than Europe itself; by eroding the European film industry's base of support abroad, American competition permanently weakened the strong pre-war European producing countries. By providing both basic data and explanatory arguments about events in this period, I hope to lay the groundwork for further, more detailed studies of individual national cinemas, film-makers and so on.

Incidentally, the reason for this essential gap in our knowledge is, I believe, because film history has concentrated on the production of films (studios, financiers, film-makers) at the expense of exhibition and distribution. In recent years there has been a trend toward exhibition history. This work is vital because it begins to tell us who saw films and in what circumstances viewings took place. But distribution still has received little attention. It, too, I believe, can reveal a great deal: it bears on how film companies made their money and controlled their markets and can also suggest what types of film various parts of the world's population could see.

What do I mean by calling American cinema 'dominant' in any given country? I am primarily interested in the degree to which audiences were seeing American films as opposed to other films. (This study is a prelude to a larger book on the major European stylistic movements of the post-World War I era. There I will be dealing with some of the same topics that I cover here in Chapters 4 and 5, but presenting the European perspective.) As an historian of style, I am concerned with the norms of cinematic practice to which audiences (including film-makers) would have been accustomed. Ideally, we would want to know what percentage of screen time American films occupied in a given country and period. Most statistics, however, come from customs and censorship records, which simply show how much footage of any type was available in the market. For my purposes, then, the American film can be considered dominant in a market when it obtained a significantly larger share than its competitors – say, 40% of the footage available, with others supplying 20%, 15%, etc. In practice, the American share was often so large that the definition becomes automatic – achieving a 70–95% share is dominating a market by any standards. Wherever estimates on shares of screening time are available, however, I will give them.

I have not discussed American exports of raw stock, non-theatrical films or film equipment. These are important in an overall view of the USA's economic hold abroad and could well form the basis of another study. Because I have only a limited space and am primarily interested in the predominance of stylistic norms, I have concentrated on theatrical films. I have also eliminated Canada from this study. The American domination was as great there as anywhere, but Canada has always been different from other foreign markets; as one commentator put it in 1926, 'conditions in Canada are so like those in the United States and access is so easy that it is regarded by the industry as part of the domestic industry.'[1] I do not condone this view, of course, but much of what I will say about the American market will apply equally to Canada. This subject also deserves a study of its own and indeed, there is much relevant information in Peter Morris' *Embattled Shadows*.[2] Finally, I shall not be making any extensive effort to explain why American films appealed so greatly to foreign audiences, since this kind of social issue would mean focusing on the reception side of the subject rather than on the distribution side and involves many questions other than the ones I try to answer here. I do hope in my work in progress on European film styles in the 1920s to deal at least briefly with this issue.

Acknowledgments

A number of people and institutions contributed greatly to this study. I am grateful to the Bibliothèque Nationale, Gillian Hartnoll and the staff of the British Film Institute Library, the British Library, Jacques Ledoux and the staff of the Cinémathèque Royale de Belgique, Arthur R. Abel and the staff of the Edison National Historic Site, the Library of Congress, the Museum of Modern Art Library, the New York Public Library's Performing Arts Research Center, the Wisconsin State Historical Society Library, the University of Wisconsin-Madison Libraries, and the Wisconsin Center for Film and Theater Research.

Thanks are also due to Charles Musser, Janet and Peter Staiger, Geoffrey Nowell-Smith and Rosalind Delmar, Gabrielle Claes and Thomas Elsaesser for providing ideas and hospitality along the way. Special thanks to Douglas Gomery and Leslie Midkiff DeBauche for commenting on parts of the manuscript and to David Bordwell for his usual invaluable aid at every stage.

1 Regaining the American Market, 1907-13

From our modern vantage point, it may seem hard to believe that the
film industry of the United States has not always dominated world
markets. For decades other national cinemas have struggled to gain or
maintain a toehold in their own markets. We are inured to the notion
that the commercial American film rules over most of the world's
screens. In fact, the American industry did not gain its initial
domination until the mid-teens. The war had severely curtailed
production in the single biggest film-producing country – France – and
the resultant gap in supplies to film-consuming countries allowed
American exporters to step in.

In the years after World War I, the success of the American film
industry in maintaining its hold abroad was attributable primarily to
its huge domestic market. Few countries in the world had enough
theatres and a big enough film-going public to amortise the films they
produced. Yet during an American release, a film's expenses were paid
off and many films might begin earning profits quite apart from
revenues coming in from other countries. No other industry could hope
for similar returns on domestic exhibition; most, such as France,
Germany or Italy, depended on exports to help amortise films which
brought in only modest amounts at home.

Yet this large domestic market had existed from almost the
beginning of public exhibition by projector. By utilising the existing
circuits of vaudeville theatres for film exhibitions, American
manufacturers tapped an existing set of outlets and audiences. And
after 1905, the expansion of the nickelodeon movement created a
rapidly growing market.[1] Compared with this, film exhibition in other
major producing countries (France and Britain) used less systematic
and developed methods. Yet France managed to seize world markets
before the USA did and Italy was a strong competitor in the pre-war
years. How was it that the USA, with its large domestic market and its
several well-established production companies, took nearly two decades

1

to move into first place – and then only when a major war was crippling its rivals? Was the American industry on its way to dominating world markets in any case?

Perhaps the main reason why the Americans got a late start into world markets was precisely the size of the home audience. The demand for films within the USA, despite a few minor early slumps, expanded from the early years of the century well into the 20s. Demand went up particularly sharply as the nickelodeon boom began in 1906 and domestic producers had to organise their output to keep up. In addition, the litigation and harassment by the major patent-holding companies, the Edison Manufacturing Co. and American Mutoscope and Biograph (AM & B), kept the film production sector in a disorganised state until the Motion Picture Patents Company (MPPC) began operating in late 1908. This led to a more stable situation for the licensed manufacturers and we shall see that widespread expansion into foreign markets began after 1908.

Within the next few years, the licensed and independent producers were able nearly to saturate their domestic market and then to expand into markets abroad. (Export usually costs more and entails more capital investment; it is thus primarily desirable when local markets have ceased to offer additional profits.) In the meantime, foreign producing companies, especially the giant Pathé Frères, had already expanded into the international market and had invaded the USA. The great demand created by the nickelodeon boom could only be met by adding imports to the domestic release schedules. By the time the American companies came to the point of organising themselves into a coherent industry, they were faced with strong competition in their own market. The pre-war period thus involved two movements: one to reduce the foreign share of the US market, the other to establish agents and subsidiary offices abroad for the sale of American films.

THE STRUGGLE TAKES SHAPE – 1907

To some extent, the strength of a company's exports can be gauged by the type of sales methods used. Economist Frank A. Southard Jr. described the forms which American sales interests in Europe typically took during the 20s: the agent or representative, the branch house, the fully controlled subsidiary, the minority interest, the concession, the contract and the licensing agreement.[2] Of these, three forms are most relevant to film before the war. A company might simply have filled orders obtained by an agent, who took whatever profits he could obtain above the producer's price. Secondly, under a licensing agreement, a company might have allowed another company abroad to sell its products on a royalty basis. Thirdly, there was the fully controlled subsidiary, in which the parent company owned a second company incorporated in another country. As a company grows in strength, it tends to move from using an agent or licensing agreement to using a subsidiary company, since the latter involves a higher investment outlay. We can also designate such sales as indirect (agents or licensing) or direct. Direct sales, though more expensive to establish, can in the long run prove more profitable, given an adequate volume of sales, since none of the revenues are turned over to intermediaries.

Before 1907, most films imported to and exported from the USA were sold by agents. For example, during the summer of 1894, the Edison Manufacturing Co. made a New York firm of exporters, Maguire & Baucus, the exclusive agent for its Kinetoscopes and films for most foreign countries. In about March of 1897, Edison apparently became dissatisfied with the volume of business being done abroad and rescinded the exclusive contract, selling thereafter through Maguire & Baucus and various foreign jobbers. This continued to be the basis for export until December of 1903, when the National Phonograph Company Ltd, an Edison subsidiary in London, began direct sales of films in Europe.[3]

Other companies' films were also sold through agents or jobbers, but foreign sales were not large or systematic. William E. Gilmore, Edison's president, investigated the European business in 1904 and wrote of 'excessive competition'; he stated that the Kinetoscope business (projecting as well as cabinet models) was showing a loss as a result of this and of low film prices in Europe. He also sought a European company to undertake the licensed sales of Edison films but was unable to find one.[4]

The first American production company to open foreign subsidiaries specifically for the sale of films was Vitagraph. Its main foreign office was established in 1906 in Paris and a London branch opened that same year. By 1907, Vitagraph's business in Britain and on the Continent was heavy enough to make printing positives abroad desirable and a laboratory was planned in Paris; by March of 1908 it was nearing completion. By that time the Edison company had taken Vitagraph and others into the pre-Patents Company licensing arrangement, the Film Service Association (FSA). Among other things, the licence permitted production companies to manufacture their own cameras. Vitagraph's model was unique at the time, with two lenses and sets of magazines in the same body, making two negatives simultaneously.[5] The second went to the Paris laboratory, to minimise delays in releases abroad. From 1909 on, as other producers established their own direct representation in Europe, they took up a similar practice of shooting a second negative for European printing; typically, however, they were to use two cameras side by side.

By 1907, two American companies, Edison and Vitagraph, had direct representation abroad; others were selling through agents. Aside

3

from Vitagraph, American brands had made only relatively small inroads into foreign markets. Indeed, its early start in foreign markets seems to have given Vitagraph an advantage abroad that it did not lose until the war; as late as 1918, an American expert surveying the European situation, particularly in regard to France, could declare: 'With the noticeable exception of the Vitagraph films, which seem to lead American films in Europe almost everywhere, there is comparatively little sale of American-made films in France.'[6] Even those companies that had European agents employed them primarily to buy European films for import and secondarily to sell their own films abroad.

Before the nickelodeon boom became apparent in 1906, most European films were sold in the USA by indirect methods. Georges Méliès' Star Films of Paris, for example, sold through AM & B prior to 1902. In November of that year, apparently as an attempt to control the problem of illegal duping of Star Films, Georges' brother Gaston opened the Star Film Agency in New York, using a second negative to supply the American prints.[7]

In July 1904, Pathé Frères' agent, J. A. Berst, arrived in the USA to establish the first Pathé office in that country. Edison moved at once to prevent the expansion of foreign companies into the American market. It was currently engaged in a number of lawsuits against domestic companies, based upon its film and camera patents. In November 1904, Edison brought suits against Pathé and Méliès under the film patent. Together, Gaston Méliès and Berst hired a law firm; they continued to operate while awaiting the decision. The suit apparently did hamper Pathé to some extent; in Berst's 1913 testimony in the anti-trust suit against the MPPC, he claimed, 'It prevented us from expending money in our business, in the building of factories and studios, and we did not dare to import many films at a time, and kept only a small office, trying to dispose of positives as fast as they came in.'[8] The suit delayed Pathé's plans to build its own printing laboratory in the USA; yet by 1908, Pathé was to become the largest single source of films in the American market. It would be one of the Edison company's chief sources of irritation during the 1907–8 period leading up to the formation of the MPPC. A brief outline of Pathé's position in general will show how the French film industry achieved its early hegemony on world markets.

Before 1901, most of Pathé Frères' profits were based upon its phonograph business. But in 1901 it stepped up its film production and soaring profits resulted. According to Georges Sadoul, by the 1903–4 fiscal year, Pathé's profits had quadrupled over their pre-1901 levels. Some of this money was re-invested in new facilities: a factory at Joinville and a colouring plant. The French market, however, was relatively small and easily supplied. This was probably one reason why

Pathé moved abroad for extra profits sooner and more extensively than did American firms. Some of Pathé's profits also went into the establishment of a far-flung network of offices in major world cities. The company began by sending travelling salesmen into undeveloped areas, selling films and all the equipment necessary to conduct screenings in regions that had previously had none. Pathé's strategy at this early stage seems to have been well-suited to the development of markets for its films. By encouraging local entrepreneurs to open theatres the firm created a demand for Pathé films. Pathé would then open a film exchange in the area, saturate the market and keep other film companies out. Up until the early war years, American observers were to report from such markets as China or the Middle East that Pathé had a virtual monopoly. The Edison company, on the other hand, seems to have handled some markets in such a way as to discourage the establishment of local theatres. In 1907, for example, Edison had a projectionist touring the backwaters of Colombia, giving exhibitions to the native population. He reported making money at it, but it was hardly an effective way to build up a stable market for Edison films.[9]

Pathé moved rapidly to open offices around the world: London, New York, Moscow, Brussels, Berlin, St Petersburg (1904–5), Amsterdam, Barcelona, Milan (1906), Rostov-on-Don, Kiev, Budapest, Warsaw, Calcutta and Singapore (1907). The 1906–8 period was the largest for Pathé's profits and investments; Sadoul has described the complex structures of horizontal and vertical integration the company built up during these years. In 1909, Pathé opened a new Melbourne office, it moved into South Africa with direct sales in early 1912 and by 1914, a Pathé ad listed forty-one offices in major cities around the world, in addition to the home office in Paris.[10]

Looking back in 1940, Charles Pathé claimed that his company's 'cinematographic supremacy in the world rested solely on a head start'.[11] Beyond this, however, Pathé Frères took that head start in numerous small markets which could initially support only one film company. The profits from these markets in turn would allow Pathé to expand further and maintain its early momentum. And, as we shall see, when the American film industry began to expand seriously into world markets, Charles Pathé transferred an increasing amount of his company's activities to the USA, allowing Pathé Frères to continue supplying its world distribution network through the war.

As Pathé was opening its New York office in 1904, the officials at Edison were exercised not only about direct competition against their own films but also about the loss of revenues from their own American sales of Pathé films. On 1 July, Charles Pathé wrote to Edison, 'For more than a year we have watched the methods employed by your company, who copy all our films which they think interesting, in

5

defiance of our rights of ownership.' He went on to propose that, since Pathé's American agency was about to open, Edison and Pathé sign an agreement not to dupe each other's films. Frank L. Dyer, of Edison's legal department, wrote to Gilmore; Dyer viewed Pathé's letter with suspicion: 'It is possible that they are putting out a feeler to secure a licence to operate in this country under our patents.' Dyer suggested that the Edison company inform Pathé of their patents claims in motion picture film and declare an intention to sue should Pathé open an agency in New York:

> The suggestion might then be made that we would make an agreement with them under which they would give us the option of copyrighting and duplicating their films in this country, paying them a royalty per foot on all films which might be duplicated. . . . The advantages of the arrangement as suggested are that we would keep Pathé Frères out of this country and would be in a position to legitimately copy their films. . . . If the arrangement is not made, and Pathé Frères establish themselves in New York, we would encounter a more active competition on their part and would have to undergo the uncertainty of a suit against them on our patent.

There is no indication in the Edison records of a reply to Pathé's inquiry; at any rate, Pathé went ahead and opened its office without benefit of any arrangement with Edison. Edison responded with its suit against Pathé. The Edison company also penalised the Kleine Optical Co. for dealing in Pathé films (by eliminating discounts and other privileges) and instructed its London office in October to stop buying the Pathé product.[12]

The Méliès and Pathé suits never came to court and in early March of 1907 the two were still the only foreign branches listed in the *Moving Picture World*. But by this point Pathé had made serious inroads into the American market. It did this in part by underselling other companies; as of April its list price for a foot of positive film was 12 cents, significantly below Edison's 15 cents per foot (with prices at 9 and 12 cents, respectively, wholesale). This difference was seen at the time as a major factor in Pathé's success: 'It is a well-known fact that if Pathé Frères had not been the first to reduce the price of film much below the average ruling price of the English and American markets, they would not have attained their present position.' (Edison seems to have felt the effect of this underselling abroad as well. The manager of the Berlin office informed Gilmore in June that Pathé's wholesale prices in Germany were a mere 6 cents a foot; Gilmore responded by ordering the price of Edison films to drop as of 1 December to 8 cents a foot in the London and Berlin offices.)[13]

The events of 1907 focused the conflict for the American market

6

between domestic producers and foreign importers and ultimately influenced the formation of the MPPC. This seems to have been the point when the nickelodeon boom was far enough advanced to attract additional foreign brands into the country. Beginning in March 1907, a series of such firms entered the American market on a regular basis. Some had sold occasional films there before, but now obtained agents or opened direct-sales offices. A glance at Chronology 1 (in Appendix I) shows that this began when the Urban-Eclipse Co. signed as its American agent the Kleine Optical Co. of Chicago. Other British companies appointed Williams, Brown & Earle, a Philadelphia-based import firm, as their agent. The Italian firm, Cines, opened a subsidiary in New York in August. Other agencies and offices followed. In August 1907, the *Moving Picture World* estimated that within the next five to six months, 1,000 new nickelodeons would be opening:

> We know of three more film manufactories that will open for business shortly and they will take care of the demand as far as home production is concerned. In addition, there are several more Italian, French and English firms about to come into the field and these will be able to fill all orders.[14]

During 1907, two key court decisions led the Edison company to believe it finally had the power to use its patents as weapons against domestic and foreign competitors. The first of these was in a camera patent suit, and it gave Edison only limited power against foreign imports (since foreign films did not involve the use of cameras in the USA). I will discuss the impact of this decision before going on to examine the second, more crucial decision – this time in a film patent case. In March, the decision in the AM & B's suit against the Edison company came down. It upheld the Biograph camera as not infringing Edison's patents, but in doing so, the decision seemed to affirm that Edison's patents gave that company control over all sprocket-driven cameras in use in the United States. (The Biograph camera used rollers rather than sprockets to move the filmstrip.) By implication, the Edison officials assumed, all perforated film would be controlled by the company's parallel patent – the one under which Edison had suits pending against Pathé, Méliès, and various domestic producers. Edison commenced a brief struggle with Pathé which would end with the formation of the MPPC.

In early 1907, Pathé was planning to build its laboratory in New Jersey in order to make its positive prints there. Apparently Pathé had interpreted the March court decision to mean that perforated film was not protected under an Edison patent; this was the view expressed in the French company's letters of that period. A printing plant would have ended Edison's hopes of gaining the agency for Pathé films, thereby controlling Pathé's growth in the USA. Therefore, during the spring of 1907 the Edison company entered into negotiations to obtain a distribution licence for Pathé's films in America.

Immediately upon the handing down of the AM & B vs. Edison decision in March, Gilmore cabled to G. Croydon Marks, a London consulting engineer and patents expert who was to handle the negotiations with Pathé. 'See Pathé Paris,' he instructed Marks. 'Do not want to drive them from American field. Willing make arrangements handle their product here exclusively giving full representation same as our own product.' Marks spoke to Pathé officials between 19 and 28 March and found them amenable to the plan. Pathé, however, took the position that the recent patent decision referred only to cameras, not film. Pathé's representatives' assumption at this point was that if Edison were to take its films for the USA, it would in turn gain an exclusive licence to sell Edison films in France. They also showed Marks the plans for their American printing plant.[15]

Marks asked for the Edison company's terms. After consulting with Thomas Edison in early April, Gilmore cabled the terms to Marks: Edison to pay Pathé a fixed rate per foot for negatives, plus another rate on positives sold; the prices to be maintained at present levels (that is, Edison, 15 cents per foot, Pathé, 12); a refusal to license Pathé to sell Edison films in Europe. Gilmore also mentioned the film patent and hinted that if Pathé tried to do its own printing in the USA, Edison would pursue its pending 1904 lawsuit against Pathé. As a result of the camera decision, he said:

We feel that we are in a position to force our competitors to come to an understanding with us so far as the manufacture and sale of films is concerned in the United States; but, as I have already stated, it is not our intention to crowd them out of doing business in this country; on the contrary, we want them to continue to do business, but we feel that we should have some recognition, as naturally this litigation has cost us a great deal of money (upwards of $40,000), but on the other hand we do not feel that we want to take the stand that no others can do business under any circumstances.

This remarkable statement – assuming as it does that Edison deserves to be compensated by its competitors for the costs of its litigation against them – suggests that Edison was by this point questioning the wisdom of its constant lawsuits. Clearly, obtaining an agency or licensing agreement for other companies' films would bring in more money than taking those companies to court; Gilmore is perhaps suggesting here that Edison would drop its suit against Pathé in exchange for its agency. As he says in this same letter, 'We are looking at this matter, however, from a purely commercial standpoint, and would therefore prefer to make an equitable arrangement with Pathé which would be satisfactory to all concerned.' Finally, Gilmore brings up the matter of the planned Pathé laboratory in New Jersey for the first time in his correspondence with Marks and instructs him to tell the Pathé officials about the wonderful facilities of the new Edison studio in New York.[16]

Apparently Pathé found Edison's terms attractive, for Marks reported on 13 April that he had obtained a friendly response. Pathé seems to have been amenable to abandoning its planned laboratory, which its representatives said would cost about $25,000 (about $256,250 by 1982 prices). Pathé still took the position that Edison's film patent would not hold up and it set forth its own terms: Edison to pay Pathé $10 (just over $100, 1982 prices) per metre of negative, plus a sliding scale on positive footage sold; Edison to take the entire Pathé output; the licence to be for the USA only, not Canada. At this point Pathé still hoped to obtain a licence for Edison films in France.[17]

Sometime between the receipt of Marks' letter in late April and mid-May, Gilmore conferred with Edison and they seem to have decided against the Pathé deal. On 21 May, Marks sent Edison's final offer to Pathé. Far from being a compromise between the two companies' sets of terms, the Edison offer promised less than had its own earlier terms: Edison to pay only a fixed royalty per foot of positive sold, with Pathé supplying the negative free of charge; Edison to have a choice of which Pathé films to handle. No mention was made of selling Edison films to Pathé. The next day Pathé sent a letter to Edison's London office, chiding Edison for reneging on negotiations which Edison had itself begun and for stretching the affair out: 'We cannot withhold from you that the refusal you have intimated to us today might have been made a month and a half earlier, which would have prevented our company losing through it some hundred thousands of francs.' The reference here is presumably to the delay in building Pathé's New Jersey laboratory. By mid-June, Pathé Frères had incorporated in Jersey City; it began building its laboratory in Brookbound, New Jersey.[18]

The full reasons why the Edison company backed out of the negotiations with Pathé are unclear. Since Gilmore's crucial conversation with Edison around the first half of May took place in person, no written record survives. Two 28 May letters from Gilmore in London, to Edison and to William Pelzer (of Edison's New York office) describe certain Pathé films as too *risqué* for the American market. Hence Pathé's demand that Edison take its entire output, at $10 per metre of negative (over $300 a reel – over $3,000 in 1982 terms) may have seemed unreasonable. But there may have been other factors. Gilmore concludes his letter to Pelzer: 'As Mr. Edison has well said these outside entanglements do not prove to be of value, and I am firmly convinced that he is right in this conclusion.'[19] Perhaps the

Edison officials decided the Pathé proposals would cost more than a possible lawsuit; perhaps they hoped to compete successfully with Pathé in the American market.

Whatever Edison's reasons for abandoning the negotiations, Pathé's distribution push during the summer and early autumn of 1907 established it more firmly in the American market. By October Pathé was able to send a new contract to all the exhibitors and renters using its films, setting forth restrictions on reselling, duping and bicycling prints (that is, transporting a single print around a number of theatres, thus getting several shows for the price of a single rental); there was also apparently a sort of block-booking clause, in that customers were forced to take all of Pathé's output or risk getting none. It was a sign of Pathé's growing power. But at just this same time, Edison finally obtained a decision in one of its suits based on its film patent; on 24 October 1907, a Chicago court declared that Selig Polyscope had violated that patent. According to Berst's later testimony, he was influenced by that decision to negotiate with Edison for a licence; those negotiations began in December. Within that month, Berst received assurances that his firm would get a licence and Pathé's Brookbound plant began printing positives. The actual licensing agreement between Edison and Pathé was not executed until May 1908, but this delay was due primarily to the necessity for translating all documents into French and corresponding with the parent firm. Berst testified in 1913 as to why he gave in to Edison:

> My reason was to be protected under the patent, and not to be endangered by that suit, which was pending, and about which we had consulted our attorneys, Kerr, Page & Cooper, many times, and who could not give us any assurances that we could manufacture or conduct our business satisfactorily in this country.[20]

By the end of 1907, as a result of the AM & B and Selig decisions, Pathé Frères had found itself in the same situation as most other domestic and foreign firms. The formation of licensing groups would dominate events in the film industry during 1908 and, incidentally, lead to the diminution of imports into the USA.

FOREIGN FIRMS AND THE 1908 LICENSING ARRANGEMENTS

Early in 1908, Edison and the AM & B set up rival licensing groups. These groups continued to operate separately for much of the rest of that year. Yet almost immediately Edison put procedures in motion that would create the Motion Picture Patents Co. Edison's broad policy in licensing other film producers was to limit the number of foreign brands allowed to circulate. The AM & B licensed those companies which Edison had refused – foreign companies or importers. When the AM & B and Edison finally agreed upon terms to form a single licensing company, most of these foreign brands were to find themselves excluded from the new group.

In December (shortly after the October patent decision against Selig) Frank L. Dyer addressed a congress of renters in Chicago, apparently convincing them that Edison had the right to control the manufacture and exhibition of films. Their agreement and that of the Chicago-based producers left the way open for the formation of the Film Service Association (FSA), a licensing arrangement similar to that of the later MPPC. During early 1908, Edison signed with a group of licensees: Essanay, Kalem, Lubin, Georges Méliès, Pathé Frères, Selig, Vitagraph and various renters. According to Sadoul, 125 renters agreed to pay the Edison company $5,000 ($51,250 in 1982 terms) a year for their licences. This money, coming on top of Edison's film sales, pushed its gross revenues past those of Pathé, even though Pathé continued to release more footage.[21]

During February, the AM & B responded by forming the Biograph Association of Licensees. It did so on the basis of the Latham Loop patent, which Jeremiah P. Kennedy, the company's president, bought from Ansco on 5 February. The AM & B charged its licensees a fee of 0.5 cents per foot, all of which was to go to a legal fund to challenge the FSA. Except for the AM & B itself, all members of the Association were importers or foreign companies: Kleine Optical (agent for Gaumont, Urban-Eclipse, Lux, Raleigh & Roberts, Ambrosio, Rossi, Aquila, Théophile Pathé, and Warwick); Cines; Williams, Brown & Earle (agents for Hepworth, R. W. Paul, and Cricks & Sharp); Graphic Cinematograph Co.; and Williamson & Co.[22]

The Edison camp's opposition to the uncontrolled importation of films was apparent from the start. In an interview in late February, the Biograph Association vice-president spoke of the Edison combine: 'To make this effective they have taken in the Pathé Company, the largest foreign manufacturer of films, and the Méliès Company, which is not so important, the idea being to give them a monopoly of the importing business, which is very large.' In general, people whose companies had been excluded from the FSA blamed Pathé for the group's lack of foreign members. A representative of the British firm, Walturdaw, which had suddenly lost its place in the American market 'considered Pathé mainly instrumental in the resolve to shut out the other foreign manufacturers.' George Kleine, shortly after Edison brought suit against Kleine Optical in March, complained that the FSA was trying to give the public an impression that it handled only domestic films and the Biograph group only imports. He claimed that in fact a considerable portion of the FSA's releases were European:

But it is certainly entertaining to observe the French rooster [Pathé's logo] strutting behind the American flag pretending to crow 'Yankee Doodle', while the listening ear hears the 'Marseillaise'; and if he could crow in words, he would probably dwell on the line: '*L'étendard sanglant est levé.*'[23]

This rhetoric was perhaps not entirely groundless. The FSA members did justify their exclusion of foreign films by belittling them. William ('Pop') Rock, of Vitagraph, declared in March that the FSA was helping the industry when it 'shut out the importation of foreign stuff that was not suitable or good enough for the American market'. Those companies which failed to join the FSA, he declared, would have to depend upon 'a lot of unheard-of small foreign manufacturers whose productions the American public will not stand for'.[24]

As of 2 March 1908, the FSA members ceased using foreign films except those of Pathé and Méliès. Biograph licences may have aided some foreign companies to stay in the American market, but they could not assure them any substantial outlet for their films. A representative of Cines complained in April that the demand for its films had shrunk by at least 75% since 2 March.[25] Some idea of the relative strength of various companies during mid-1908 is hinted at by an interesting document in the Edison archives. For the period 1 to 30 June Edison's legal department sent a man to visit film theatres in New York City and various New Jersey towns; the result was a chart of how many films of each brand, licensed and unlicensed, had been shown in those theatres. The survey covered thirty-nine houses in New Jersey and sixty-seven in New York, with a total of 515 films seen in one month. Of these, the brands shown were (giving the number of films and the percentage of the total):

FSA: Pathé (177/34.2%); Edison (45/8.7%); Vitagraph (82/15.9%); Kalem (32/6.2%); Selig (26/5%); Lubin (40/7.7%); Essanay (42/8.1%); and Méliès (14/2.7%).

Biograph Association of Licensees: Gaumont (11/2.1%); AM & B (15/2.9%); Nordisk (8/1.5%); Cines (13/2.5%); and Urban-Eclipse (10/1.9%).[26]

These figures constitute a small, possibly unrepresentative, sampling. Yet, taken very generally, they suggest the success of the FSA in cutting down the market for the Biograph Association's films. Of the total films shown, 45% are foreign, 55% domestic. Pathé's share is over one-third of the total and about 76% of the foreign films.

The rival factions did not share the market peacefully. Following the period of licensing, the struggle heated up once more. The AM & B brought suit against Edison in late February and shortly thereafter Edison took Kleine Optical to court. At the same time, the Biograph side gained another major member by licensing the Great Northern Company (the Danish firm Nordisk's American subsidiary, referred to by its Danish name in the report above), when it opened its New York office in March. But Biograph nearly lost three other signatories that same month when Cines, Gaumont and Urban-Eclipse attempted unsuccessfully to jump ship by joining the FSA.[27]

These events made it clear that the two licensing organisations, the FSA and the Biograph Association of Licensees, had not solved the problem of excessive competition among film producers. Using patent litigation and other extreme methods, the major film companies were spending their resources in trying to put each other out of business. Yet that approach to competition in the marketplace was already outdated by 1908. The formulation of the MPPC, which tried to establish an oligopoly in film production, was more in keeping with the trends of American business of the period.

Edison, the AM & B and their licensees formed the MPPC in 1908, in the wake of the great merger movement of the decade 1895–1904. During this era, business was becoming Big Business, encouraged by a number of factors. The Sherman Anti-trust Act was passed in 1890, in an attempt to limit the growth of huge companies, trusts and other combinations which might be in restraint of trade. (This was the law under which the MPPC and its companion distribution firm, the General Film Co., were finally dissolved in the mid-teens.) During the 1890s, however, courts interpreted the vaguely worded Sherman Act very broadly. Cartels as such were held to be illegal; that is, collusion among separate companies within an industry to do such things as fixing prices was not permitted. But the Act was not used to discourage various forms of combination in which individual companies joined together in other fashions, such as by merging or forming holding companies. For example, the Edison General Electric Co. merged with one of its rivals, the Thomson-Houston Electric Co. in 1892 to form General Electric. In addition, certain state laws permitted forms of combination locally; New Jersey, where the MPPC incorporated, had such laws. The loose interpretations of the Sherman Act, in combination with other factors, actually encouraged the merging of smaller companies into larger ones during the first years of the Act's existence. The biggest wave of mergers occurred from 1895 to 1904, but the practice had by no means stopped by 1908. By 1910, 'Many of the nation's most influential big businesses had been created either through vertical or horizontal growth, or through a mixture of the two.' Indeed, the basic structure of the twentieth-century American economy was in place by this point.[28]

This move toward combination and bigness changed methods of

13

competition. Before the merger movement, a larger number of firms within a single industry might compete by extreme price-cutting until the weakest firms dropped out of the market. But with larger companies sharing a field, prices were more likely to be agreed upon to some extent. Products could be differentiated by other means, such as brand names and advertising. The MPPC did in fact establish a set schedule of prices for its licensees' films; similarly, it is perhaps not insignificant that the star system as a means of product differentiation and a basis for advertising emerged in the years after the MPPC's formation. One economic historian has summed up the business pattern during this century's first decade:

> Because the anti-trust laws threatened, and because it was much easier and more reliable, big firms seldom tried any more to drive competitors out to secure most or all of the market. Instead, producers settled for a fairly steady share of the market, avoiding price competition, and secured the benefits of an economic world much more stable than the one which had produced big business.[29]

The two early licensing groups and the MPPC itself were logical attempts, given the business practices of the day, to bring stability into the film industry and to give control of the film market to a relatively small number of producers. But in order to make an oligopoly work, the companies that comprise it must have the ability to discourage the entry of new producers into the market. In some industries this is easier than in others. In this period, mergers and oligopolies tended to work best in industries involving highly advanced technology which could create economies of scale. That is, if an industry depends to a great extent on expensive and complex equipment, the cost per item of output will tend to fall as the number of the same item produced increases. New firms will find it difficult to enter the market, since a large initial investment is needed to achieve the same economies of scale and compete with existing firms' prices.[30] In film-making, this was to become a major factor in sustaining the oligopoly structure that emerged during the late teens and 20s in Hollywood. Since a number of companies (Famous Players-Lasky, Loew's, Fox, First National and so on) already had large studios, expensive equipment, and highly salaried stars, it became extremely hard for new firms to enter the field and gain a significant share of the market; such costly equipment and staff were practical only for productions of relatively large numbers of films. But in the years that followed the MPPC's formation, the expenses involved in film-making were not great enough to discourage new firms from forming and the market was still expanding fast enough to accommodate new brands of films. To sustain a successful oligopoly among its licensees, the Patents Co. needed another means to

14

discourage entry. Its means were the various patents owned by its members, which were pooled on the formation of the MPPC.*

The Patents Co. might have succeeded in controlling a significant share of the market if its barrier to the entry of other companies into the American market had been more effective. But there were several problems. First, there were alternative cameras that did not use devices covered by the MPPC's patents (and independent companies often used infringing cameras in spite of the risk of litigation, sometimes disguising them as other, non-infringing brands). Other film companies could operate or import into the USA with few restrictions, as the rise of the independent movement beginning in 1909 demonstrates. Secondly, the basic patent – the Latham Loop, on which the MPPC depended – was struck down by a court decision in 1912, allowing other companies to enter the field at will.

The MPPC also attempted to increase its hold on the American film market by creating the General Film Co. in 1910. General Film went beyond the oligopoly structure that existed in the production wing of the industry; it was an attempt to monopolise completely the distribution area by buying up all the major exchanges in the country. This concentration of distribution would also provide the MPPC with economies of scale. But the era of hands-off treatment of big business was undergoing considerable change. Theodore Roosevelt's administration had instituted a harder line on trust-style activities in business. In 1903, Congress had created the Department of Commerce and Labor to investigate business practice and prosecutions began to go forward during Roosevelt's term, increasing in William Howard Taft's administration and continuing up until the USA's entry into World War I in 1917. In particular, two crucially timed decisions in 1911, breaking up the Standard Oil Co. and the American Tobacco Co., set guidelines for future anti-trust prosecutions. Beginning in 1912, the government brought the suit which would end the MPPC and the General Film Co.; the decision was handed down in October 1915, with the Opinion specifically citing the Standard Oil case as a precedent.[31]

During its existence, however, the Patents Co. had many long-reaching effects, including a continuation of the FSA's attempts to control imports. As we shall see, these attempts were somewhat successful.

* One tactic we might expect the oligopolistic MPPC to employ would be to restrict supply in order to raise the price, and hence the profit, per unit. Yet there is little indication that the Patents Co. tried this. Some of the companies in fact increased the number of reels released per week over the next few years; similarly, the prices fixed upon the formation of the General Film Co. in 1910 held steady. Perhaps the expanding market and the frequent entry of new, unlicensed firms made it impossible for the MPPC to manipulate supply to its advantage.

15

Officials in the Edison Co. may have envisaged the creation of a licensing agreement along the lines of the MPPC as early as 1 February 1908. The Edison archives contain a hand-written outline headed 'Proposed Scheme', carrying that date. Among its provisions were a few that would affect imports. The first suggests that Biograph be admitted as a licensee under the Edison patents. (This would change, of course, with the acquisition a few days later by the AM & B of the Latham patent; that company would then only consent to equal status as a co-licenser.) The next section states:

Kleine to be reorganized as Licensee limiting importation to 5,000 feet of new subjects per week for entire list of foreign mfg. [sic] as advertised, including Gaumont. In case any foreign manfg. drops out, the amount of film imported to be correspondingly reduced in proportion to his importance as shown by Kleine's output since Feb 1/08.

Next, the outline says that others among the Biograph licensees would be admitted on the same basis as Kleine, but with imports limited to 2,000 feet per week; these companies would be Williams, Brown & Earle; Cines and Great Northern.[32]

At this very early stage, it would seem that Edison had no objection to licensing virtually all the companies importing films into the USA under the AM & B licences (since most of these were represented by either Kleine or Williams, Brown & Earle). But over the next few months, the plans for the licensing company changed, eliminating most of the imported brands. Possibly Pathé insisted on this move; it was still expanding quickly. It opened a Chicago branch in early 1908 and Charles Pathé spent the summer in America planning the creation of an exchange system outside the FSA. Around the beginning of September, Edison talked him out of this plan.[33] Possibly Edison had to offer concessions regarding other foreign companies to keep Pathé within the fold. And possibly the AM & B officials, once they had a position alongside Edison heading the MPPC, would no longer feel any obligation to support the foreign importers which had made up the bulk of their Association. At any rate, the AM & B representatives met from May to June 1908 and the resulting plan eliminated most foreign companies.

On 29 July, the AM & B, Edison and Armat (a patent-holder associated with the AM & B) signed an agreement which gave them and companies connected with them protection from litigation. This presumably ended Edison's suit against Kleine (as a Biograph licensee), as well as the AM & B's against Edison. At about this time, the plan for the MPPC was sent out to the licensees which were to be admitted and the company was incorporated on 9 September 1908. It was largely owned by the AM & B and Edison companies and was empowered to license film producers on the basis of patents pooled by the two stockholding firms. The MPPC's provisions restricted imports. Pathé had a licence and could import and make films without limitations. Only one importer, George Kleine, had a licence and the firm could bring in only 3,000 feet of film per week (that is, negative film, the equivalent of three one-reel films). It could deal in two brands: Gaumont and Urban-Eclipse. Before the agreement, Kleine had represented nine or ten foreign firms and averaged more than 3,000 feet per week.[34] (Possibly one reason the MPPC planners wanted to include Gaumont was because it manufactured a non-infringing camera, which it could presumably have sold to independent firms if left outside the licensing arrangement.)

Typically, historians of this period list Méliès among the foreign firms in the Patents Co. when it went into operation by signing the licences for the various members on 18 December. Pathé and George Kleine were, however, the only foreign company and importer to receive licences on 18 December. Accounts of the period usually claim either that Méliès received its licence at the same time or refer vaguely to a licensing arrangement concluded some months later. But studies of the MPPC and of Méliès alike fail to explain the reasons for and effects of the delay. The actual events had relatively little impact on the foreign film's place on American markets, since Méliès was contributing only a small amount of film weekly. These events did, however, affect Méliès' Star Films considerably and are indicative of how important the American market was to foreign companies.

The Méliès company was effectively barred from the MPPC for about nine months through no direct fault of either Georges or Gaston. On 31 January 1908, the brothers received an FSA licence from Edison. On 18 June, Gaston obtained permission to form the George Melies Corp. in Illinois; the original licence was then transferred to this corporation in September. When the formation of the Patents Co. occurred on 18 December, its officials planned to include the Melies Corp., but Chicago-based licensees objected on the grounds that some Melies stock had been sold to an unlicensed exchange operator in Illinois by the Melies Corp.'s vice-president. This nullified the September agreement with Edison. The MPPC revoked the old Melies licence and withheld the new one. There followed a period of conflict, with the Melies Corp. instituting a lawsuit against both the MPPC and the Méliès brothers on 21 May 1909 to get its promised licence. The case dragged on for some time, with the decision going against the Melies Corp. In the meantime, Gaston was granted a new licence, effective 16 September 1909, in his own name rather than in that of the Chicago corporation. This entitled him to make films and release them in alternation with Star Films made by Georges in Paris.[35]

The chronology of these events would seem to explain why Star Films' Paris studio closed down during the approximate period January to September 1909. Paul Hammond's filmography for Méliès lists no films released by either Georges or Gaston in 1909 until October. Recent accounts of Méliès' career note this gap but attribute it primarily to a sudden decline in the popularity of the trick genre in the USA, flooded with Star Films' prodigious output of 1908 (estimated at 67 films, against 9 in 1909).[36] Yet there is no apparent reason why the popularity of Méliès' films should decline so precipitously to nothing in late 1908. On the other hand, it seems significant that the studios closed just after the denial of the licence in December and that both Gaston and Georges brought out their next films in October 1909, the month after the new licence went into effect. This suggests that Méliès had by this time become highly dependent on the American market.

Aside from this temporary problem, the foreign companies within the MPPC continued to operate successfully for the next few years. Pathé remained the most important producer in the American field. In the spring of 1909, the *Bioscope*'s American correspondent declared:

> Both Trust and Independent manufacturers have Pathé-fright. In other words, the quality of the Pathé picture is far and away ahead of that of its competition.
>
> This brings about three results. The public like Pathé pictures; the older manufacturers are trying to compete against them; the newer ones look upon them as the standard, which they hope some one day to reach. From this state of affairs there has arisen a condition of mind which one can only call Pathé-mentia.[37]

By May of 1909, Pathé's plan to set up a studio for production in the USA was public knowledge. This plan may have resulted from an apprehension that the MPPC would succeed in its lobbying efforts to raise the tariff, being debated in Congress that summer. It may also have come about because Pathé wished to tailor its production to the lucrative American market by introducing local colour. This, at any rate, was its stated reason for opening studios at that time in New Jersey, as well as in Germany and Italy. (Pathé's policy was to produce in the various countries where it had offices and by this time many of the films it distributed were made outside France.) Whatever its reason, Pathé's American studio opened in April of 1910; its first release – like many of its American productions, a Western – was *The Girl From Arizona* on 16 May. As of 1911, Pathé's share of the MPPC's profits was the highest, followed by Vitagraph, Edison, Selig, American Biograph, Essanay, Lubin, Kalem, George Kleine, and Méliès. (In 1910, Pathé's share had been second, behind American Biograph;

presumably its American production helped boost it into first place.)[38] As we shall see, however, Pathé extensively reorganised its American strategies just before the war began and that move would profoundly affect its place in the American film industry.

The formation of the MPPC was the main factor in the struggle for the American domestic market before World War I. Without its restrictions, foreign companies would presumably have continued to enter that market after 1907 as the demand for films increased. Such companies would have shared the market with growing numbers of domestic firms, coming into existence for the same reason. But with the MPPC excluding all but a few foreign firms, the others faced an uphill struggle to regain their American distribution.

THE INDEPENDENT MOVEMENT'S FOREIGN ALLIES

Most of the European firms excluded from the Patents Co. retired at least temporarily from the American market. Aside from Méliès, no importing company was to receive a licence after the initial formation of the MPPC (although George Kleine did make one change in the companies it represented). As Chronology 1 (in Appendix I) shows, no new agents or subsidiaries came into being until late 1909. Apparently only the Great Northern Co. weathered the storm. In May, the *Moving Picture World* was offering congratulations: 'The Great Northern Film Company occupies the unique position of being the one great importing film house, which through recent changes, combinations and affiliations, has absolutely preserved its independence.'[39]

Given the MPPC's refusal to license more than a few foreign film brands, most European producers chose to side with the various independent groups in the USA. Upon the initial formation of the FSA and Biograph Association of Licensees, representatives of all the significant European producers had met in Paris, on 9 March 1908. Attending were officials for Gaumont; Urban-Eclipse; R. W. Paul; Warwick; Lux; Rossi; Aquila; Théophile Pathé; Cricks & Martin; the Graphic Co.; Walturdaw; Raleigh & Roberts; Ambrosio; Nordisk; Cines; Berlin Kinematograf; Hepworth; Clarendon; Williams, Brown & Earle; and Kleine Optical. The meeting considered the FSA's effect on European imports. A unanimous vote approved the AM & B's efforts to keep the American market open; those attending subscribed $15,400 ($163,702, in 1982 dollars) to the cause, empowering an international committee to act in the group's interests and to provide information at future meetings. This meeting had little effect; Sadoul has chronicled in some detail how additional meetings later that year and in early 1909 ended primarily by providing a forum for Eastman and Pathé to battle for the European raw-stock market.

Yet, however ineffectual it may have proved, the March 1908

meeting in Paris was at least symptomatic. By this point, according to Sadoul, over three-quarters of the big European producers' profits were coming from the American market and this provided the impetus for the Europeans to struggle for their place there.⁴⁰ The meeting also ended with the firms agreeing to side with the independent group against the trust rather than trying some more direct strategy – say, forming their own alternative releasing group in the USA. This was to be their approach for a few years, until it became apparent that American independents also had little interest in promoting foreign films.

The first independent group to challenge the MPPC formed during January and February of 1909. This was the International Projecting and Producing Co. (IPPC), under the presidency of J. J. Murdock, a prominent member of the Western Vaudeville Managers' Association. The new firm planned to begin by importing European films; in about three months, using an allegedly non-infringing camera and projector invented by vice-president D. W. McKinney, the IPPC would commence production in the USA. A British film dealer, Will G. Barker, was in America at this point and threw in his lot with the IPPC; he signed over the agencies of a number of British companies to the Murdock firm: Wrench; Hepworth; Clarendon; Cricks & Martin; R. W. Paul; Williamson; and Walturdaw & Warwick. Barker outlined his purpose upon his return to Britain: 'I took up the cudgels with the Independents to fight for their rights', and to keep the American market open to American films. The orders he brought with him were the most lucrative to be seen in two years, he declared.⁴¹

The IPPC began releasing on 22 March 1909; from the beginning it was apparent that the firm could not live up to its goals. Although it claimed to be the exclusive agent for anywhere from eighteen to thirty-two European companies, its actual releases were small. The *Bioscope*'s American correspondent wrote in April: 'There are complaints that films from your side of the Atlantic are not delivered in sufficiently large quantities to meet the demand.' A few weeks later he betrayed increasing irritation: 'You people, however, in England seem invincibly stupid in catering for this market. You don't, or won't make the pictures, although you can; and, if you do, you won't take the ordinary business means for selling them, describing them, and advertising them.'⁴² The IPPC never did begin production on its own and it was soon to decline in the face of competition from other independent organisations.

During its brief life of about one year, the IPPC did manage to keep some place on American markets for European films. But probably more significant in the long run for maintaining importation was Murdock's triumph over the MPPC in the matter of the tariff. In the spring and summer of 1909, Congress was debating the Payne–Aldrich

Tariff, the first major change in American import duties since the 1897 Dingley Tariff. Tariffs were at this point the main source of revenue for the federal government (the income tax being still a thing of the future) and the Dingley Tariff had instituted a twelve-year period of extremely high *ad valorem* rates on dutiable goods (averaging about 49% as of 1900).[43] The rate on films coming into the USA was 25% *ad valorem* (typically about 1.5 cents per foot for positives), plus 65 cents per pound celluloid tax (with one pound equal to about 200 feet).

The MPPC set out to have this tariff raised in the 1909 bill. Given that the film duty was below the average, the goal was not an unlikely one. In April, the licensed producers submitted an affidavit stating that the American industry needed to be protected by a high tariff, since the cost per metre of negative produced in the USA was higher than in Europe. J. J. Murdock lobbied against the MPPC position; his success was attributed at the time to his social and financial standing, deriving more from his vaudeville connections than from his work in film. The tariff passed on 5 August 1909, retaining the same *ad valorem* rate and eliminating the celluloid tax, thereby reducing the overall duty. Table I summarises the import duties for the silent period, giving an estimate of the average tax on a reel of film.[44]

TABLE I

Film tariffs in the silent era

Tariff and date	Duty rate	Average cost of importing 1000 feet	Average cost in 1982 dollars
		(prices as of date of tariff)	
Dingley, 1897	25% *ad valorem* and 65 cents per pound of celluloid	$18.00 (pos)	$206.71
Payne-Aldrich, August 1909	Neg: 25% *ad valorem* Pos: 1.5 cents per foot	$15.00 (pos)	$159.50
Underwood-Simmons, October 1913	Neg: 3 cents per foot Pos: 1 cent per foot	$30.00 (neg) $10.00 (pos)	$290.10 $96.70
McCumber-Fordney, September 1922	Neg: 3 cents per foot Pos: 1 cent per foot	$30.00 (neg) $10.00 (pos)	$171.57 $57.20

The relatively low tariff on film adopted in 1909 (the average on all dutiable goods was 42%) made it possible for imports to continue. Indeed, the duties fell again in 1913; at that point the Underwood–Simmons Tariff generally relaxed protective duties (reducing the average *ad valorem* rate to only 29%). Film duties remained at that level through the 20s. Whatever success American firms were to have in excluding imports from the domestic market, government tariff policy would play virtually no role in the struggle.

During the summer of 1909, when the tariff was being debated, the independent movement was gaining some momentum. The Patents Co. had served injunctions against various producers, exchanges and exhibitors shortly after its formation; by the summer it became apparent that these were not enough to stop independents from operating. More small firms entered the field, cutting prices below the fixed rates charged by the MPPC members. This lured theatres to drop their licences to secure the cheaper independent films.[45] A series of independent organisations arose, struggling over the portion of the market left uncontrolled by the MPPC.

A second independent firm, the Film Import and Trading Co., came into being in September as a rival to Murdock's declining IPPC. Film Import and Trading also depended almost entirely upon foreign brands, although it was the last independent company to do so. It was said by late September to have control of twenty-three European agencies formerly held by the IPPC; Murdock apparently retained only a few of the relatively unprolific British brands. The independent side was reportedly: 'practically split into two factions, the Murdock faction and the non-Murdock faction. The non-Murdock faction controls most of the imported film, and some of the home-manufactured film, so that they are very strong.'[46]

Yet another group formed in September of 1909, the National Independent Moving Picture Alliance. This was not a company, as the two import firms were; it was a loosely organised group containing Film Import and Trading, the Great Northern Co. and a number of other importers and domestic companies; Murdock was elected its president. This new group was an attempt to control sales practices and to lay down guidelines for pricing; its goal seems to have been to introduce some of the stability into the independent faction that the MPPC had gained for its licensees.[47] The Alliance had, however, little effect and although by late 1909 the independent ranks had grown, they still offered little coherent opposition to the MPPC.

Soon the flimsy structure which the independent movement had built up during 1909 collapsed. At the end of that year, the *Moving Picture World* noted that the IPPC was virtually out of business and that the Film Import and Trading Co. was now the central factor opposing the MPPC. Yet in April 1910, Film Import and Trading filed for bankruptcy. The National Independent Moving Picture Alliance had accepted Murdock's resignation in February and had ceased to be a factor in the independent field.[48]

Before going on to look at the effects of the more coherent independent movement of 1910 upon imports, it may be useful to estimate the impact of the MPPC upon the foreign film in its early period of operation. Any attempt to compare specific quantities of domestic vs. foreign film is probably impossible. The US Department of Commerce did not keep records on film footage imported before mid-1910. Schedules in trade papers do give numbers of titles released, but each company sold a different number of prints of each film. Hence our figures must be very rough. Sources from the period give estimates which suggest that between 1909 and 1912, the MPPC controlled from 66 to 75% of the total market.[49] Granted these figures are rough, but they indicate that during this period the independents, and hence most foreign firms, were working with between one-quarter and one-third of the market. (This also suggests that, in spite of the growing number of independent firms, their survival depended less on seizing a larger share of the market than on an expansion of its total size.)

What of the foreign films within these two factions? Table A.I (Appendix II) details the number of short films in the regular weekly release schedules in the USA for selected periods between April 1907 and October 1914. (The table does not list features or any films released via states rights, whereby the exclusive rights to distribute a film within a given territory – usually one or a few states – would be sold to local exchanges.) Table A.I does not give any indication of the number of prints sold, which limits its usefulness. Pathé, for example, reportedly had a standing order for 160 prints of each film in the USA in 1910, at the time of the General Film Co.'s formation.[50] It probably sold more prints than most domestic producers, while other foreign film companies would sell fewer. Nevertheless, given the absence of systematic data about footage sold by each firm, an accounting by number of titles is perhaps the next best thing.

By this measure, we can see that the foreign film was doing well in the American market in 1907. The events of 1908, with the various licensing agreements, caused this to fluctuate noticeably, but without an overall decrease in the foreign share. In Table A.I, I have listed the number of titles and percentages of the total release for all foreign films and then the same information for the licensed foreign films only. During 1909, the licensed foreign films made up an average of about three-quarters of the total foreign release (tending to support the estimate that the MPPC controlled about that proportion of the market). But beginning in early 1910, the licensed share falls sharply and typically remains at less than one-half of the foreign total for the next year and a half. (Pathé's share of the market was so great that the estimates of licensed percentages are undoubtedly too low in terms of footage sold; yet the proportionate drop from 1909 to 1910 reflected in the table should hold regardless of this.)

The independent movement gained considerable strength in the spring of 1910 through the formation of the Motion Picture Distributing and Sales Company (hereafter the Sales Co.). Organised by officials of two major independent manufacturers, the Independent Motion Picture Co. (Imp, Carl Laemmle's production firm) and the New York Motion Picture Co., the Sales Co. was to serve as a distribution agency through which the independents could sell their films. It included foreign brands: Great Northern (which had been operating its own office all along); Lux, Eclair (both of which had just opened New York offices); Cines (releasing irregularly); and Ambrosio, and Itala (each of which had the New York Motion Picture Co. as its American agent).[51] A comparison of this list with the foreign brands being released in the USA before the formation of the MPPC reveals a distinct shift in nationalities represented. While French and British films had featured most prominently among the earlier brands, Italy had replaced Britain by 1910. It was well on its way to being America's second rival, after France, for world film markets. During the intervening two years, the British film had acquired a reputation for poor quality. British films had only occasional minor successes in the American market for the remainder of the silent period; only in the early sound era, with such films as *The Private Life of Henry VIII*, did the British film regain any significant reputation in the USA.

Shortly after the formation of the Sales Co., a group of producers broke away, resolving to release their films separately. They formed the Associated Independent Film Manufacturers. Interestingly, all the foreign companies with their own American offices (Eclair, Lux, and Great Northern) joined this maverick group; possibly they suspected that the Sales Co. would become an organisation parallel to the MPPC, limiting the amount of importation. The president of the Associated Independent Film Manufacturers was Paul H. Cromelin, who was in 1914 to open one of the first major import/export firms, Cosmofotofilm. In a 1914 article he looked back at the events of mid-1911, when the Associated Independent group of companies gave in and allied themselves once more with the Sales Co:

When the writer left for London in the summer of 1911 there was no way by which a motion picture play, no matter how excellent, could get a showing in the United States, except by license from the 'trust' [MPPC] (which was not obtainable), or through the then existing other combination known as the 'Sales Company'. True, a print might be sold here and there but for all practical purposes ordinary competitive conditions were non-existent.

24

That summer, the Sales Co. reincorporated to accommodate the members of the Associated Independent Film Manufacturers; it demanded that the Association's members distribute only through the Sales Co., set a schedule of prices and charged a distribution fee. It was in effect opposing the MPPC by using similar 'trust' strategies. At this point, the Sales Co. included these foreign brands: Eclair, Ambrosio, Film d'Art, Lux, Great Northern, and Itala.[52]

The Sales Co. was seen as sealing off most foreign films from the non-licensed portion of the American market. In early 1911, a member of the Barker Motion Picture Company commented on his inability to sell in the USA a film which had been a considerable success in Britain: 'The Patents Company licensees have to be reckoned with on the one hand; the Sales Company on the other. It is the policy of these two concerns to as far as possible exclude the imported product.'[53] After the formation of the Sales Co., numerous articles in journals like the *Moving Picture World* and the *Bioscope* discussed the issue of the closed American market failing to reciprocate the open British one, of which American films were currently gaining a lucrative share.

The Sales Co. provided a relative stability for the independent market and the situation remained largely unchanged for nearly two years. Foreign firms not in either the MPPC or the Sales Co. could sell films on an irregular basis via the states rights distribution system. Usually they did this simply by selling the American rights to a film to a small import firm, which in turn handled the states rights sales. This was obviously a less stable means of selling, since there were fewer theatres open to such films than to the two national organisations and the releases were on an irregular basis.

During this period, a few changes occurred. In November 1911, Gaumont left Kleine Optical and hence the ranks of the licensees, to do its own independent distributing. Kleine replaced this brand in January 1912, by becoming the agent for Cines. In April 1912, the Sales Co. began to break up. One group of American firms split off to form the Mutual Film Corp., with the purpose of acquiring a chain of exchanges. Another new distribution group, the Film Supply Company of America, acquired the rights to several Sales Co. brands; this was the only company to include foreign firms: Gaumont American, Great Northern, Lux, and Eclair (in addition to its domestic brands: Comet, Reliance, Solax, Thanhouser, Majestic, and American). Finally, the remaining firms in the Sales Co. (Rex, Republic, Imp, Powers, Champion, Nestor, and the New York Motion Picture Co.) left to form the Universal Film Manufacturing Co. in mid-1912; it contained no foreign companies, although it did pick up the agency for Ambrosio when that Italian firm opened its own New York office in September.[54]

The impact of the Sales Co.'s disintegration upon foreign films'

25

position in the American market is difficult to assess. Certainly each new realignment that formed seems to have been less dependent on foreign brands than had its predecessors. In early 1913 the *Bioscope* again attacked the 'closed market' policy in the USA, pointing out that the independent factions – Universal and the Film Supply Co. – were increasingly reluctant to take foreign films.[55] As Table A.I (in Appendix II) indicates, there was a slow decline in the proportionate share of the regular release market held by short foreign films from the approximate time of the Sales Co.'s formation and increasing after its break-up in the spring of 1912; this decline lasted until the beginning of the war. In July 1910, the Department of Commerce and Labor began keeping customs figures on film imported and exported. (Prior to that month, films were measured as part of a more general category of photographic goods.) Chart 1 in Appendix III shows the footage for imported film, with only positive included until July 1915. For the four years from mid-1910 to the beginning of the war, this chart shows a somewhat different pattern from Table A.I, shown by number of titles. Despite a slump in mid-1913, the trend was generally upward until one month before the war began. Comparing these two sets of data, we can perhaps conclude that the foreign film's proportionate share of the American market was shrinking, but that more footage was actually being sold. A number of foreign firms – Itala, Ambrosio, Copenhagen, Gloria, Nova, and Pasquali – opened offices or signed agents in the USA (see Chronology 1 in Appendix I). But these new importers were outstripped by the numerous independent domestic producers which came into being during these same years. Given the continually expanding market for films, it is plausible that the foreign companies' sales could increase, while their proportionate share of the market decreased or remained constant.

Also aiding foreign firms to increase their sales in America was the rise of the feature film. The first really major release of a foreign feature during this period came with *Dante's Inferno* in 1911, sold through an exclusive distribution contract with the Monopol Film Co., which disposed of it via states rights. The higher admission prices such features could command led to further imports and expanded domestic production. As Cassady points out, the companies that made or distributed these films were often new firms, separate from those that dealt primarily in short films. Adolf Zukor's Famous Players in Famous Plays (formed in 1912), the Jesse L. Lasky Feature Play Co. (1913) and others came into the field to specialise in features. Zukor started his new company by successfully importing the French feature, *Queen Elizabeth*, starring Sarah Bernhardt, which he claimed to have helped finance.[56] In cases where the foreign producer had no American office, an American firm would buy the American rights and rent direct or sell via states rights. The court decision of 1912 nullifying the MPPC's

26

Latham Loop patent ended the threat of litigation and encouraged the entry of these new firms into the market.

The foreign film, then, had made some progress toward recovery from the blow dealt it by the formation of the MPPC in 1908. The MPPC's attempt to control the American distribution field through the General Film Co. had been only partially successful. But it had certainly helped to limit imports – although this worked only because the independent factions adopted a similar strategy. The Europeans still saw the Patents Co. as one of the key factors opposing them at the time when, on 15 August 1912, the US government brought suit against the MPPC under the Sherman Act. The charges related in part to imports:

> The interest of defendants in forming the new company and in entering into the license agreements was to control, restrain, and monopolize all branches of commerce among the States of the United States and with foreign nations relating to the motion picture art, and to exclude others therefrom.[57]

The Europeans followed the case with considerable interest. About halfway through the trial, the *Bioscope*'s American correspondent predicted an open market for foreign films:

> At last the freedom of the American market is at hand. Pictures are beginning to be sold, not by reason of a monopolistic hold by certain groups of the producers, but chiefly on their merits. Less than a year ago a sale of twenty copies was almost unheard of, even for the best productions; today a sale of twenty copies is no longer regarded as phenomenal. All productions of merit, whether made here or abroad, find a ready market, even in present conditions, and as soon as the final dissolution of the organised monopolistic groups has taken place the American market will be the best in the world.[58]

Whether or not the dissolution of the MPPC and the General Film Co. would have created a largely open market for European films is a moot point. Even had the war not occurred, a new, more lasting oligopoly was beginning to take shape in 1912–15; Universal, Paramount-Famous-Lasky, Loew's and Fox were all in the early stages of their formation. These might effectively have kept imports to a minimum in any case. But by the time the lower-court decision against the MPPC came down on 1 October 1915, the war had so altered the foreign film's situation in the USA as to make the event largely irrelevant to importers.

2 Crossing the Herring Pond, 1909-15

In early 1909, shortly after the formation of the Motion Picture Patents Co., American producers began a systematic push into foreign markets. This movement continued until the war began; at that point, there was a brief lull, due to uncertainty as to the length of the hostilities and as to the best means of distribution. Even during the first months of the war, however, American producers and distributors foresaw that they could seize the opportunity to place their films in a permanently dominant position on world markets. As Chronology 2 in Appendix I shows, within a short period, American firms had reorganised their European branches (in some cases moving operations from Paris to London) and were again opening new offices or contracting new agencies.

The expansion of American distribution abroad went on at a rapid pace until the mid-20s, when it abated somewhat. This was partly because the basic structure of the Hollywood oligopoly of companies was substantially complete by that time. There were three 'majors' leading the industry: Famous Players-Lasky (with its distribution/exhibition branch, Paramount), MGM (formed in a merger in 1924; its distribution/exhibition branch was Loew's) and First National. Five 'minors' existed: Fox, Universal, Warner Bros., United Artists and the Film Booking Office. United Artists was a separate type of company, since it did not actually produce films; it distributed them for a few elite independent producers led by Fairbanks, Pickford and Chaplin. Several of the majors and minors were in the late stages of vertical integration; that is, they produced, distributed and exhibited their own films. Paramount, Loew's, Universal and Fox were acquiring theatres and the First National theatre group began regular production in the early 20s.[1] As they expanded at home, these companies generally created foreign distribution outlets as well. When Warner Bros. bought Vitagraph in 1925, it obtained the latter's extensive series of foreign offices. A few smaller, recently created or independent firms were still in the process of expanding abroad. But on the whole, the main expansion that had begun in 1909 was over; by the mid-20s most firms had representation in virtually all viable markets.

28

Although in 1908 Vitagraph, the leader in foreign distribution, had opted for Paris as the headquarters for its foreign laboratory, most firms chose to work through London. Beginning in the spring of 1909, the American members of the MPPC went about arranging distribution there – Essanay gaining its own office, Edison opening a separate film office for the first time, Vitagraph still operating the one it had opened in 1906 and American Biograph, Lubin, and Selig signing with an agent. During 1910, firms from the independent ranks began to follow suit, though most of these would work through agents for the next few years. In the meantime, the Patents Co. members and their agents were establishing additional branches on the Continent.

London continued to be the centre of American foreign distribution between 1909 and 1916; even after its decline in that capacity, it retained its role for the European distribution of American films. Even as the American film grew stronger abroad, the British production sector was declining. Britain had enjoyed a strong export position only in the early years of the century; the nearly total exclusion of British firms from the Patents Co. undoubtedly helped to disrupt this. But by acting as the re-exporter for American and other foreign films, dispatching them to all parts of the globe, British distributors and renters found quite a lucrative field – until the war intervened.

Britain was at the time a logical country to choose for the function of agent/re-exporter. It was traditionally the largest market for many American goods and this was certainly true of films. Aside from the USA itself, Britain had the greatest number of theatres – reportedly about 2,000 in 1911, with 300 of these in London alone.[2]

The system of distribution was entirely different from that used in America. In the USA standing orders and exclusive contracts tied theatres to whichever film service – licensed or independent – they chose. This meant that each producer sold about the same number of prints of each film. Trade journals, especially abroad, called the USA a 'closed market'. In Britain, on the other hand, an open-market system prevailed. Producers sold their films to renters, who in turn distributed them to as many theatres as they could. Since there was seldom an exclusive contract with any theatre for a film, that film might be rented to a number of theatres in the same district. The renters and theatres would all scramble to get popular titles as quickly as possible, since the potential audience would soon be exhausted by this simple form of saturation booking. Theoretically, it would have been more profitable for renters to charge higher fixed fees for smaller numbers of prints, thus extending the usefulness of each title and lowering costs. But with the open system, nearly twice as many titles came into the market as

29

were needed and there were many renters catering to the theatres. An exhibitor who could not rent the desired film immediately from one renter could either turn to another renter who was willing to buy more prints of the same film or could simply rent a different title. With the star system not yet well-established and short films still the rule, there was less possibility of renters differentiating the products they sold; one film could substitute for another with relatively little difficulty. An American firm or its agent could thus sell many copies of a single film. Under such a system, the renters bore the high expenses of obtaining a large number of prints whose earning life was likely to be short; the selling firm reaped the extra profits.

As a result, Britain was an attractive place to locate a laboratory where a firm's second negative could be shipped for all foreign printing. Other factors encouraged this tendency. Before 1915, there was no tariff on film imports. Also, the British shipping system was the finest in the world. American shipping facilities were, in contrast, weak. Available tonnage had declined during the Civil War and there had been little government incentive thereafter for shipbuilding; the many other expanding fields of manufacture had drawn the necessary capital. The percentage of American exports carried in domestically owned vessels had fallen from 35.6% in 1870 to a mere 9.3% by 1900. American goods were carried primarily on British, French, Japanese and German ships. The demands of commerce with a far-flung empire had led Britain to maintain a large fleet; a reliable estimate suggests that at the end of 1913, British ships carried about 52% in value, 50% in volume, of the world's seaborne trade.[3] Furthermore, British businesspeople had knowledge of international commerce and could cope with the different currencies, languages and other special problems involved.

Such facilities and skills were placed at the disposal of the inexperienced American film firms. In 1910, the *Bioscope* noted the shift in emphasis within the British film industry: 'Slowly, but surely, the English film manufacturers are going in for film hiring, and to all outward appearances are finding that there is more scope for their energies in that direction than in producing films.'

This strategy may have been profitable in the short run, but it helped create problems that were to plague the British film industry for years. By downplaying production in favour of distribution and exhibition, the British firms left the field open for foreign films; with so little screen time being devoted to native production, it became increasingly difficult to interest investors in making British films. French and Italian firms took generous shares of this market, to be sure, but the Americans gained more quickly. One American government official stated in 1911 that American films made up from 60 to 70% of the films imported into Britain. The figure of 60% was given in a number of consular reports over the next two years. This probably reflects either the American share of imports (rather than of the entire market) or estimates of footage sold and screen time occupied by American films. In terms of the number of titles released in Britain, as listed in the pages of the *Bioscope* (see Table A.II in Appendix II), sample weeks show the American share rising from about one-quarter to just under one-half of the British market. Certainly by the second half of 1911, all the major American firms had representation in Britain and British agencies were snapping up each new independent firm as it came into existence. In 1912, a prominent agent placed the average number of American prints sold in Britain for each film at between five and thirty; a good sale would be closer to 100 and a very popular film might sell up to 200 prints.[4] Within three years, the American film had successfully crossed the Atlantic Ocean – which trade papers of the period frequently referred to as 'the herring pond'.

Although the American firms moved in steadily to capture a substantial share of the British market, they seem to have been less adept at extending their advantage to other markets abroad. Much of the evidence from trade papers and customs statistics of the period suggests that the American industry was content to allow their British colleagues to handle the business of exploiting those other markets and skim off a share of the profits. Although a few American firms opened branch offices in major Continental cities, they seldom did their own distribution there; rather, they sold the rights for one or more countries to local companies. Until the middle of the war, many American offices abroad existed primarily to sell rights and to supply the quantity of prints ordered by the foreign firm taking care of the distribution.

Given the USA's lengthy commercial domination of the world, it seems odd to look back now and realise how naïvely the pre-war film export situation was managed. Apparently in selling the British rights of their films, many firms would, for a relatively low additional fee, simply throw in the rights for, say, the Continent or the British colonies or the Far East or even the world outside North America. This situation aroused little comment at the time, but part way through the war, American firms began to try dealing directly elsewhere and frequently found themselves undersold on the same or similar films by British companies.

In 1916, the American agent who sold *Civilization* abroad deplored the custom of including the rights for the British colonies in the sales of the rights for Great Britain. Metro's foreign representative noted the same problem with the Far Eastern market a year later: 'Through including or "throwing in" in their London transactions the rights of their films for the Orient American manufacturers are underselling themselves.' He suggested that 'the remedy is for America to limit the

31

London agent to his field of operations and not throw in the whole world outside of the United States and Canada.'[5] The main reason for this pre-war state of affairs appears to have been the convenience of handling only one set of foreign rights. The American film industry was still expanding and its officials had little experience or knowledge of far-flung markets. In 1919, the *Moving Picture World* analysed London's former place as the distribution centre for American films:

> The American producer had at his very doors a market more than sufficient to show him a tremendous return on his investment – and this market was infinitely more easily reached than was the foreign market. He knew the domestic market and didn't know the foreign one. He could deal intelligently with the domestic distributor on the essential matters of price, censorship, etc., but he was forced to admit that he didn't know what his wares were worth abroad or why some of his pictures were impossible for foreign exhibition. London, with a well-oiled organisation, established primarily for the purpose of carrying on trade in all lines with the many English colonies, which, in turn, were local distribution centers, was the logical city in which to sell anything intended for the foreign trade by the 'job lot' process. The price London was willing to pay, whether large or small, represented pure 'velvet' for the American producer. In the earlier days, there was little concern in this country whether the price paid for the rights of a picture for the foreign territory represented the maximum possibilities for the picture or not. A transaction with London interests was easily made, and all concern over the foreign fields was easily avoided.[6]

Thus, outside the most conveniently reached foreign markets, most of the sales made around the world were indirect.

A comparison of Charts 2 and 3, in Appendix III, shows that the vastly larger portion of American exports were going to Britain. The British chart (Chart 3) shows raw and exposed stock combined to mid-1917, while the American exports chart (Chart 2) separates raw from exposed after mid-1913. On the latter chart, it becomes apparent that American sales of exposed film remained remarkably steady during the pre-war years; the main fluctuations that appear there, with large rises in early 1912, mid-to-late 1913 and early 1914, correspond closely to the shifts in American raw-stock exports. Up to the beginning of the war, the American film industry's average monthly film exports were: first half of 1912, 2,675,465 feet; 1913, 2,692,487 feet; January to July of 1914, 2,645,829 feet. Such steady shipments at a time when American firms were expanding their business abroad helps confirm that very little selling was done except through London. In all probability, the exported films were often negatives, from which additional prints could be struck for British agencies selling them in other parts of the world.

Although sale through London agencies was perhaps not the most profitable method of distributing films in the long run, it did allow the American product to reach far-flung and smaller markets. There were only a few ways exhibitors or distributors in such markets could get films, since there was little or no native production. They could order them directly from the producer, depending on descriptions in trade papers to judge the quality of the film – this was a relatively minor means of selling and buying. More frequently, a local distributor would order groups of films from large firms specialising in export to distant countries. In South Africa in 1912, the largest theatre owners would receive regular shipments of films by post from export companies in London with whom they had standing orders; often these included American films. They would run these, then rent them out to smaller theatres in the country. Another common ordering procedure arose as the number of theatres and larger distributors grew in each country. The distributor, sometimes associated with a theatre chain, would open a buying office in London; buyers could then attend trade shows and order whatever number of prints the home market could absorb. In 1913, for example, the South American Feature Film Co. opened an office in London, to buy British and other films for South America.[7]

But some small or undeveloped markets could not afford many new prints. In India in 1910, for example, there were few permanent theatres – one in Calcutta, one in Rangoon and four in Bombay; other locales were served by about seventy touring cinemas. Pathé was the only distributor with direct sales there and it would not rent, only sell. The main theatres would buy Pathé films direct and sell them used at half-price to the travelling shows; some new topicals and used prints were obtained via the post from London. An even smaller market, Syria, in 1912 used films leased from firms in Paris and Rome, but received them only after they had been shown in Egypt. The policy of moving into such small markets with direct sales had little chance before the war, since Pathé retained its firm hold. An American consul in China pointed out in 1911 that 'A well-known French company had a practical monopoly on the market.'[8] From its offices in Hong Kong, Singapore and other key Far Eastern cities, Pathé could supply the few theatres in the surrounding small countries.

Nevertheless, films other than Pathé's made their way into these distant markets – mainly through London. There grew up a thriving business in 'junk' prints. Again, London was its logical centre; with so many prints being shown simultaneously, a great many used copies would be unrentable within a period averaging about ninety days. An analyst commented in 1914:

Because the life of a film is so short in England, hirers often pursue the practice of selling 'commercial stuff' to continental agents – thus, a subject is reincarnated, as it were, placed in circulation in some foreign territory and thus it pursues a profitable career. This evil has grown up into a good sized leech that bleeds the continental revenue of many American manufacturers.[9]

The 'junk' film travelled to the most distant markets. Special companies existed in Britain to cater to theatres in markets too small to support the purchase of new films. Such companies circulated flyers listing titles and noting condition, price per foot and number of copies on hand; the firms also printed advertisements in British trade papers that circulated abroad. The Actograph Co., London, for example, ran a nine-page ad of this type in 1910 in the *Bioscope*, selling film at a minimum fee of $1\frac{1}{2}d$. per foot; over two pages were devoted to Pathé prints, a half-page to Gaumont, one-third of a column to American Biograph, with a few Seligs and Lubins, and a very few Essanays, Edisons, and Kalems. (The rest were British.) In 1912 the Philograph Film Service had on hand 500,000 ft. of used film beginning at $\frac{1}{4}d$. per foot.[10] Needless to say, none of the money from such sales found its way back to the producing firms; yet there was little criticism of the practice before the war. Indeed, it was not until the mid-war period, when the American industry moved toward direct dealing around the world, that exporters began to decry the effects of the London trade in used films.

THE AMERICAN POSITION JUST BEFORE THE WAR

The USA's delegation of much of its world distribution to firms in Britain makes it difficult to assess the American film's position in world film markets in the early teens. Many of the prints sent abroad do not appear in the Department of Commerce customs figures, since they were made in Britain. (The British Board of Trade published re-export statistics, but these began only in 1915 and they include non-American films as well, with no way of determining the origin of the footage.) There are two central questions which one would wish to ask about this period: how strong was the USA's position in foreign markets and was that position improving at a significant rate even before the war began? We cannot find definitive answers, but there are many bits of evidence from the period which may allow us to make at least tentative judgments. Trade journals and official American government reports gave many details on the film industries of every important market in the world. A summary survey here of these markets may serve to give a cumulative view of the USA's situation; it should also, incidentally, provide a general look at world film distribution in these years just before the war.

Britain

We have already seen how the American film companies moved into Britain during the period 1909–12 and gained an estimated 60% of film sales. What was the situation in 1913 and 1914, just before the war? There seems to have been a slight decline in the popularity of American films during 1913; the *Bioscope*'s year-end summary declared: '1913 has been notable for the very greatly increased popularity of Continental films, as compared with American productions.' The main gainers were Pathé, Cines, Pasquali, Gloria and Ambrosio – all but the first being Italian brands. The American consul in Sheffield found that the vogue for Westerns was dying down in favour of Italian, French, and British films. (Complaints of the lack of variety in American Westerns were beginning to surface in many parts of the world at about this time.)[11]

In 1914, one British expert attributed the recent decline in American films' popularity to a lack of progress in their quality:

> When your producers began to invade the London market, their stuff was far away superior to that being turned out by producers of other countries, but the one mistake of your manufacturers was that they had been too content to rest on their past laurels. While they were doing this, the production side of Europe began to wake up, and it developed to such an extent as to threaten to oust American films from first place.[12]

The European 'developments' probably included the spectacular *mise en scène* of the Italian films of recent years. The low production costs of hiring extras and building sets allowed companies to make films which could compete successfully in world markets; this was one big factor in Italy's pre-war challenge to American and French films.

In 1914, the *Moving Picture World* compared the American and British markets in detail. This excellent description is worth summarising at some length, since it reveals the strengths that made the British market attractive to begin with, and the weaknesses that would, about two years later, cause the American exporters to change their sales policies in relation to Britain. In the USA, about 200 films went on the market per week, of which perhaps 130 had been sold by standing orders before they were even shot. In contrast, close to 350 subjects were offered in Britain weekly, but none would be sold before a trade showing to the renters and exhibitors. Only about 150 might actually be sold and released. This compares with 160 actually released in the USA (some states rights films, particularly foreign, would find no takers in the USA); about 90% of films released in the USA were of domestic make. At the beginning of the war, Britain had about 47% as great a population as the USA (about 46,000,000 vs. 98,000,000); its

35

land area, however, was only a small fraction of the size of the USA. Britain had only about a quarter the number of theatres (4,000 vs. 15,000), meaning that each theatre served more people (about 11,500 people in Britain, vs. 6,500 in the States). Because of this density of theatres and population, competition was very keen among British exhibitors. That is, because people in a given area had more theatres within easy reach, they could see a film in an early run; then other theatres in the area would have less potential to show it successfully on a later run. In the US, conversely, a title might be months old and still not have played in theatres within reach of some segments of the widely distributed population. Thus in the US prints had a longer life; while in Britain distributors had to supply larger numbers of prints (due to the high demand for first- and second-run bookings). These prints would then be shown intensively and have a short rental life.

Such a policy would help explain the relatively large consumption of films by the British market. The *Moving Picture World*'s estimate put the amount of footage sold in the USA at only roughly twice that sold in Britain. But in spite of this difference in footage, the short market life of a print in Britain meant that nearly as many individual titles would be sold there as in the USA. That is, with four thousand theatres booking from the one hundred exchanges in Britain, each exchange served an average of forty theatres. If half the exchange customers booked the film for three days (bi-weekly changes were customary), the basic life of a film would be sixty days. Given some lag time between bookings, the actual life of a film would average ninety days. But Britain also had more major first-, second-, and third-run theatres than the USA. These wanted new films as soon as possible and the hirers had to purchase a large number of prints. One of the most important importers, J. Frank Brockliss, had recently sold seventy-two prints of one Lubin film and over 100 of the popular Imp film of *Ivanhoe* (of special interest because it was shot on location in Britain). Every exchange worth its salt had one or two copies of these films, but, as a result, no bookings were possible after the first two weeks. The exhibitors and producers made money in such circumstances, but the exchanges suffered. (This problem would bring about modifications in the British distribution system in the second half of the teens, with manufacturers beginning to rent direct on an exclusive first-run basis by district.)[13]

Europe
After Britain, Germany was the USA's best market before the war. In early 1911, American officials in Germany reported a recent increase in the use of American films. By the beginning of 1912, there were approximately 1,500 theatres in Germany. An open-market situation existed, as in Britain, but with less centralisation. Film companies had representatives in Berlin, but typically the agent would travel to show

the films to local renters. These bought the prints outright and rented them to theatres. By this point a dozen American firms, mostly the licensed producers, had representatives in Germany and in most districts at least one American film appeared on each programme. Figures on new films released in a few periods in later 1912 and early 1913 indicate the sources by country (see Table II).

TABLE II

Sources of new films in Germany in 1912 and 1913

Country of origin	Month of November 1912, 413 new films		Last week of December 1912, 107 new films		First half of January 1913, 197 new films	
	Number	%	Number	%	Number	%
USA	130	31.5	33	30.8	59	29.9
Germany	56	13.6	10	9.3	23	11.7
Italy	114	27.6	29	27.1	52	26.4
France	67	16.2	19	17.8	37	18.8
Britain	31	7.5	10	9.3	17	15.9
Scandinavia	10	2.4	6	5.6	9	4.6

These consistent percentages suggest that the American film firmly held a larger share of the German market than did any other foreign country. In 1913, a *Moving Picture World* observer commented on the stability of the market: 'Almost all American manufacturers are represented in Berlin and if comparatively few of their products are advertised in the trade journals the cause must be sought in a well established market which takes care of itself.'[14]

But in countries that had a stronger production sector than did Germany, the American film did not fare as well. During the years 1909–12, Vitagraph was the only successful American company in France; other companies sold occasional films from London, but these played mainly in the large cities. Vitagraph's John Bunny was considered one of the few foreign stars known in Paris. As of 1912, the Parisian renting business was shared by only three main firms: Gaumont, Pathé and the Agence Générale. Gaumont and Pathé acted in part as agents for other brands and the Agence Générale was simply an agency for a variety of other firms. Vitagraph films, for example, played regularly in the Gaumont Palace Hippodrome in Paris; the Agence Générale at one point purchased five copies of a particularly popular Vitagraph. By late 1913, however, the hold of the three distributors on the French market was weakening as other firms were entering the field. This offered the possibility that a greater variety of foreign films would make their way into France. *The Battle of Elderbush Gulch* was a big success in Paris at that time and Selig's Tom Mix series became quite popular. But American films were still seen primarily in the larger towns; the major French firms continued their hold elsewhere.[15]

Italy was also a difficult market. In 1912, there were about 1,240 theatres in the country. Reportedly, rentals of 22,000,000 lire ($4,281,822, or $41,405,218 in 1982 dollars) were paid for foreign films that year and 13,000,000 lire ($2,530,167, or in 1982 terms, $24,466,714) for Italian; most of the foreign films would have been French. The *Moving Picture World*'s observer in 1913 characterised the Italian market as a small one, with sales restricted to an average of only five or six copies.

In such circumstances, the Italian producers could not amortise their films at home and were heavily dependent on export. The only American brand firmly established in Italy was Vitagraph, which had an agency there; it also sold occasional Rex and Solax films. Edison also had a representative and a theatre owner imported some Selig and Kalem films. But even one of the biggest American features of this period, Selig's *The Coming of Columbus*, sold only seven prints. There were two basic reasons for this: more new films came on to the market than were needed and prints were sold by a sort of 'states rights' system, with only five districts to be supplied. Competition was keen among a few major companies – Gaumont, Pathé, Eclair, Cines, Ambrosio and Vitagraph. Indeed, as the Italian film gained abroad, it seems also to have decreased the American share of its domestic market. Just before the war, reports declared that fewer American films were being shown in Italy than in previous years.[16]

Outside these major European markets, the success of American films apparently depended largely on the ease of transportation and commerce with Britain. Branches and agents in London did quite well in selling to Belgium and Holland, for example; the sales in these two small countries were reported to be nearly equal to those in Italy. As of 1910, Denmark was said to produce films long enough (two to three reels) nearly to fill its own programmes; import was a minor factor. But Norway, with no production of its own, imported most of its films from France and the USA. American action films were popular in Norway in early 1914, but the market was too small to warrant direct distribution. Films were sold to the twenty theatres in Christiania (Oslo) by representatives from Copenhagen; these prints in turn circulated to smaller theatres until they wore out. In general, American films were doing well in the smaller markets of north-western and northern Europe and in Germany.[17]

But southern and eastern Europe were still largely supplied by

France and Italy. In Spain, Barcelona was the centre of distribution; being on the Mediterranean coast, it could easily receive prints from either country. As of 1907, it was getting most of its films from France and Italy, some from Germany and only an occasional American film. By 1911, some American brands were becoming known – mostly the licensed firms, Vitagraph, Edison and American Biograph. Italian films were used most, followed by French and American. The editor of a Spanish trade journal summarised the main brands: 'Pathé's have for a long time been the best known, although latterly they have had to meet the competition of brands such as Eclair, Vitagraph, Itala, and perhaps also Ambrosio.' Some German firms were becoming known; Nordisk was just beginning to export to Spain. In 1912, the Motion Picture Sales Agency of London (representatives for Lubin, Kalem and American Biograph) opened a Barcelona office. This may have had some effect, since the following year an American official found American and Danish films breaking into Pathé's near-monopoly in the Seville district. But in 1914, the same official noted that only the very best American films were able to compete with Pathé, Gaumont, Nordisk and the Italian brands.[18]

The eastern European countries were of little importance to American firms. In 1910, films were reported to be popular in the Balkans. As with many smaller countries, there were still few theatres – ten in Belgrade, a few in other areas. As usual, Pathé dominated the field; films were obtained from its Austrian and Hungarian branch houses. In 1913, Hungary was getting films from Trieste and Budapest. Italian films were common, as were films of Pathé and Nordisk. American brands were known, with Vitagraphs most common and an occasional Kay-Bee or Bison 101 Western coming in. Greece was at this point an undeveloped market, with no theatres yet opened for the exclusive showing of films. (Small markets around the world often followed the early practice in the film-producing nations, by initially showing films in existing legitimate or variety theatres; in warm countries open-air theatres were also used.) As of 1913, some big French firms had recently opened branch agencies; only a few American films made their way to Greece.

One *Bioscope* article from 1913 gives a more precise indication of the USA's place in eastern European markets. The author had researched the number of films of each production company that were imported into Romania during 1912. Of a total of 1,472 films, he found this breakdown: Pathé, 426; Eclair, 186; Gaumont, 393 (giving France a 70.7% share); Cines, 58; Pasquali, 31; Savoia, 32; Itala, 28 (Italy, 10.1%); Kalem, 38; Thanhouser, 26; Vitagraph, 83; Lubin, 52; Edison, 24; AB, 18 (the USA, 16.4%); B and C, 16 (Britain, 0.9%); Messter, 13 (Germany, 1.1%); and Heron, twelve (unknown, 0.8%). Assuming the distribution patterns for most eastern European countries were similar, we can infer that France far surpassed the USA in this region before the war.[19]

The same was true for Russia, which was one of the more lucrative European markets. In 1911, there were about 1,200 theatres there; this was not a large number relative to the population, but it allowed a sale of at least a dozen prints. These came into the country as positives from European agents. As of 1911, French and Italian producers, with representatives in the major cities, carried the field; the only American brands shown were Vitagraph, Edison and American 'Flying A'. Through the next few years, consular officials in Moscow and Odessa stressed the necessity for American firms to obtain representation in Russia: 'There is no doubt that many films made in the United States would meet with good success if properly introduced, but as it is they are all sent through exchange agents in Europe and as a result France and Germany are better known than the United States.' Such urging aroused little response. In 1913, the main brands being used in Russia included Pathé, Nordisk, Cines, Gaumont, Gloria, Deutsche Bioskop, Eclair, Itala, Echo, Ambrosio, Denmark, Tanagra, Continental, Film d'Art, Vitagraph, Eclipse and Milano. Just before the war began, about 90% of the films shown in Russia were imported and although there are no figures available, we can assume that only a small share of these were American.[20]

Central and South America
The pattern of competition American films encountered in Europe makes considerable sense, given the geography and the established film production in certain key countries. But when we look at other markets, it is apparent how inexpertly organised the pre-war American export business was. Central and South America present some striking examples of how the American methods failed to adapt to local market conditions. If the American film industry could not control markets so close to itself, how could it succeed in the Far East or in Africa? Yet even directly adjacent Mexico obtained its films primarily from European distributors.

In 1911, Mexico had few permanent theatres – a small number in Mexico City, one in Vera Cruz. The rest of the country saw films in travelling exhibitions. Pathé dominated the market; the showing of an American film was a rare occurrence. Even Panama, with its close ties to the USA (the Panama Canal was currently being built) obtained only about one-half its films from the USA in 1914. In 1912 a theatre owner in Durango, Mexico, told why he showed mostly French films:

He attempted to import all his films from the United States, but ... the length of time required and the uncertainty of regular shipment made the venture a money-losing proposition. He further stated that

40

the explanatory matter was all printed in the English language, an innovation which proved anything but popular.

Time and again during the period one finds similar complaints from various far-flung markets about the use of American films with the original English-language intertitles. The attempt to translate all films into local tongues seems to have begun only partway through the war.[21]

There were also consistent complaints during this period that American films were too expensive when purchased from the USA. For example, in late 1913, a theatre owner and distributor in Colon, Panama, declared that he showed about 85% American-made films. Up to October of that year he had obtained these from the USA; but it turned out that he could get American films cheaper by buying them from London firms and he had switched over. This price differential remained in force for some years and we have the spectacle of American films crossing the Atlantic in negative, being printed and the positives being shipped back once more into the markets of Central and South America. Indeed, it was easier at this point to ship goods from Britain to South America than from the USA (in part because Britain's dominant position in supplying South America with coal necessitated frequent sailings). Only with the major changes that took place in shipping and world commerce during the war was it feasible for the American film supplies to gain the advantage in these markets.[22]

There were other problems to contend with in Central America and the Caribbean region. Many markets were just too small for American firms to consider them worth pursuing. A Philadelphia theatre chain in 1913 investigated the exhibition possibilities in Puerto Rico, but its representative concluded that there was little to be done there in the near future, due to the small population and the poverty of the people; tent theatres were showing used prints at the time. Also, French firms had moved in early and picked up what little business was to be had. Pathé and Eclair had branches in Mexico City and Guadalajara, from which they supplied the widely scattered theatres of Mexico.[23]

The large South American market would, during the war, become a major factor in the USA's takeover of world markets and later in its retention of control. European firms dominated South America before the war; the income from it and similar markets allowed the French and Italian firms to amortise expensive productions which would not pay for themselves in those countries' domestic markets. Without such foreign markets, the Europeans would make smaller profits and have less capital to invest in lavish, competitive films. But American firms failed to gain any substantial place in the pre-war market. In 1910, the four part-time film theatres in Bogotá, Colombia were reportedly obtaining virtually all their films from French and Italian companies.

As of 1911, a major importer in Montevideo, Uruguay, supplying Brazil as well, used European films almost exclusively, obtaining only a few scenics from the USA. In 1912, a major Brazilian importer hired the French firm of Aubert as his European buyer. By 1914, there were two major exchanges in Lima, Peru. One bought no American films; the other dealt in a few – mainly Tom Mix Westerns.[24] In Central and South America, the American film had a smaller share of the market than in Europe; importers depended primarily upon Continental brands. When they did obtain American films through London exporters, these might well be used prints, bringing no income to their original producers.

Australia and New Zealand

Few foreign markets succumbed so thoroughly to the American film during the war as did Australia and New Zealand. While the American share of the British market reached a maximum of about 90% by the 20s, in Australasia the estimate invariably given was 95%. Although British firms initially had a considerable hold on this market and fought to retain it, the American film was well on its way to taking over even before the war.

The Australian market had developed late, but swiftly. After the initial visit by the Lumière programme before the turn of the century, little had been done in the way of exhibition. But by early 1908, there were six local dealers in cinematograph equipment, as well as a branch of Pathé (although the latter did not open its regular film office in Melbourne until the following year); these catered to the growing fad for the movies. In 1909, the *Moving Picture World*'s Australian correspondent reported from Sydney:

> The Edison Manufacturing Company have a branch here, but their films are seldom seen on the screen. Now and then you see one with the brand on, but there is no doubt that the Continental makers have got the pull. Lately a lot of Lubin's films are being shown in this city, and good work they are.

The Edison 'branch' was probably either a phonograph sales office or an Australian agent. When Pathé opened in Melbourne later that year, it took over as the sole agent for Edison, but few of the latter's films were shown. As of 1910, an American official found that the number of American films imported was only one-seventh the number of British and less than one-half the number of French; but 'the United States is now making more progress in Australia than any other nation, and the demand is becoming general for American films in preference to English or French makes'. In September, a British consul confirmed this trend for the *Bioscope*; another article commented with some

42

apprehension that Britain's hold on the Australian market was now primarily in the area of exhibition equipment.[25]

One factor in popularising the American films was the major exhibition and distribution network of American entrepreneur J. D. Williams. In 1911, Williams owned the largest theatre chain in Australia, as well as the International Film Service, which distributed British films and the MPPC members' films. Few unlicensed American brands were being shown in Australia yet; this was probably because films came through London, where the independent firms were just getting established. Partly as a result of Williams' efforts, American films were becoming popular in Australia as of 1911; as in many areas of the world, Westerns were the most successful.[26]

New Zealand distributors also obtained their films through London. In late 1911, an observer wrote to the *Moving Picture World* declaring that over one-half the films shown were American. Vitagraph, AB, Edison and Lubin led the field, with a few Seligs and independent brands in use. The American consul in Auckland confirmed that 50% of the imports were American.[27]

In 1913, Charles Spenser bought the exchanges of the Greater J. D. Williams Amusement Co., thus taking over control of the film business in Australia. (Williams went on to various enterprises abroad, including being one of the founders and the first general manager of First National.) Spenser hired a buying agent in New York, helping establish a more direct supply of films into Australia. Indeed, once the war began, Australia was one of the first markets to which American firms shipped directly. Along with South America, it was a key market for gaining and maintaining the American hegemony.[28]

India and the Middle East

American films proved slower at invading another large part of the British Empire – India. We have seen that prior to 1913 India could only support a few permanent theatres, supplied mainly by a Pathé office and by used prints obtained from London. This situation changed little over the next two years. By 1912 Bombay had gone from four theatres to five; Pathé was still the biggest supplier. Other brands that showed occasionally were Itala, Cines, Urban, Gaumont, Edison, and Vitagraph – mostly in used prints. More theatre construction took place in 1913. Calcutta gained three and there was at least one in Madras; their patrons were mostly Europeans. But the USA made no inroads into Pathé's control; an occasional Edison film came in from London or New York. A consul in Bombay suggested that an American dealer in used prints might do well.[29]

The only significant market for films in the Middle East at this point was Turkey, which covered a good deal more area before the war than after. In 1910, its scattered theatres received films from Italy and

France. Permanent theatres were on the increase, with ten in Constantinople by mid-1911; Pathé had a representative there. A few British and American films supplemented the French and Italian ones. In 1912, American films were reported to be popular in some areas of Turkey, though they were still far outnumbered by Continental brands. As of 1913, the business in American films was growing.[30]

The Orient
Despite the USA's success in Australia and New Zealand, it made no similar advances in the Pacific markets to the north. The Orient gives perhaps the best indication of any major area as to how thoroughly Pathé had saturated world markets before the American export drive began; it also provides further evidence that distribution through London re-exporters initially undermined the American producers' move into new markets.

As of 1912, in the Straits Settlements, for example, Pathé had a virtual monopoly. There were only three theatres in Singapore and six in the rest of the Malay Peninsula. But Pathé maintained an office in Singapore, from which it could also supply the surrounding small countries. Other brands, such as American Biograph, did make their way into the market – but these, too, were sold by Pathé. In 1913, there were twelve to fourteen theatres in all of Malaya; brands in use included AB, Pathé, Gaumont, Itala, American Kinematograph (Pathé's American-made films) and Comica. Theatre owners claimed that ordering American films directly from their manufacturers was impossible, since the prices were nearly double what London exporters asked for the same films. In 1915, two small exchanges had opened in competition with Pathé and these supplied some American films, presumably also obtained via London.[31]

China was potentially a vast market, but it had few theatres before the war. These were primarily in the port cities and catered to the European population. In 1911, Hong Kong had six theatres, which dealt mostly with Pathé's local agency. An American official reported that some American films were used but were obtained mostly through European exchanges. American firms had not yet bothered to go after Chinese business. Pathé also monopolised the small port cities' business, such as in Swatow, with its two theatres. Only one American firm had a representative anywhere in the area which could supply such towns – Lubin, with an agent in Manila. Shanghai and Canton each had three theatres as of 1913 and, again, Pathé controlled them both. Indeed, Pathé-Phono-Cinéma-Chine, with its branches in Calcutta, Bombay, Hong Kong, Tientsin and Shanghai, was in a position to supply the whole region.[32]

Japan was a more flourishing market, but the American position there was equally minor. At the time of the opening of the first

44

permanent film theatre in 1903, most of the films shown were obtained from Pathé, Urban, Warwick and Gaumont. Yoshizawa and Co., the owner of that theatre and the first producers of films in Japan, opened an office in London in 1908 to buy European films and equipment. A second production company and distributor, Goshi Kwaisha Fukuhodo, opened a similar London branch in 1910. As of 1911, a Yoshizawa representative said, both firms 'are endeavouring to introduce into Japan American, Italian, and other films, which hitherto have not largely been imported'. In 1912, the American consul at Yokohama found few American films playing and there is little evidence of growth in that market before the war.[33]

The only Oriental market in which the USA had a considerable standing at this point was, not surprisingly, the Philippines – its only colony in the region, acquired in 1898. In 1911, Manila had about 25 theatres, mostly run by Americans and favouring American brands. But one exhibitor complained that 90% of the prints from American exchanges were worn almost beyond being showable, with splices, torn sprockets, ends and titles missing and 'Every subject taken on a very, very "rainy" day.' Even such prints were difficult to obtain regularly; exhibitors would buy whatever they could from sources all over the world. This exhibitor suggested the reasons for this neglect:

> Every exchange and factory of repute in the United States had been so rushed with business that the former could not consider the question of rentals [abroad] until their own circuits had been supplied, while the latter, apparently, were too busy to consider the sales, owing to the points of policy and territory not having been looked into.[34]

This relegation of the Orient to the status of a 'junk' market would eventually end as the USA looked abroad for alternatives to European markets lost during the war.

Africa
Throughout the period this study covers. the African continent was the least significant market for American films. Egypt was completely dominated by French film interests. Few other countries were developed enough to warrant attention. The major exception was South Africa. In 1910, the film business was in a primitive condition there, with no distributors operating. As in India, three big theatre owners in Cape Town would simply buy films directly from Europe or the USA and sell the used prints to smaller theatres. For example, the Elite Picture Palace began running all of Edison's releases as of late 1910, obtaining them from Edison's London office. As of 1912, there were forty theatres in the Johannesburg district; the methods of

distribution were similar to those in Cape Town. But in mid-1913, about eight film exchanges merged to form the African Film Trust, controlled by I. W. Schlesinger, an American; this company would dominate the South African film business for years to come and would aid in the move to an increasing dependence on American films. (This situation resembles the one we have seen at work in Australia, where another American built up a major distribution/exhibition chain using American films.) Already in 1913 'Among the films popular in South Africa are a good many of the American make: Vitagraph, A.B., Kalem, Lubin, Nestor, Rex, Solax, and many others.'[35]

We may now return to our two basic questions. What was America's position in world markets? And was the USA moving into world markets at a significant rate before the war? Prior to the war, American films were clearly predominant in only three major markets abroad: Britain, Germany and Australasia. In a few others it may have been headed in the same direction – for example, in South Africa and small northern European markets like Belgium, Holland and Norway. But we still find a large portion of the globe served almost exclusively by French, Italian, and British firms – South America, much of Central America, the Middle East and India, the Orient, Russia and eastern Europe, and the Mediterranean countries. The USA certainly had the advantage of the largest domestic market for amortising its films, but Italy and, particularly, France had offset that advantage by capturing a larger overseas market among the smaller, more easily saturated areas. Perhaps the Americans would have gained the upper hand ultimately, but it is not clear that they were making substantial progress in that direction in the early teens.

THE FILM INDUSTRY AND THE GENERAL EXPORT SITUATION

The American film industry's push into foreign markets began in earnest in 1909. It came in the midst of a general increase in American commerce abroad. The American economy had grown hugely since the end of the Civil War and foreign trade participated in this growth. In the period 1900–13, exports had grown by 76%, imports by 113%. Despite the greater growth in imports, the balance of trade was in the USA's favour; one of its biggest surpluses came in 1913. Moreover, the types of exports were changing. While foodstuffs, and particularly grain, had made up 39.8% of the total exports in 1900, their portion fell to 20.7% by 1913. But exports of manufactured goods, in which category films would fit, rose from 35.4% in 1900 to 48.8% in 1913. The rise in the total value of exports is apparent in Fig. 1.[36]

As trade increased, the USA moved into wider markets. In the 19th century its main markets for foodstuffs had been the richer nations of

FIG. 1

Changes in the total value of exports, 1891–1931

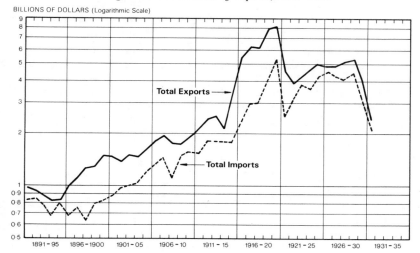

BILLIONS OF DOLLARS (Logarithmic Scale)

Europe, primarily Britain. Early in this century, sales to Germany, France and Italy were on the rise. But more significantly, Europe's share of overall American exports was declining. In 1900, Europe was 74.6% of the USA's market; by 1913, the share was down to 59.9%.

> During the last decade of the 19th century there had been fear among the European producers that Europe would be commercially 'Americanised', but during the early years of the 20th century it became clear that the commercial struggle between Europe and the USA centred not on the European market, but on the undeveloped markets throughout the rest of the world.[37]

This diversification of markets would prove essential in the American film industry's takeover; certainly there can have been few product areas in which the struggle ended in such complete success for the USA.

In general commerce, the move into broader world markets proved a necessary accompaniment to the shift toward the export of more manufactured goods. In manufactures, as well as specifically in film, the Europeans had their own industries; they needed fewer American goods in this area than in raw materials and foodstuffs. While in 1912, 60.9% of all American exports went to Europe, only 30.8% of finished manufactures went there. But the move into non-European markets went slowly, since European countries had already established themselves in such markets during the 19th century. The USA was most successful in developing North American markets, less so in South

47

America and Asia, and even declined in a few markets; during the period 1900–13, the changes shown in Table III occurred in the USA's share of each region's imports.

TABLE III

Changes in the American share of imports, 1900–13

	1900 %	1913 %
North and Central America	13.5	25.0
Canada	60.0	63.4
Mexico	50.6	53.9
Cuba	44.2	52.8
British West Indies	26.5	42.9 (1910)
South America	2.8	6.0
Argentina	11.8	13.8
Chile	12.5	13.0
Orient	4.7	4.7
China	7.5	8.5
Japan	20.9	15.8
India	1.7	3.8
Australia	12.2	11.6

American firms encountered a number of obstacles in these markets – essentially the same problems film exporters faced. European exporters were already established there; there was widespread European investment abroad; the Europeans had superior shipping facilities; European firms often made goods for specific markets (note here the American film exporters' failure to translate intertitles); European banks had networks of branches abroad to supply credit; European firms were more likely to establish direct-sales offices; they were more willing to extend long-term credit; lower production costs in Europe led to lower prices; and European firms had more knowledge of local packing regulations and needs. Since the turn of the century, American industry had been moving to correct these problems by using some of the same methods. Perhaps most importantly, though there was a continued dependence on sales through agents, the use of export departments and foreign branches was increasing. By 1913, the upcoming Panama Canal opening stimulated American shipbuilding; more available tonnage on non-European routes would greatly facilitate the export of goods to other markets.[38]

48

On a small scale, the American film industry was following these trends, though in a somewhat laggardly fashion. Other American goods were being made and handled by established, well-organised industries which had long since saturated their home markets. Film companies, faced with the necessity of expanding at home and abroad at once, usually took the easier route by limiting their direct representation to the few largest markets, selling via agents elsewhere. This meant that French and Italian competitors continued to hold major places in world markets. But the American film industry had done well for itself, moving within a few years into second or third place. Along with the rest of the American economy, the film industry would be catapulted into the leading position by the war's radical alteration of existing conditions.

THE AMERICAN POSITION IN THE FIRST YEARS OF THE WAR

The war spread over Europe in the week of 28 July to 4 August 1914. On the first day, Austria declared war on Serbia. Germany followed on 1 August by declaring war on Russia and on Russia's ally, France, on 3 August; it invaded Luxemburg on 2 August and Belgium on 4 August. On 4 August, Italy declared its neutrality and at midnight, Britain declared war on Germany. Other countries began allying themselves with either side, a process which continued until, by the end of the war, most of the world's nations were at least nominally engaged in the hostilities.

The ultimate effect of the war on the world's supply of films was to reduce greatly the production of the leading European countries, France and Italy, and to allow the American exporters to take over the markets which those countries had supplied. Reactions in the American trade press just after the beginning of the war indicate that members of the industry quickly foresaw the possibility of such a takeover. In September, the *Moving Picture World* accurately predicted that: 'Within the next year or so the demand for American films in Europe will be large enough to justify a greater "invasion" than Europe has ever known before.' (Appropriately, this invasion metaphor became almost universal in discussions of expanding the American film trade abroad.) It also suggested the methods by which American firms could, and indeed later did, extend their control over markets abroad:

The real problem in Europe will be the problem of distribution. . . . Every country in Europe has peculiar conditions which require expert treatment. The prospective of increased demand for American-made films will greatly smooth the way of distribution, but much remains to be done. It may be questioned, for example, whether the distribution via London is in all cases the best.

49

Whatever has been done up to now in extending the sale of the American film in Europe has been done via London. There is no doubt that more distributing stations on the continent will be needed in the future.[39]

A few commentators also realised early on that a key to American takeover would be the supplying of films to non-European markets formerly dependent on French and Italian films. The editor of *Export American Industries* pointed out in October:

> While the source of supply formerly dependent upon the rental markets is gone as a result of the European cataclysm, it will be possible for them to re-establish their former relations with European film manufacturers after the war is over and the countries involved have recovered from its disastrous effects. But this is merely a possibility, and just how likely affairs may take that course depends entirely on American film producers. In other words, the latter should not merely look to the present, but should build for the future.

This was to be the USA's strategy in the second half of the war, in the long run enabling it to hold the world market after the war. Articles also began appearing in trade papers giving specific advice on how to export more effectively. In a November essay bluntly entitled 'Cashing in on Europe's War', the export manager for the Nicholas Power Company urged readers to consider neglected markets in Asia, Oceania, Africa and Latin America, giving a rundown on the differences between direct and indirect dealing with such markets.[40]

There is no question that many in the American film industry realised immediately the possibilities which the war opened. They knew also, in theory, what should be done to take advantage of those possibilities. But the industry was in no position to act instantly to take over world markets. As we can see from Chart 2, in Appendix III, total American film exports took a slight dip after the war began; they began to climb significantly, if sporadically, about eight months later. We might expect to find such a pattern, with difficulties in shipping, the loss of markets within the European war zone and the lack of direct-sales facilities abroad, helping to delay a major American push abroad. Chart 2 makes the timing of the takeover clear: during the second half of 1915 and especially in early 1916, American export increased and we can assume that the actual move to dominance on world markets occurred then.

France
At the beginning of the war, French production was completely

50

decimated. The French trade papers ceased publication immediately. But fortunately John Cher, the excellent Paris correspondent for both the *Bioscope* and the *Moving Picture World,* kept close tabs on the situation and reported it to those journals. The French film industry began to suffer a slump even before hostilities actually broke out. People were taking their savings out of banks and hoarding them; theatre attendances fell sharply. The theatres closed down completely when the mobilisation orders came. As of 16 August, things were improving in Paris; the Pathé Palace re-opened; Gaumont and Pathé had re-established their topicals services. Eclipse, which had been responsible for printing Selig films in its Paris lab, managed to send a batch of prints to London.[41]

Cher interviewed the various French producers, giving a good picture of the industry just after the war's beginning. The Red Cross had taken over most of Eclair's facilities and many of the company directors were in uniform; only the Eclair *Journal,* the company's newsreel, was continuing to appear. Cosmograph had ceased production altogether, its studios serving as barracks; the office still operated, but the head of the company was in the army. Gaumont's Paris office was still open. Pathé's staff was mostly in the military; all but one-twentieth of its French facilities were being used as barracks. But Charles Pathé declared confidently: 'We've got sufficient films in stock to assure the regular release of weekly programmes for the next six months. You can reassure your readers that the firm of Pathé Frères will continue to supply their customers throughout the world.' (As we shall see, Pathé did so only by shifting its base of operations almost entirely to the USA.) By late August Pathé was hiring amateur camera operators to keep its newsreel service going. But the scarcity of French topicals meant that the distributors had to depend increasingly on American newsreels.[42]

Pathé's remark about having six months' worth of negatives on hand suggests another reason why the Americans could not immediately take up the slack left by the decline in French production. French companies continued to operate for some time on such backlogs. At first, many had hopes that the war would only last a few months and there was a belief that it might not disrupt the world's film commerce too greatly in that time. Also, Italian film-making did not fall off so precipitously. There were 23 Italian companies producing early in the war. But even though the country was officially neutral, that status was shaky. Mobilisation was going on and production conditions deteriorated from the start.[43] Danish and British production kept up fairly well during the early part of the war. Hence there was an interval of about eight months when American films simply maintained their pre-war levels or even declined.

51

There were two main reasons for the slight dip in exports at the beginning of the war. Although the USA was not at war, it was effectively cut off from some of its European markets; most film dealing with Germany went on through London and other means of reaching that market had to be found. But the more immediate problem in the early weeks of the war was the lack of shipping facilities. This resulted in short-term uncertainty about whether American branches and agents in London could keep up supplies at all.

At the very beginning of the war, British shipping came to a near standstill. Most lines cancelled their August sailings. On 4 August, the State Insurance Office opened to insure cargoes carried on British ships; its purpose was to avoid the price inflation in Britain that would result from the high premiums charged by private companies. The scheme benefited non-British companies using British ships. In actuality, the danger from enemy attack proved relatively small in these early weeks. Britain had the strategic advantage at sea from the beginning of the war, just as Germany had it on land. By the end of 1914, Britain had cleared the seas of German commercial and military vessels. There were, however, real setbacks to British shipping that affected trans-Atlantic trade. Britain needed ships for military purposes and early in the war pressed about 4 million tons into transport duty. Certain ports were designated for military purposes; others had part of their facilities reserved for military use. (Such actions would result in occasional delays in the American film companies' trade.) By mid-August, shipping lines went back into operation. During the first six months of the war, general imports into Britain were down only about one-quarter from the six months just prior to the war.[44]

The London offices and agents of American brands had only slight problems with supplies at the beginning of the war. The *Bioscope* surveyed some of them. Bishop, Pessers & Co. declared they had Balboa negatives on hand and expected no interruption of service; J. Frank Brockliss promised the same for his brands for August and September. Thanhouser could go to the end of the year; Vitagraph had lost 40,000 feet of negatives in transport, but had replacements on the way. American Film had negatives through their 28 September release. Only the Pathé Frères Cinema Ltd had major problems; no negatives were coming from Paris and hence there was some delay in release dates. But Pathé negatives were coming from New York without difficulty. With the initial shipping delays minimised, the American firms simply took to keeping negatives on hand further in advance, to offset any delays or losses in shipping. Edison, for example, hastily sent 30,000 feet of negatives to London in the last two weeks of August.[45]

These large American negative inventories and shipments took the place of the imports which failed to enter Britain from Continental producers. The *Bioscope* expressed a somewhat nervous gratitude for the USA's aid:

> Unprepared for the sudden cutting off of our sources and supplies – outside America – we were threatened with a film famine during the early days of the war. America seized the opportunity which presented itself, and though her action was purely a business one, we must realise our indebtedness to American firms who stepped into the breach. With fairly large stocks in hand and the way open – thanks again to our Navy – to throw large consignments hastily across the Atlantic, they stood in a favourable position.

The author also predicts a return to normal, with European producers catching up – a hope based on a shorter war than ultimately materialised.[46]

During the period August 1914 to April 1915 there was little change in the position of American films on the British market. Once the transportation uncertainties of the early weeks were settled and the extra supplies of negatives received, the British war slogan 'business as usual' applied to the film industry. Theatre attendances remained good due to the high level of employment, the desire of the public to see newsreels and the need for escape.

The Rest of Europe

Since the USA was officially neutral, it could continue to supply films to Germany, through Scandinavia. One observer reported early in the war that Berlin theatres were mostly open, with Danish and American films still popular. In April 1915, the American consul in Breslau found American dramas, comedies and Westerns doing well; *Judith of Bethulia* had just completed a successful run. He suggested that 'Dealers should also supply every house with a colored slide of the American flag to be shown at the end of every American film.' There were no reports of difficulties in getting films into Germany, despite the blockades, and American film exporters continued to regard it as a good market until early 1916.[47]

Elsewhere in Europe the American films did poorly during these first eight months of the war. Belgium was completely cut off, with its theatres converted into Red Cross centres. At the beginning of the war, Swiss theatres had to close for lack of supplies; the ties with Paris, Berlin and Milan were all cut off. Spain also experienced a reduction in imports from Britain, France, Germany, Italy and the USA; distributors resorted to re-issuing older films. By early 1915, American films were still having little success in Italy; the war scare and economic hardships were affecting theatre attendance.[48]

Transportation difficulties made eastern Europe, including Russia, almost impossible as a market for American films during the war.

Central and South America
The situation changed little in Latin America as well. As of about March 1915, American consuls reported that French films still dominated in Mexico; in Costa Rica, French and Italian films were the most popular, with a few American Westerns showing.[49]

The American film industry became interested in the South American market as soon as the war began. It was the one area mentioned universally in trade paper articles on the possibilities of taking advantage of decreasing European supplies. Compare these discussions, all of which appeared in the trades within the first few months:

> Attention of the American producers is directed to the South American market which will be seriously affected by the suspension of the Continental companies . . . It is just possible that the failure of the customary supply may induce our South American neighbors to consider our product.

> When peace reigns once more in Europe, one of the first harbingers of the return to normal living will be the re-opening of the picture theaters. And their programs will be made up of American-made films. Then will come the greatest prosperity the American manufacturers of motion pictures have ever known. With their South American market not only established, but developed way beyond its present capacity; with the European market forced to rely almost exclusively on their productions; and with the domestic market bigger than ever, American-made films will not only lead the world – they will constitute it.

> Indications point to a picture war in South America and already several 'independents' have an invasion of that territory under way in an endeavor to get control of the situation now that the war has cut off the European supply of films.[50]

But in spite of this attention and optimism, it was not until 1916 that American firms really succeeded in South America. In the first half of 1915, distributors and exhibitors were able to get supplies from Europe. Films entered Argentina through Buenos Aires, where two major companies controlled much of the business: Max Glucksmann, Pathé's agent, and the Sociedad General Cinematografia, Gaumont's agent. They also handled other brands of film and there were small importers. Although French films were most popular, Vitagraph, Edison, Lubin,

Broncho, Thanhouser, Selig, and Kalem films found some use. Rio de Janeiro was Brazil's central distribution point; agents there represented Pathé, Eclair, Gaumont, Roma, Celia, Pasquali and Nordisk. Other brands in use were Itala, Ambrosio, Aquila, Gloria, Messter, Monopol, DKG, Deutsche Bioskop and Lion's Head. Not a single American firm had a representative; the few American films came via Europe. A consul in Brazil expressed cautious hope: 'In spite of the war, films are still being received from Europe, though in smaller numbers and more irregularly, so that the present should be an excellent opportunity to increase the use of the products of the United States.'[51]

Paraguay got its films from Buenos Aires by river and hence used mostly European brands as well; some Vitagraphs and Universals made their way there (and were still being shown with English intertitles). The same was true for Uruguay; the two big Buenos Aires distribution firms had branches there. But supplies were beginning to fall off by about March 1915 and theatres were depending on re-releases. The American consul in Montevideo urged, 'The popularity of American films is unquestioned, and manufacturers not already in the field should not delay if they intend to enter.' Colombia, on the other hand, was showing virtually all French films. An American official investigated why and found that most of the films the American firms had bothered to send were poor genre pictures: 'Stop using Colombia and the rest of South America for a "waste basket" in which to dump the plays the American public refuses to see.' He also found those American films which were translated used bad Spanish.[52]

Australia and New Zealand

On the other hand, the Australian market for American films continued to improve. Within two weeks of the war's beginning, American firms were turning to more direct dealing: 'Australian buyers, though already getting many of their American pictures by way of San Francisco and Vancouver, are perfecting arrangements to get more by those routes.' New Zealand's import figures for 1914 and 1915 also show an increase in direct shipments:

	1914	1915
From the USA	£12,155	£21,888
From Britain	£16,507	£22,715

Much of the film coming from Britain would be of American make, but the larger gain for the USA shows that fewer shipments were being made via London. An Australian import tax imposed in early 1915 failed to reduce the flow of American films. As of April, about 70% of the films in use were reportedly American. By this point, several major distributors – West, Spenser's, the Greater J. D. Williams Amusement Co., Amalgamated Pictures and Pathé Frères – had merged to form Australasian Films, a firm which dominated that market until challenged in the late teens by American direct-sales branches. As we have seen, Spenser's, Williams, and Pathé were all largely dependent upon American films and that tendency continued in the new firm.[53]

Other Markets

The situation in other distant markets remained little changed during the first months of the war. India still depended largely on used film from Europe. About 40% of China's films were 'junk'; only about one-quarter of the total film used there was American in the early months of the war.[54]

THE FOREIGN FILM IN THE USA DURING THE WAR

In Chapter 1, we saw how the foreign film was making something of a comeback in the USA just before the war, partly as a result of the sale of feature films on the states rights market. But as Chart 1 in Appendix III shows, with the approach and beginning of the war, imports fell off; they continued generally to decline until after the war. Indeed, there was a lag of more than a year before imports began to increase significantly again, resulting from the interval necessary for European industries to rebuild their production in adverse economic situations. The brief resurgence in the last third of 1917 probably resulted from two factors: the temporary decline in American production after the USA entered the war in July and the creation of a backlog after the introduction in July of import/export restrictions. But apart from this, the war caused a gradual reduction in the significance of foreign films in the American market.

Chronology 1 (in Appendix I) shows that early in the war those producing countries which had so far been little affected by the war continued to move into the USA. Several Italian firms opened branches (for example, Savoia) or signed agents (Gloria and Milano) in early 1915. Hepworth's American branch was still active, as was Great Northern. But by late 1915, most of these firms were in trouble. In December, both Ambrosio and Hepworth sent representatives to trade-show films and met with only slight success. Such films sold on only an occasional basis thereafter. Great Northern was the last foreign company to continue regular releases while depending entirely upon imported films; it declined and was out of business by the war's end. After 1916 there were no branch or agency openings noted in the trade press; business from abroad depended increasingly upon the growing number of import/export agents in New York, who bought up seasonal outputs or single films, mostly for sale on the states rights market.[55]

The only foreign companies which prospered in the USA to any extent throughout the war had begun producing there already. Three French companies had set up their own studios and begun releasing films before the war: Eclair, Gaumont and Pathé. Eclair continued to operate for about a year, independently of the parent French company – too independently, as it turned out. One official of the American branch had reorganised it into a series of smaller firms under a holding company in an effort to reverse the original company's losses. In September of 1915, the French Eclair sued to bring its subsidiary back to its original form; this in effect knocked the American branch out of the market permanently.

Gaumont was more successful, though on a small scale. The chronology of events is somewhat unclear. Gaumont apparently divided its American operations in mid-1910, continuing to release only its French films through George Kleine. An American studio opened in Flushing under Herbert Blaché. It seems to have made a small number of films before the war. As of 1 January 1912, Gaumont left Kleine and began releasing independently through its American branch. When the war began, the Flushing studio was initially disrupted by the call-up of its French personnel. But Gaumont advertised for scenario submissions early in 1915, indicating an intention to step up production. By the time Léon Gaumont paid his first war-time visit to the USA in April 1916, the American branch was doing its own films and was also responsible for several series for other companies: the *Mutual Weekly*, a scenic series called *See America First*, and *Kartoon Komics*. At this point Gaumont was releasing via Mutual, but went over to states rights sales about two years later. All in all, Gaumont's war-time work in the USA kept it established in the market, but it gained no substantial place there.[56]

Pathé's activities during the war are of considerably more interest, since it had been the single largest company on the American market as of 1911. Given its break with the General Film Co. in 1913, it could conceivably have moved into the ranks of the independent feature companies and become one of the majors in the post-war Hollywood oligopoly. It did not do so, apparently because of some fundamental miscalculations Charles Pathé made.

The year 1913 was a turning point for Pathé Frères. In February it acquired the Film Service, a British distribution firm, and began renting directly in Britain. During the year, Charles instituted a new policy in Europe, phasing out production and instead releasing independently produced films. In January 1914, Charles came to the USA to institute the same approach. Then, in May, Pathé broke with the General Film Co. ranks. Which side really desired the split is not clear, but the move fits in with Pathé's goal of becoming a distribution firm. J. A. Berst testified at the MPPC trial that he had initially opposed the formation of the General Film Co.; he was persuaded to participate in it but had never been satisfied with the arrangement. These views may have been hindsight, but they may help to account for Pathé's move away from the MPPC. Possibly, too, Berst and Charles Pathé foresaw the outcome of the case and wanted to establish a new distribution system. Whatever the reasons, Pathé launched its offensive in May by running ads accusing the General Film Co. of breaking its contract by refusing to distribute the newsreel, *Pathé Weekly*. Pathé then set out to establish its own exchanges in the USA to circulate the newsreel.[57]

During 1913, Pathé had established an American subsidiary, the Eclectic Film Co., to distribute features. Its founder, Arthur Roussel, was the one who arranged for the production of *The Perils of Pauline* (released from April to December of 1914). In July 1914, Pathé switched its American operations over to its European system of only releasing films produced by other companies – except for *Pauline*, which Pathé made under contract to Eclectic. Charles persistently touted this system, comparing his firm to a book publisher. When the war began, Pathé was still releasing some films, probably its French product, through General Film. The number of weekly releases declined in late August and September; in October, the licensed programme replaced Pathé with David Horsley's Ace Comedies. That month Pathé transferred its main office from Paris to London; the war was going badly and it seemed that Paris might fall. Charles announced in London that, due to the variety of sources from which Pathé obtained negatives, the loss of the French studio's product would not prevent Pathé from supplying its world exchange system. The variety of sources was no exaggeration; Pathé had for years built its large release schedules from a hodgepodge of film brands, shot all over the world. In early 1913, the brands included: American Kinema (Pathé's American-made films), Belge Cinéma, Comica, Eclectic (again, its own American films), Germania, Holandsche, Iberica, Italian Art, Imperium, Japanese, Modern Pictures, Nizza, Pathé, Russian, SCAGL (a French company in which Pathé had an interest), Thalie, and Thanhouser. But Charles' prediction that these sources would keep his company going proved too optimistic. A number of the countries involved were cut off by the hostilities; others failed to maintain supplies. By a month into the war, Pathé's English release programme depended on its own American Kinema films and a few minor American independent brands (for example, US Comedies, Denver, Chicago, Michigan).[58]

In October, Charles went to the USA from London. Sadoul has interpreted his actions as a sacrifice of the French film industry's interests to those of Pathé's stockholders. According to Sadoul, Pathé Frères had ceased to grow by the beginning of the war. Its capital had risen from 5 million francs in 1907 to 30 million in 1912–13, but the

58

1914 profits were almost the same as in 1908. Dividends had fallen sharply. But the share of Pathé's profits that came from the American market had grown since 1908 to over 50% (the French share was only 10%). What Charles did, Sadoul claims, was to leave the French industry in a shambles by opting to concentrate on the American market.[59]

Charles had to contend with a crisis in the USA. As a result of the break with the General Film Co., Pathé had no distribution for its non-feature programme and was near bankruptcy; there were rumours of a sell-out to Fox. But Pathé borrowed to open an exchange network. By November 1914, Eclectic had broadened its operations and was releasing Pathé narrative films, newsreels and *Pauline*. In January 1915, Charles announced the formation of a new company, Pathé Exchange, to replace Eclectic. By March the national network had grown to twenty-two exchanges.[60]

For the remainder of the war Pathé flourished on the policies Charles had originated. The serials were a tremendous hit everywhere they showed. Similarly, Pathé's concentration on shorts proved profitable. Harold Lloyd's lengthy series of comedies, produced by Hal Roach, were released and re-released by Pathé. By the late teens, Pathé Exchange was known as the main distributor of independent serials and shorts. In the short run, the approach was a success, carrying the company through the war. But in the longer run, the companies which emerged in the post-war era as the leaders of the American industry were those which concentrated on features and which built up their holdings through vertical integration. Charles Pathé had chosen to do neither. His preferred product, the serial, declined in status and popularity by about the time the war ended. In effect, serials were B products by the 20s and not so profitable as they had been. Similarly, though shorts continued to be a staple part of film programmes for decades to come, they were seldom as prestigious or lucrative as in the mid-teens. Without a strong grounding in the feature area, Pathé Exchange remained simply one of the biggest firms in the less important independent wing of the industry. Pathé also swam against the stream by dropping most of its production side. The firm had originally been one of the earliest and most extensively vertically integrated film companies in the world; it made projection and production equipment, produced films, distributed them and even began making its own raw stock – something no American firm ever tried. In France, it also began buying up theatres at about the same time that the major theatre chains were forming in the USA. Yet Charles Pathé, with his book-publishing model, chose to back away from this strategy. Had he fully maintained the vertically integrated structure of the pre-1913 period and moved into features as well, it seems quite possible that his firm could have emerged from the war in a position to challenge such strong rivals as Famous Players-Lasky and First National. As it was, his failure to do so may have lost him one of the last chances any foreign firm would have to establish a significant and lasting hold in the USA. In 1921, its American stockholders and management acquired control of Pathé Exchange from the parent company in Paris.[61]

3 Cashing in on Europe's War, 1916-18

'This war was made for America.'
Léon Gaumont, 1916[1]

THE GENERAL AMERICAN FOREIGN TRADE SITUATION DURING THE WAR

The decades leading up to 1914 were largely prosperous and stable for the leading industrial nations. The gold standard was still in use, making it easier to control currency fluctuations and to make payments between countries. London was the world's financial centre, based on Britain's position as a strong creditor nation; the fruits of the industrial revolution and a worldwide empire made this leadership possible. In spite of the USA's high exports and favourable balance of trade, it was still a debtor nation. Foreign investments, particularly from Britain, France, Holland and Germany, had been attracted by the tremendous prosperity in the late nineteenth-century USA; railroad securities and various industrial stocks promised a high rate of return.[2]

Just before the war, the USA seemed the likeliest candidate to overtake Britain as the world's most powerful nation. Its export surpluses would eventually have counteracted its foreign debt to the point of making it a creditor nation. But the war hastened the process considerably. As soon as war broke out, foreign investors rushed to sell off a large portion of their holdings in the USA. American investors, spurred by profits from the wartime export boom and eager to develop new markets abroad, invested heavily in non-European areas. And, in spite of the nation's neutral position, as of October 1914, the American government permitted private banks to loan money to the Allied nations to finance the war effort. In addition, once the USA entered the war, the government itself extended credits to these countries. By the end of the war, the USA held substantial debts abroad.[3]

The USA's position was also strengthened by a wartime export boom. As Fig. 1 (on p. 47) shows, after a slight dip in the early months of the war, total American exports soon climbed rapidly, reaching a peak in the late war and early post-war periods. This

61

enormous increase resulted from two main factors: the demand for munitions and foodstuffs by the Allies and the American move into export markets which the industrial nations of Europe could no longer supply adequately. These same causes would aid the film industry in its export push.

Britain entered the war with an inadequate supply of armaments for a protracted conflict. Most officials involved in planning war strategy expected a quick German defeat. But the conflict went badly and during the winter of 1914–15, the various belligerent nations began to order armaments, foodstuffs and raw materials from the USA. These orders ended the initial decline in American exports and stimulated capital investment in armaments manufacturing. Prior to the war, the USA had no munitions industry of any note, but during 1914 to 1916 major companies like Du Pont rapidly built new plants or converted old ones. By the time of the American entry, a substantial industry had grown up. The USA began to replace such traditional sources of grain and other foodstuffs as Australia and South America. In order to maximise the use of its merchant fleet, in 1917 Britain's government adopted the 'Atlantic Concentration', dictating that ships obtain supplies along the shortest routes. This pulled ships from distant areas of the world and concentrated them on the shorter North Atlantic routes; thus the USA (and Canada) became Europe's major suppliers. In 1914, the USA held a 25% share of British imports; by 1918, that share had risen to 49%.[4] And since British shipping was so extensive, that country was co-ordinating most of the supply lines for the Allied countries as well as for itself.

As the war effort taxed the industrial nations of Europe, their exports decreased. Also, the Atlantic Concentration meant that Britain and other countries were unable to ship goods to distant locations as extensively as before; such markets had to be abandoned to the competition from rising exporters like the USA and Japan. In 1913, for example, British exports had been 80% as great as its imports; by 1917 they were down to 40%. Overall, Europe's place in the world economy eroded during the war. In 1913, its share of world production was 43%, by 1923 it was 34%.[5]

The long-range success of the USA resulted not simply from a rise in manufacturing and exports, but also from the build-up of the facilities for supporting export: shipping and financial organisations. The export boom in armaments and foodstuffs greatly stimulated shipbuilding in the USA. We have seen that before the war American goods went abroad in British, German, Japanese and other ships. But during the war, the British government took control of much of that tonnage, and American exporters found it more difficult to get space. German vessels had been driven from the seas and even vessels of neutral countries were subject to delays because they could be diverted and searched by the British. As a result, there was an increase in shipbuilding in the USA. By 1918, it accounted for over half of all production by Allied and neutral nations. Indeed, in 1917–18, the USA was able to send about one-half of its men and *matériel* across the Atlantic in American-owned ships. But the great shipbuilding effort was mostly a response to greater commercial needs and it increased after the Armistice. Japanese building was also substantial; much trade in the Far East and India went over into Japanese hands. American shipping lines replaced British ones in the traffic between North and South America (partly because South American buyers had to substitute American coal for European). Both Japanese and American companies developed new services crossing the Pacific.[6]

The USA's expansion into the international financial scene also came during and just after the war. The Allied nations had an elaborate borrowing system among themselves, but before the American entry, Britain was the principal financier of the war. Its loans could be used by the Allies for making purchases in other countries and much of the money ended up paying for American goods. But once the USA got into the war, it took Britain's place as financier. From 1914 to April 1917, the USA shipped out about $7 billion in goods; only $2.4 billion of these were paid for by credits from various sources. But during the USA's participation in the war, it exported $10.3 billion in goods and gave out $7.3 billion in credits from the government. For Britain, the financing was a strain, but the USA was in effect financing the export of American goods, which promoted industry and agriculture. Shortly after the war, New York replaced London as the centre of world finance. American banks opened branches abroad during the war, giving sales offices the opportunity to extend credit more easily to customers – an important point for American film firms trying to establish direct-sales offices.[7]

In general, the war had the effect of decentralising the international economy, which was no longer so strongly dominated by Europe. In addition to North America and Japan, South America experienced a wartime boom, with export surpluses strengthening the various currencies.[8] Greater prosperity would tend to make these countries a market of interest to American film exporters, since the population could afford to pay the higher prices necessary for the rental of newer Hollywood films.

LONDON VS. NEW YORK AS THE USA'S DISTRIBUTION CENTRE

A comparison of Charts 2 and 3 (in Appendix III) shows that, as the American move to hegemony occurred from mid-1915 to early 1916, the bulk of film footage was still going to London. Even the sudden increase of January 1916 (the largest monthly shipment of the silent

63

period) consisted almost entirely of film destined for Britain: 49,432,065 of a total 53,991,697 feet. (Since 1,004,675 feet of raw stock left the USA that month, it could have accounted for only a small portion of the increase in sales to Britain.) British imports for the next four months also correspond closely to the total American exports. But as of June 1916, significant disparities between the two charts appear; the considerable export jump in December shown on Chart 2, for example, does not appear in the British chart. During the second half of 1916, the American film industry was sending larger portions of its wares elsewhere; the trend signals the decline of London as the centre of American world distribution. What caused this change? We might expect to find contributing factors in the areas of transport difficulties, British government regulation of import/export or the growing recognition within the American industry of the advantages of direct sales to non-European markets.

It would seem at first glance likely that the war at sea, and especially German submarine activities, might help explain why American firms turned away from the North Atlantic routes for foreign trading. But there is little correspondence between these two sets of events. The first declaration of U-boat war on 4 February 1915 initiated a period of pressure that culminated in the sinking of the *Lusitania* in May; thereafter American government complaints caused the Germans to moderate their activities. That summer, Paramount's business manager found that Paramount films were going, via London, to such distant Oriental markets as the Straits Settlements without interference. On 8 February 1916, Germany intensified its submarine attacks, keeping the pressure on until the autumn of that year. Yet American exports, most of which were still going to Britain, were high in the spring and fell off later that year; this period of lowered U-boat activity corresponds with the beginning of the shift of American trade away from London. The declaration of unrestricted submarine warfare, on Allied and neutral vessels alike, came in February 1917 and there followed the worst months of losses to U-boats of the war. In June and July, Britain began regular use of the convoy system to the USA and elsewhere; losses fell off to less than 1%. Yet the largest American shipments of the year correspond to the height of the submarine war and the monthly footage falls off as the seas were becoming comparatively safe.[9]

The trade papers reported remarkably few losses of film shipments at sea during the war. During the worst period of U-boat activity in 1917, Essanay lost fifty prints of its first Max Linder comedy, destined for Britain. In mid-1918, the Fox company declared that it had not lost any films in transit, merely experiencing a few delays. At about that time, a batch of *My Four Years in Germany* prints went down on a torpedoed merchant ship bound for Britain, but this was exceptional. The American Film Co. and Paramount both claimed to have lost no

64

footage at all during the war.[10] The evidence suggests that the sporadic submarine war had relatively little impact on American decisions about film export.

Regulations enacted by the British government had various effects on American exports to the country. During the war the government acted to discourage the importation of films, especially from the USA. On 1 October 1915, it imposed an import duty on American films. Later, in March 1916, it moved to limit exports from Britain by demanding that they qualify for a licence and in May 1918, similar licensing restrictions were applied to imports from the USA. The primary purposes of these regulations were to raise money for the war effort through the tariff, to discourage nitrate cellulose from falling into enemy hands and to limit the amount of British currency leaving the country in the film trade with the USA. To a certain extent all these measures succeeded in their purposes – but the licensing provisions also contributed to Britain's loss of the re-export trade.

The British tariff on luxury goods, including films, was imposed on 29 September 1915. The initial rates were $\frac{1}{2}d.$ per foot of raw stock, $1d.$ on positives and $8d.$ for negatives (working out to about 1 cent a foot for raw stock, 2 cents for positive and 16 cents for negative). William Selig gave the inevitable American businessman's response: 'One thing is almost certain, the people of Great Britain who view pictures will, in the long run, pay the increased duties.' They apparently did indeed; as of November some American branches in London were reported as raising their prices to cover the costs of the tax. British exporters were worried that the tax would reduce re-export business. They met with government officials in October to request a rebate of taxes on films re-exported, pointing out that the business was worth about £500,000 a year ($2,430,000, nearly $23 million in 1982 terms). These efforts succeeded; by the end of the year, firms exporting footage that had previously been taxed as an import were allowed a rebate.[11]

The initial reaction to the tariff within the British industry was a fear that the re-export trade would go elsewhere. In October, the *Moving Picture World* stated: 'A British contemporary sounds a note of alarm for the benefit of the British government. It is all in reference to the import tax which has been imposed. Our contemporary fears lest "the centre of the world's film market" will be transferred to some other city than London.' In December, the *Bioscope* commented on the situation: 'Looking back on the progress of the Trade during the past few years, the development of London's position as the film market of the world is, it must be admitted, due entirely to the policy of admitting to this country all films free of duty.' But these pessimistic views did not take into account the fact that Britain was still the USA's best foreign market. The *Moving Picture World*'s British correspondent wrote in November:

The American contingent in London regards the impending taxation with marked indifference, an indifference the staunchest patriot must admit is engendered only from a sound conviction that they are still on 'terra firma' and that the imposed duty will, in comparison with the increased turnover, prove to be a mere peppercorn.

At about this point British importers were lobbying for a reduction in the tax, and they obtained one in mid December. The tariff on raw stock dropped from $\frac{1}{2}$ to $\frac{1}{3}d$. and on negatives from 8 to 5d. (about 10 cents).[12]

Rachael Low has given the 1915 tariff as the main factor in the decline of the British re-export trade. But this was probably not the case. The biggest shipments of the entire war period from the USA to Britain occurred in the half-year following the tax's imposition. Had it been to the American firms' disadvantage, they would surely have ceased sending negatives to Britain, substituting shipments of only the positive prints needed for the British market itself. When the tax was first in effect, it was 1 cent per foot on raw stock, 2 cents on positives, 16 cents on negatives. Assuming the American films were printed on imported raw stock, a sale of at least sixteen positive prints would make the importation of a negative worthwhile. (That is, the extra cost of importing a negative and the raw stock to print positives would be 17 cents per foot to make the first print and 1 cent per foot for each additional print. The extra cost for importing positives printed in the USA would always be 2 cents times the number of feet. The cost becomes lower on the negative and raw stock after the sixteenth print.) One British importer reported that sales were down in Britain in late 1915; only about ten prints of a film were needed in the market.[13] But given that an additional six prints could easily be sold from London to the colonial markets, Latin America and those European markets still open, the sale of sixteen prints was not implausible. And with the December tariff reduction on raw stock to $\frac{1}{3}d$. and negatives to 5d., the break-even point for importing negatives was a sale of anything over seven positive prints. The tariff would seem in fact to have encouraged the importation of negatives, as opposed to batches of positives and the printing of positives in Britain. Once the negatives were in Britain, re-export was convenient.

There is little evidence of adverse reaction to the tariff from American firms. Joseph R. Darling, the Fox lawyer who had planned the case against the Patents Co. and was now engineering Fox's move into world markets, commented in an interview: 'I don't think it will have a detrimental effect on our business. . . I haven't heard of any objections to the tax; there are some grumbles, but one expects them and does not regard them seriously.' The American position in Britain was simply too lucrative for the tariff to affect it to any great extent. The *Bioscope* analysed the number of British-made and foreign titles released, both on the open market and by exclusive contract, during the month of January 1916 (see Table IV).

TABLE IV

British and foreign titles released in Britain in January 1916

Week ending	British-made	Foreign-made
8 January	14	136
15 January	15	136
22 January	8	128
29 January	16	128
	53	528

Only about 9% of films on the British market were made domestically and the American film was gaining a larger share all the time. (Italian and French films were in decline and Britain had just banned Danish film imports to prevent German films from slipping into its theatres.)[14]

On 17 March 1916, the War Trade Department ordered a ban on unlicensed exports of all motion pictures. The ease of obtaining these licences depended upon the destination of the films. For neutral countries doing business with the Central Powers, licensing was difficult; these included Norway, Denmark, Holland, Greece and Sweden. To ship to these countries, the export firm had first to obtain a certificate from a trade organisation within the country. The reason for the decree was to prevent indirect trading with the enemy. Film was an especially dangerous commodity, consisting as it did of nitrate cellulose. The Allied blockade of Germany was never complete. Imports and exports continued on neutral ships through the Baltic; Sweden in particular carried on trade with Germany. Since the beginning of the war, imports into neutral countries contiguous to Germany had grown tremendously; for certain commodities American shipments to those areas had doubled or trebled. In March 1915, Britain and France issued the Reprisals Order and began seizing some goods if they were assumed to be destined for a hostile country; by the end of 1915, all nitrates were on the list of goods to be taken. Germany was wholly dependent on imports for nitrate, which became very difficult to obtain as soon as the war began. Where formerly gun cotton (the raw material for nitrate film) had been used in the manufacture of explosives, the

Germans turned to nitrate cellulose as a substitute. The British feared, probably with reason, that some films making their way into German hands could end up being used for this purpose.[15]

Unlike the tariff, this licensing decree does seem to have adversely affected re-exports from Britain. In May, the *Moving Picture World*'s British correspondent stated: 'The London exporters of second-hand films, and there is now quite a community, are being inconvenienced in their business through the State restriction of celluloid export to such a degree that not a few of them appear to think the effect of the legislation will be to drive them entirely out of business.' That summer the head of Selig's London office described the situation there:

> We cannot export a film without a license from the Government, and this is not a matter of a day, but of a week or ten days – and sometimes months. If you want to send a film to Holland, before you can apply for your license from the British Government, your customer in Holland must go to the Dutch Government and obtain from the Netherlands Overseas Trust a guarantee that the film is not going to be re-exported; and in order to protect that guarantee the customer has to put up with the Netherlands Overseas Trust, a deposit equal to the value of the film which is coming into the country.

In March, Selig's representative had declared the foreign share to be about one-half of the total business done in its British offices. Selig had orders for 46,000 feet for Japan, 48,000 feet for Spain and the Philippines, 64,700 feet for France, 72,000 feet for Scandinavia and Russia (films for Russia were now going via Scandinavia) and 14,000 feet for Africa. Clearly the new British regulations made dealing with the countries of north-eastern Europe and Scandinavia extremely difficult and those areas provided a substantial share of at least some companies' overseas orders.[16] We have seen already that the decline in Britain's proportion of total American film exports began in June 1916, a little over two months after the licensing decree.

During 1916, 1917 and early 1918, the American export trade shifted gradually away from London, centring in New York City. Then, in May of 1918, the British government imposed one final restriction. The order went out that no American film was to be imported without a licence from the Board of Trade; each order had to be individually justified. There was little response in the trade papers of either country; perhaps the re-export trade had declined enough by this time that the order made little difference except to the supply of films for the British market. The *Bioscope* assumed the reason for the order was to save shipping space, but it pointed out that few commodities brought in higher import duties for the amount of space occupied than did films. (A more pressing reason was probably to keep British currency, by now suffering inflation, in the country.) The British export chart (Chart 3, in Appendix III) shows one last spurt of shipments in May (since the regulation applied only to films ordered after the fifteenth of that month), with a precipitous decline thereafter. The American exports, on the other hand, although they dipped after the May peak, did not fall off as badly; clearly by this point the USA was dealing more directly with its other markets.[17]

Beginning in early 1916, the trade presses of both countries debated the 'London or New York' question. The *Moving Picture World* in particular proselytised for direct trade with non-British markets, providing much information to American firms and putting out special export issues.* In January 1916, it editorialised against London as the USA's sole distribution centre:

> There are importers of American films in London who represent American films in every country of Europe, and a good many Asiatic countries, and who have never left London, except for occasional short trips to the continent. London has until now fixed the number of copies absorbed by the rest of Europe. London laid down the rule, for instance, that Holland and Belgium use one copy each and that Italy was rarely good for more than five copies. London practically regulated the sale of American film in Germany and Russia and Australia.[18]

This is an early expression of a feeling that Britain had not only co-opted American business in these markets, but had done so in an inefficient, unambitious manner.

American firms and foreign buyers seem to have agreed. As we have seen, by the summer of 1916, Britain's share of American exports showed signs of decline. In December, the *Moving Picture World* noted that Australian and Latin American buyers were establishing branch offices in New York. In March 1917, it gave some reasons for the increase in direct trade with South America:

> Our American banks have very greatly increased their connections

---

* The *Moving Picture World* added its first regular column on foreign trade, 'Our London Letter', on 24 Aug. 1907 and its 'Foreign Trade Notes' on 7 Sept. 1912; it began reprinting all American consuls' reports on film on 3 Oct. 1914. It added a successful Spanish-language version, *Cine-Mundial,* on 20 Dec. 1915, reaching 4,000 readers in Central and South America, Spain and Portugal, and the Philippines. [W. Stephen Bush, 'Here is "Cine-Mundial"', *MPW,* 18 Dec. 1915, pp. 2,154–5.] Judging from the correspondence columns, it appears that the *Moving Picture World* did have a considerable readership in most parts of the world and acted as a kind of forum for discussions of issues concerning foreign trade.

in foreign countries. The shipping lines running out of New York to South American points are steadily adding to their fleets and increasing the number of sailings. As this country is producing more than half the world's supply of films, does it not seem reasonable that the export trade in films should be largely centered in New York?[19]

American facilities and know-how were finally beginning to catch up with the ambitions the American film trade press had expressed in the first months of the war.

In 1916, the British recognised the trend. The *Bioscope* published its first 'Special Foreign and Export Supplement' issues on 11 January and 12 July 1916. The January issue noted the decline in London's 'junk' film trade. As more theatres were built in a country, the demand for used film would decline. The current junk markets were considered to be the West Indies, Dutch East Indies, Malay Peninsula and parts of South America. Both Japan and India were now going to New York rather than London for their prints. As late as April 1917, the *Bioscope* responded defensively to several American trade-press articles 'to express our unshakeable conviction that London is still, and will remain, the "film clearing-house of the world." ' But by July it admitted:

> Until a short time ago London was the acknowledged and undisputed centre of the film world – the international exchange through which practically all dealings in film were conducted. To-day this supremacy is threatened. We are faced with a danger of the world's film export trade leaving Great Britain for America.

The July export issue noted the loss of John Olsen and Co., the buyer for the largest distributors in Scandinavia; Olsen had moved his firm from London to New York and other companies were doing the same.[20]

One problem the American industry faced in its competition with London was the fact that foreign buyers could often get the same films cheaper in London. In November 1916, the *Moving Picture World* noted that one American company had recently sold a serial to Argentina, only to lose the deal when it was discovered that a print purchased from London had already played there; the American firm had to pay shipping both ways without a sale. Joseph Monat, of Monatfilm, Paris, had recently come to New York in hopes of finding lower prices on American films there than in London; in fact he found them higher. But the situation was changing. In December one major American exporter declared that, although it had been cheaper to print positives in Britain than in the USA, a recent price rise for raw stock in Britain made the costs about equal (although the balance eventually tipped once more in Britain's favour).[21]

The May 1918 regulation demanding the licensing of American imports dashed any remaining hopes of Britain's regaining the wartime export trade. In August, the *Bioscope* concluded that for the fiscal years of 1916 to 1918, the USA's direct, non-British sales had increased by two-thirds, while its exports to Britain were down by over one-fifth. A British exporter, Lionel Phillips, reviewed the world situation in an article in the *Kinematograph*, reprinted in the *Moving Picture World*: British sales to Japan had dropped to almost nothing when the principal buyer for that market moved to America; Australia now bought only topicals from Britain; South Africa was getting 80% of its films from the USA; Scandinavian buyers had removed to New York; South America was virtually closed to British firms; American representatives had recently visited India and sold whole blocks of their companies' films; France and Italy were open, but had only a limited capacity to absorb films. Phillips ended by exhorting British dealers to rebuild London's place. To this the *Moving Picture World* replied snippily: 'If Mr. Phillips really wishes to keep in touch with the world markets and maintain his position as an exporter of films on a large scale he should establish his headquarters in – New York.'[22] Some of his compatriots had already done so.

After the war, the British looked hopefully for signs of a shift back toward London. But by that time the general commercial problems in the USA that had initially turned exporters to London had been solved. The issue was really settled for good by 1916. And post-war economic difficulties – primarily inflation – in Europe were to make it even less likely that buyers would return to London when they could operate in the flourishing situation that existed in the USA.

AMERICAN EXPANSION ABROAD

The big increases in American exports during 1915 and early 1916 resulted primarily from the decline of the industries of other nations. It was simply a matter of more orders coming in; American firms were not yet developing new markets or changing their distribution methods. Had the war ended in mid-1916, the American film would have been in a much stronger position than before the war – yet it would not have been guaranteed any long-term hold on world markets. From 1916 on, however, American firms adopted new strategies, dealing directly with more markets, opening more subsidiary offices outside Europe and thereby establishing a control which other producing countries would find difficult to erode during the 20s.

Non-European markets would be the key to the new strategy. An examination of Chronology 2 (in Appendix I) shows that during this period American firms were signing agents and opening new offices in

71

a greater variety of locales. The pre-war companies were still operating, but our main concern is with those relatively new feature-film companies which would develop into the majors and minors of the 20s Hollywood oligopoly. During the second half of the war, these companies were Famous Players-Lasky (resulting from a merger of the two companies in July 1916), Universal, Goldwyn (of the three companies that later formed MGM, the one with the best overseas distribution) and Fox. Each firm pursued a different approach to expansion abroad. By grouping the events relating to each into brief chronologies here, we can see these approaches more clearly.

Universal, the first of these companies to have established itself abroad, had distribution facilities in London and Europe already. But the key events in its post-1915 dealings reveal an interesting pattern:

1916 – Japanese and Indian branches open; September 1916 – Singapore branch opens; February 1917 – Java branch opens; June 1918 – now has twenty foreign branches, including Manila.

After the war the next major branch openings would be in Mexico and Australia. Universal was the only American company to concentrate initially upon the Far Eastern market as its means of moving toward a worldwide direct-distribution network. It was the first, for example, to open a branch in Japan; Tadao Sato has spoken of Universal's Bluebird brand films as the first popular and influential group of American films to reach that country.[23]

A parallel pattern emerges in Fox's dealings abroad. Fox had no foreign agents or offices before late 1915, but at that point it moved swiftly to open its own distribution branch offices, largely bypassing indirect sales through agents:

October 1915 – Fox's first foreign branch opens in Montreal; December – branches open in Argentina and Brazil; February 1916 – a chain of exchanges in Britain is organised; April – Fox's Australian subsidiary is formed; April 1917 – recent openings in Norway, Sweden, Spain and Portugal, Uruguay and Paraguay; October – agencies sold for the British colonies, Peru, Bolivia, Chile, Central America; Late 1918 – French subsidiary opens.

Fox's avenue of entry into large-scale exploration was South America. Its first foreign branch outside North America was in Rio de Janeiro and it continued to expand its operations in Latin America until by early 1919 it had offices or representation in every country except Colombia. Fox moved into the lucrative British market quickly and also began direct dealing with Australia. Since South America and Australia were the two key non-European markets in the American wartime takeover and subsequent control, this strategy put Fox in a strong position abroad. Indeed, during the 20s, Fox was probably proportionately more powerful in foreign markets than in the domestic film-making hierarchy.

Famous Players-Lasky, which, with its distribution arm, Paramount, was currently growing into the most powerful film firm in the USA, expanded abroad in a less concentrated fashion. Even before the merger, Famous Players and Lasky used the same representatives abroad. In July of 1914, Samuel Goldfish had opened a London office for both, but he sold the rights for other European countries to agents. For much of the war, Famous Players-Lasky continued to work through agents in most areas:

> April 1916 – signs South African agent; May – signs French agent; July – Famous Players-Lasky merger; February 1917 – signs agent for Argentina, Paraguay and Uruguay; March – acquires controlling interest in Australia Feature Films; June – John Olsen buys Scandinavian rights; January 1918 – signs agent for West Indies and Central America; February – French agent, Gaumont, expands to cover Switzerland, Belgium and Egypt; *c.* October – recently opened Chilean subsidiary.

Famous Players-Lasky was perhaps less eager to invest a great deal abroad to open offices because it was expanding so quickly in the American and Canadian markets – opening exchanges and buying up theatres. Certainly in the 20s the company was powerful abroad and gained more direct-sales facilities. But it is notable that the two subsidiary offices Famous Players-Lasky opened in this period were again in the two key markets – Australia and South America. Famous Players-Lasky beat the other American firms into Australia when it bought into Feature Films Ltd. This was a small exchange chain at the time, competing with the powerful Australasian Films Ltd. Within three years, Paramount had built it into one of the largest exchange and theatre chains in Australia. By 1920 the staff had grown from its initial 4 to 100; its head claimed that Paramount's share of the market had gone from 6% to 60%.[24]

A latecomer to this group, Goldwyn opted for quite a different strategy. Samuel Goldfish, who had engineered Famous Players-Lasky's initial move abroad, was now renamed Goldwyn. He repeated his earlier actions on a grander scale:

> March 1917 – begins world-wide publicity campaign for new company; October – opens export department; March 1918 – sells rights for Australia, New Zealand, Scandinavia, Chile, Bolivia, Peru, Ecuador, South Africa, India, Burma, Argentina, Uruguay, Puerto

Rico, San Domingo; negotiating Italy, Spain, France; April – sells British rights.

In this way Goldwyn, a new company, was able to move quickly into a variety of markets. In 1920, it would opt for direct distribution in Britain and would gain agents for Australasia and the Far East; this extensive distribution system would later be modified to serve MGM.

Whatever strategy each company employed, they all shared one trait – all avoided a dependence on London and thus gained greater control over various world markets. With this pattern in mind, we can return to the individual markets and determine more specifically how and when the American film industry came to control each.

The Far East and India
Despite Universal's 1916 branch opening in Japan, the American film made slow progress in that market during the war. Two firms had extensive control over distribution and exhibition in Japan and Korea – the Nippon Katsudo Shashin Co. and the Tennen-Shoku Katsudo Shashin Co. As of 1917, these companies would buy films as cheaply as possible on the London open market, show them in their own first-run theatres, and rent the used prints to smaller theatres for as little as 2 cents a foot. Such cheap rentals tended to keep other distributors out of the market; this problem was a lingering result of signing Far Eastern rights over to London firms. In 1916, French, Italian and British dramas were still the most common in Japanese theatres; American comedies were used and the serial was beginning to be popular in Japan – Kalem's *The Hazards of Helen* was a hit. But the major American brands of features remained too expensive for Japanese theatres. (This may help explain why a cheaper American brand, Universal's Bluebird, could have had an early success there.)[25] Nevertheless, with declining supplies from European producers, Japan depended increasingly on American films; Universal paved the way for other branch offices which opened there in the early 20s.

By 1916 American films were making some headway in China. The theatres were still mostly in the port cities, although a few now catered to the native population. In early 1916, an American official in Canton reported the brands most in use were Keystone, Trans-Atlantic (that is, Universal), Eskay [sic], Pathé and Vitagraph, with films coming from London or New York to exchanges in Hong Kong.[26] American films were gaining popularity, but the market was too undeveloped to warrant extensive attention; Pathé still controlled much of it.

Universal's Singapore branch, opened in 1916, and its subsequent moves into other small countries seem to have given it some significant share of that area's business. A theatre manager in Singapore reported that three firms were supplying theatres – Pathé, Universal and

Australasian. Universal handled more than its own films there; it had successfully imported the Italian epic *Salammbo* shortly after its branch began operating.[27]

Singapore was an important distribution centre for surrounding countries. Australasian had a relatively weak position; Universal and Pathé essentially competed for the bulk of the business. The increasing American share of this market and the considerable decline on the parts of France and Britain are apparent from the list of imports to the Straits Settlements, by percentage of total value, for 1913 and 1915 to 1919 (see Table V).[28]

TABLE V

Imports to the Straits Settlements

Source	1913 %	1915 %	1916 %	1917 %	1918 %	1919 %
Britain	48.5	42.1	41.4	37.4	32.3	33.0
France	19.8	11.5	6.8	8.6	2.4	8.2
Germany	9.2	–	–	–	–	–
Australia	8.0	10.3	1.6	4.4	0.9	0.8
British India	5.1	1.1	4.2	–	–	–
Italy	0.8	0.4	2.6	–	–	–
Hong Kong	0.7	–	4.2	4.2	3.5	9.2
Dutch India	–	12.9	4.8	5.0	3.7	8.1
Japan	–	1.6	4.1	3.4	6.8	11.4
Malay States	–	–	–	3.4	2.5	–
South Africa	–	–	–	–	2.0	0.5
Siam	–	–	–	14.9	19.5	4.3
USA	0.5	14.1	19.0	12.4	26.1	27.3

Note: these figures are somewhat misleading, since some of the films coming from other countries would also have been of American make – especially those from Australia and Britain. Used prints circulated among the smaller markets and would have made up the bulk of imports from India and Siam.

Singapore was a distribution centre for nearby countries, such as Siam; in Table VI there is a comparable list of the latter's film import sources by percentage of value.

Although the American share increases relatively little, the French and British shipments decline considerably. Films coming in from Singapore, as we have seen, must have been mostly from the Universal and Pathé branches there. Other markets where Universal established

75

TABLE VI
Siam's film import sources, 1914–17

Source	1914–15 %	1915–16 %	1916–17 %
USA	0.5	5.9	3.3
France	31.6	22.2	1.1
Hong Kong	0.2	0.6	0.2
Japan	5.7	2.3	3.8
Singapore	34.8	54.5	71.5
Britain	24.4	14.0	13.9

branches showed progress as well. In 1917, it was sharing the market in Java with Pathé, Eclair and several independent exchanges. American films were reportedly the most popular in that market. But there were still major problems to be solved in Eastern markets. Duping was difficult to prevent and used prints still dominated most markets.[29]

Pathé still largely controlled the Indian market, which also purchased films from Britain. Pathé's *Exploits of Elaine* serial was a hit, as it was in most countries. Chaplin and Keystone comedies were also popular. By April 1917, Universal had an office in Calcutta.[30] Within the next few years, however, India would rapidly fall under an almost complete domination by American films.

Central and South America
We saw in the previous chapter that during the war the American film industry had high hopes for South America as a replacement for the European market. But the move into that market did not occur for about two years. In February of 1915, a South American commentator pointed out that European producers had established a market in South America; in 1914, Argentina imported $44,775 worth of European films and only $4,970 of American films. Other large countries used about the same proportions, with smaller countries getting even fewer American films. The main problem, he stated, was the distributors, who wished to keep American films out of the market because cheaper films were available from Europe. He advised direct dealing with theatres to bypass these middlemen, the granting of credit and the translation of intertitles into good Spanish. The advice was good. Apparently American films had difficulty moving into South American markets even when European supplies dwindled. In late 1915, Colombian theatres were reportedly using mostly French and Italian films, in spite of the efforts of some American producers to

break into the market. The reason given was that American companies typically sent second-hand or inferior prints which looked poor in comparison with the European brands. Once European supplies lagged, Colombian theatres closed down or offered live acts in combination with films, rather than turn to American supplies.[31]

The established South American distribution firms were also major obstacles to an American breakthrough. The *Moving Picture World*, which took a particular interest in promoting the film trade in Latin America, reported at the end of 1915 that only about 15% of the films used there were of American origin: 'Strong combinations which we would call independent exchanges held a dominant position and in Chile and Brazil controlled perhaps seventy per cent of the business. The combination bought next to nothing in the American market. It was in turn influenced and at times controlled by leading European producers.' But it advised: 'This is the best time to reach out for the South American market. Banking facilities are better than ever before; transportation has been vastly improved; the old prejudice against the Yankee is rapidly dying out.' Despite gradual improvements, however, the film industry faced the same problems in Latin America as did manufacturers of other products – the lack of American banking facilities to extend credit and the problem of shipping facilities. In addition, the film exporters had not yet mastered the techniques of selling there. The chief of the Bureau of Labor in Puerto Rico wrote to the *Moving Picture World*: 'In our opinion, the transportation on foreign vessels, the long installments for payment, etc., which American commerce encountered, are of secondary importance as compared with the greatest cause preventing American commerce from getting its legitimate share of the business' – that is, that American salespeople still insisted on dealing in English.[32]

We have seen how American exports in general expanded during the war; during this period the government encouraged exchange with South America. On 10 December 1915, South American representatives attending the International Trade Conference in New York toured the Vitagraph studio there; they heard J. Stuart Blackton tell them that the South American film field had been greatly neglected and promise that Vitagraph would pay particular attention to it thereafter. A few months later, in April of 1916, the International High Commission met in Buenos Aires to discuss American–South American trade; the American section took with it a programme of Mutual, Universal, Vitagraph, Lubin, Thanhouser and World films, all provided by exporter Paul C. Cromelin. These were shown at the conference and to the public in Argentina.[33] In concentrating on South America, therefore, the film industry was following a shift in general American trade.

But the way was still blocked by two strong South American

distribution firms. In May 1916, only 12% of the films used in South America were of American origin. These two firms controlled most of the nineteen exchanges in South America and they were in a position to dictate to the theatre owners; in fact, they owned some theatres, mostly in Argentina. Because of this, they could obtain their films cheaply in Europe and ensure that theatres would use them.[34] The solution to this problem was direct dealing, with American firms setting up exchanges and renting to theatres themselves; but this took a considerable investment and knowledge of the market.

The tide turned in the second half of 1916. In June came the announcement that one of the biggest South American buyers was transferring its office from London to New York. In October, a new agency, the Empress Peliculas d'Luzo de America do Sul, opened its main office in Rio de Janeiro, with a policy of handling only high-grade American films.[35] But perhaps the main breakthrough came at about this same time with the direct sales of two American features – *Civilization* and *The Birth of a Nation*.

The advent of expensive American feature films in the mid-teens seems to have led to a new method of selling abroad. Rather than simply selling the rights to such films to agents, American companies sometimes sent representatives abroad to negotiate high prices in individual countries. In a sense, this procedure was a transition into the later method of dealing directly in a variety of countries, rather than through agents in a few key locations. *Civilization* was the first film which the trade papers reported as being sold in this way. One representative, for example, went to Japan and sold seven prints for the Oriental territory. He reported that he had to hurry to beat the spread of duped prints, which typically appeared in the Orient shortly after a film premièred. By late 1917 *Civilization* had completed a successful run in Calcutta. J. Parker Read Jr. was in charge of the sales in Central and South America. He found it necessary to tour all the countries separately, copyrighting the film in each to prevent duping. It took him six months, but he obtained $20,000 for the Argentinian rights and the same for Brazil and Uruguay (about $150,000 in 1982 terms); this was a record price at the time. Early in 1916, a Famous Players representative spent four months in the South American market, showing *Tess of the Storm Country*, *Carmen* and other films, directly to theatre managers, who professed themselves amazed at the high quality of American pictures; reportedly they had been shown only inferior American pictures by the controlling distribution companies.[36]

The first trade-paper article to crow over American progress rather than railing against an indifference to South American markets was a report on the success of *The Birth of a Nation*: 'Let's give credit where credit is richly deserved. In this case the laurel wreath belongs on the brow of David W. Griffith – a brow now thoroughly used to such floral decorations.' According to the *Moving Picture World*, 'the landslide came with Griffith and with Griffith's South American standard bearer, a capable young man by the name of Guy Croswell Smith. Now all South America talks about the marvellous Yankee pictures. They want to see more of them.' Smith had taken *The Birth of a Nation* to Buenos Aires in the winter of 1915–16 and had shown it at the Teatre de la Opera to tremendous response; it ran for over 200 performances. This success repeated itself in Chile, Peru, Bolivia and Uruguay. By the time Smith was preparing to return to South America with *Intolerance*, he had extensive advance bookings. From late 1916 on, South American theatre owners and audiences became aware of the quality of recent American films; the distribution monopolies became less significant as direct dealing increased.[37]

By December 1916, the *Moving Picture World* was gloating over the results: 'The Yankee invasion of the Latin-American film market shows unmistakable signs of growing serious. It may before long develop into a rush as to a New Eldorado.' It pointed to the newly formed South American Film Service Corp. of New York, which controlled eighty-one cinemas in Buenos Aires; this firm had contracted to handle Metro, Universal, Vim and various independent features. Some firms were still allowing their British agents to handle South American rights, but others, like Fox and Mutual, were controlling their own sales, through American agents or South American offices. One correspondent reported late in 1916: 'What little there is left of French and Italian films in this country proves how complete had become the American invasion of this market.' Fox, with its own South American branches just open, reported an enormous business.[38]

By early 1916 the American hold on South American markets was apparent. An American consul found American films playing on virtually every programme in Buenos Aires' 130 theatres. Reportedly 60% of Argentina's 1916 imports came from the USA. Department of Commerce export figures for Brazil, which had been negligble from 1912 to 1914, showed a slight rise in 1915 and another noticeable rise beginning in about December 1916. (Unfortunately, figures for Argentina, the other main point of entry to distribution in South America, were not kept separately until mid-1918, but they show an already-developed market.)[39]

The American dominance in the large markets took time to filter down into the outlying areas served by importers in Brazil and Argentina. In the spring of 1916, American films were reported to be the main ones used in Chile, but they still competed with significant numbers of Italian and French pictures. Importation was only gradually switching from London to direct sources in the USA. But in Ecuador, most of the films still came from France, Italy or Spain, with only an occasional one coming from the USA. In May, one of the most powerful South American distribution chains, the Sociedad General Cinematografica, was beginning to break away from Italian sources and to depend increasingly on American films (particularly Famous Players, Lasky, Pallas, Morosco, Triangle, and Vitagraph). Brazil had gone over to American films almost entirely by this point. The *Moving Picture World*'s Latin American specialist declared:

American manufacturers two years ago shipped their films to London and thought that they were covering the export field, blissfully ignorant of the fact that their Spanish-speaking neighbors would have had a shock if anybody had told them that we were producing here something else besides crude 'cowboy stuff'. Some good American pictures found their way there, but the Southerns did not know it. In nearby countries like Cuba and Mexico, even the importers were under the impression that Selig was a London firm, Vitagraph Parisian, and that the studios of Thanhouser were located in the suburbs of Berlin.

Between the first three months of 1916 and the same period for 1917, official Argentinian import figures showed an almost complete switch from European to American sources.[40]

By May of 1918, most of the major South American exchanges had buying agencies in New York. Some exporters were worried about the post-war prospects, but the *Moving Picture World* assured them that the chairman of the American Shipping Board promised weekly service to Rio de Janeiro, Buenos Aires and Caracas by 1920 and two steamers were already leaving the west coast for Valparaiso. There were similar plans for shipping to Central America. It would not be necessary to go back to dealing through London for markets so close to the USA. Shortly after the war ended, *Scientific American* reported: 'Leading South American film men declare they will never go back to dependence upon European markets, as they have found the American films greatly superior to European productions.'[41]

The same sequence of events occurred in other Latin American and Caribbean countries, with American films gaining a hold only in 1916. As of 1916, Curaçao, in the Dutch West Indies, had only recently had its first two theatres open, using mostly French films. Guatemala City saw Pathé, Gaumont, Itala, Roma, Torino, and Nordisk films, with a few used American prints coming through. There were two theatres in the North Honduras district; they obtained most of their films from Guatemala City. American films were simply too expensive there, running $23 a night in rentals; European films could be shown for about $18. Panama was showing a fair number of American films by 1916.[42]

As American films filtered into these countries, they gained popularity. A *Moving Picture World* description of exhibition in a Puerto Rican movie theatre suggests the impact that some American stars must have had. The theatre had been using Italian and French dramas, but in the winter of 1915–16 showed *Tillie's Punctured Romance*, introducing Chaplin to audiences: 'It is easy to imagine what a relief this is after suffering two reels with Madame Fulana de Tal, the famous Hungarian artiste, while she tries to decide whether to poison her husband with arsenic.' By late 1916 Puerto Rico had gone over almost entirely to American films. The Dutch West Indies were still supplied with European films, coming via Caracas, Venezuela; of Panama City's three theatres, one used only Spanish and Italian films, while the other two got their supplies from New Orleans. (In the Canal Zone, the YMCA was showing American films, including *The Birth of a Nation* and *Civilization*.) Mexico remained the most problematic of the Latin American markets. Due to the civil war there, both economic problems and the difficulty of shipping kept American firms away. By early 1916 Mexico's currency had dropped off to less than one-fifth of its pre-war strength in relation to the American dollar; later that year the currency was stabilised and the *Moving Picture World* hinted that Mexico was ripe for American entry. But after the USA went into World War I, the American government placed very strict limitations on exports of films to Mexico and it was not until 1919 that conditions settled down enough to make it a viable market.[43]

Australia and New Zealand
As we have seen, American films were well on their way to taking over Australia and New Zealand during the early part of the war. By mid-1916 an official of one large import and distribution company estimated that there were about 600 theatres in Australia. Most films came directly from the USA; only 'the small stuff' came from Britain. In December 1917, an American consul reported the number of theatres had risen to 800; the programmes were much like those in the USA and averaged about 95% American-made films. During 1916 there was one theatre in the central distribution city, Sydney, called the Lyceum-Triangle; it showed Triangle films and put out a newsletter for its customers – the *Triangle News*. One big Sydney exhibitor, visiting the USA to study exhibition methods, declared that American films were virtually the only ones known in Australia. And in November of 1917, the biggest distributor, Australasian Films Ltd, with its seventy Union Theatres joined the First National Exhibitors' Circuit (the large American distribution/exhibition chain), enjoying the same status as that organisation's American members. As of 1918 Australasian had rights to Triangle, Select, World, Vitagraph, Pathé, and others, in addition to First National; it distributed to the Fiji Islands, the Far East, New Zealand, British New Guinea and Java. By

81

the end of the war, Universal and Paramount films were the top American brands there – as we might expect, given their early concentration on western Pacific markets. An American exporter declared that virtually every picture produced in the USA eventually made its way to Australia; the only other product in use was a small supply of British topicals.[44]

New Zealand followed a similar trend. In Table VII, the shift in sources for imported films between 1914 and 1918 is apparent.[45]

TABLE VII

New Zealand imports in 1914 and 1918

Source	1914		1918	
	Value ($)	% of total	Value ($)	% of total
Britain	80,331	43.6	16,234	3.9
Australia	27,057	14.7	15,178	3.6
USA	59,152	32.1	386,253	92.1
France	16,770	9.1	–	–
Other	1,012	0.5	1,678	0.4
Total	184,322		419,343	

Note: these are the sources of the prints, not necessarily the countries where the films were made; much of the footage coming in from Britain and Australia would have been of American origin as well, especially in 1914. Such evidence makes very plausible the estimations during the period, which consistently place the American control of these markets at about 95% by the end of the war.

Britain

We have already looked at the British market to some extent in dealing with the decline of London as the centre of American world distribution. Here we need only consider a few other events that affected the British domestic market specifically. In the summer of 1915, Essanay's London office made the decision to stop selling its films to renters on the open market; beginning 30 September it would rent its product directly to the theatres on an exclusive-contract basis only. The reasons Harry Spoor, head of the office, gave for the switch were the recent move from shorts to features and the immense popularity of Essanay's newly acquired star, Charlie Chaplin. Sold on the open market, too many Chaplin prints would go out of Essanay's control (and the unspoken assumption was probably that used prints would undercut profits in non-European markets). The system amounted to block-booking, since Essanay forced each exhibitor to take three reels of its films each week in order to get the Chaplins. Exhibitors were hard hit, since fewer of them could show Chaplins first-run and since they had to take some unwanted films. There were reports of protests among local branches of the Exhibitors' Association, but Essanay went ahead with the plan.[46]

Although Essanay itself was soon to decline and disappear, its new policy marked a general turning point in the British distribution system. Over the next five years, that system turned completely around, so that theatres contracted sometimes for one or two years in advance, for films which had not yet been previewed, or even made. Britain went from being one of the most flexible, open markets in the world to one of the most rigid, closed ones. The system perpetuated the American firms' advantage, since it kept the theatres tied to their larger outputs, eliminating open playdates into which other countries' films might slip. (The 1927 Quota Act was to outlaw block-booking.)

In late 1915 the *Bioscope* began analysing what the American takeover meant for British production; the British film-maker's

> market is so restricted by circumstances that he simply cannot afford to spend so much money on his pictures as his American rival. In consequence, it is inevitable that through no fault of his own his work must often be inferior to American work upon which money has been lavished by manufacturers possessing practically limitless sources of profit.[47]

This plaint, which would be repeated many times, summed up the situation in which the British film has remained ever since. During the post-war period, when other producing countries – Germany, France and the USSR in particular – sought distinctive alternatives to Hollywood film-making which they could afford on smaller budgets, the British producers opted for the most part to imitate Hollywood; without sufficient capital, the results were a series of pale copies which

TABLE VIII

Value of films shown in Britain in 1916

Source	Value ($)	Percentage
USA	3,885,000	78.8
Britain	483,500	9.8
France	337,500	6.8
Other	221,550	4.5
Total	4,927,550	

simply could not compete on the international market.

How much of the British market did American films actually control? Returning from a trip to Britain on Triangle's behalf, Roy Aitken estimated the share at about 75%. Figures on the value of films shown in Britain during 1916, given by the *Moving Picture World*, suggest that this was quite an accurate guess (see Table VIII).

American consuls surveying various districts during 1917 made similar estimates. By the end of 1917, a Bristol paper claimed that 90% of the films in that area were American, and that figure was consistently given in the immediate post-war era as well.[48]

Europe

Germany, which had been such a good customer for American films before the war, took advantage of the elimination of French, Italian and British imports to build up its own industry. At first American imports continued. But in the spring of 1916, the *Reichkanzler* put out a list barring certain dispensable goods, including film; the stated purpose was to improve the country's balance of trade and strengthen its currency. An exception was made for the Danish firm Nordisk, which had invested heavily in distribution and exhibition within Germany. Older prints of American films seem to have continued to circulate, but the market was effectively lost for the second half of the war. Not until the 20s would the American firms succeed in regaining significant distribution there. Indeed, the American industry knew little about what was going on in German film circles. When in 1918 reports reached the USA that a 'Universal Film Co.' had been started in Berlin (that is, the Universumfilm Aktiengesellschaft, or UFA), there was considerable indignation and Carl Laemmle issued a statement that this new firm had nothing to do with *his* company.[49]

Germany also exercised a considerable control over the neutral and occupied markets surrounding it. As of 1916, Holland was reportedly using more films from France, Italy, Germany and Denmark than from the USA. A similar situation existed in Switzerland, which had obtained about half its supplies from France before the war. By the end of 1916, an American official surveyed the situation in some detail and reported that the German and the Italian film each controlled about one-quarter of the market, the French only 20%, with Nordisk, American brands and a few Swiss films dividing the remaining 30%. (American films were sent in from Paris, primarily to the French-speaking districts, via Geneva.)[50]

In Scandinavia, American films made some headway. They were reported as predominant in Norway in later 1916. Even Denmark, with its well-established native production, began to use American brands increasingly at about this same time; an American consul noted in November that American imports had recently seen greater use, with all the major companies' works being shown. And in mid-1917, shortly after he opened the New York branch of Olsen & Co., the major buying firm for Scandinavian distributors, John Olsen confirmed this:

It was only about a year ago that we discovered an increased demand for American pictures. Prior to that time our patrons wanted only the Italian and German pictures. They said the American pictures were too jerky and speedy. Last season [that is, autumn 1916 to spring 1917] we made arrangements for Triangle pictures and these, I think, paved the way for others. Now American subjects are in the greatest demand, and have practically eliminated the old pictures.

But American films did not obtain a complete hold on these markets. Denmark retained its close ties with the German industry. During the war, Sweden built up its native production, taking advantage of its neutral position to export; this, in combination with the decline in French and Italian imports, permitted a brief flowering of the Swedish film from the mid-teens to early 20s. Apparently American exporters also experienced some interruptions in shipping to Scandinavia after the American entry into the war. But, as we shall see, American government efforts were to aid in promoting the Hollywood product in Scandinavia in the last year of the war.[51]

While American exports declined in Germany and met with limited success in northern European markets, they increased in France and Italy and in those markets which had formerly depended heavily upon these two producing countries – for example, Spain.

In both France and Italy, the turning point seems to have come in 1917. As of mid-1915, an American consul found half the film used in the Florence district to be Italian, with 25% French, 15% German and a small percentage American. Italian production virtually closed down in July of that year, just before the Italian declaration of war on Turkey on 25 August; much of the film-making personnel had been mobilised. But by late September the industry had resumed production and kept going with some success for the duration. Indeed, for a while the interruption of imports into the country gave a boost to Italian production; one observer reported in October: 'Film producers are growing in Italy like mushrooms. Every day sees the opening of new studios. In two months we have noticed the Paris, Re, Fulgor, Sphinx, and I hear a few more are still building studios.'[52]

During 1915 and 1916, Italy continued to produce films and to compete with the American industry in* world markets fairly successfully – more so, apparently, than France was able to do. In the autumn of 1915, the *Bioscope* suggested that Turin might be taking over

Paris' earlier position as a centre of world film trade. Production was nearly at pre-war levels, although transportation made export somewhat difficult. A year later, a Cines Co. official declared that, although Italian films had lost their place in the British market, they were doing well in southern European countries and in South America. The *Moving Picture World* claimed at this same time that Italian production had in fact increased by about 25% in the past two years, with the main foreign market being South America. (This tallies with what we have seen occurring in the South American markets, with American firms not winning the battle with Italian and other European firms until late 1916.)[53]

In December of 1916, American films were still having trouble competing on the Italian market because Italian dealers found them too expensive compared to native productions. But during the next year, the Americans began to succeed noticeably in Italy. In July 1917, an Italian writer found that 'There has been the danger of an American invasion, but, compared with the enormous variety of interesting native productions, American films are really very few.' Only Famous Players-Lasky and Vitagraph had made any impact. But by September, Triangle was reported as being very successful in introducing its first film, *The Coward*, in Italy; it and *Intolerance* helped to show the Italians the quality of American films. In October, Italian productions were said to be declining in number compared with Triangle and Famous Players-Lasky films.[54]

Italy's main problem was its rapid loss of ground in South America by this point; without the income from that market, producers had greater difficulty in amortising films and hence in reinvesting in new projects. Shortly after the Armistice, the *Moving Picture World* summarised the situation:

> During the past two years, Italian pictures have ceased to be an important commercial factor in Latin America, and despite the indifference of the American manufacturers in general, does not seem to be able to hold her own in Spain and Portugal. She is even threatened in her home market.[55]

A table of Italy's exports during the war (with raw and exposed film totalled together, but the bulk of the footage being exposed film) shows that exports peaked in certain key markets, including France, Brazil and Argentina, by 1916 (see Table IX). After 1917 exports declined for all destinations; total exports declined steadily throughout the war.[56] By late 1917 American competition had reduced Italy's overseas markets and made considerable inroads within that country as well.

In France, the first few months of the war had been the most disruptive. By late August the German offensive had pushed

TABLE IX
Italy's exports, 1914–19 (in kilograms)

Destination	1914	1915	1916	1917	1918	1919
Austria/Hungary	12,379	–	–	–	–	–
France	16,394	21,566	24,531	16,214	11,513	17,172
Germany	6,196	–	–	–	–	–
Britain	27,382	3,658	3,650	3,556	2,351	1,671
Russia	2,248	1,513	10,487	3,936	–	–
Spain	5,611	14,445	11,717	11,941	10,506	8,394
Switzerland	1,962	4,416	5,044	3,427	1,862	9,042
Brazil	12,077	10,122	6,513	4,217	3,387	1,429
Argentina	8,284	11,421	8,212	4,908	2,651	2,489
USA	3,347	4,364	2,103	2,587	1,507	463
Other	8,722	30,686	13,710	13,712	13,156	15,642
Total	104,602	102,191	85,967	64,498	46,933	56,302

dangerously close to Paris and the French government withdrew to Bordeaux. From October to November, the German 'race to the sea' occurred. This offensive halted near Ypres, in western Belgium; all along the front began the trench warfare which was to characterise the combat on land. The front was stable, with most of Belgium and much of northern France in German hands and the battles that followed would fail to shift it significantly until early 1917. By 7 December 1914 the Paris Bourse re-opened and later that month the government returned to Paris. Life in the unoccupied areas of France began to recover somewhat and to adjust to wartime conditions.[57]

French film production recovered to a degree during 1915 and distributors could depend to some extent on the backlog of pre-war negatives. But the French market also began to absorb more American, Italian and British films than it had in the past. During 1915 and 1916, a number of American stars and films captured the popular and intellectual audiences of France for the first time. The French fascination with these films would carry over into the post-war period, when many of the major critics and film-makers would be influenced by them. The Pearl White serials, the first Chaplin comedies, Thomas Ince's productions and Cecil B. De Mille's *The Cheat*, all took Paris by storm; they were followed in the next years by the early films of William S. Hart and Douglas Fairbanks, which gained an equal hold on the French imagination.

By 1916, the trend was apparent in various parts of France. In St Etienne, American films had increased in number and regularity on cinema programmes; in February the first American serial had arrived and was playing at several theatres. The same was true at Le Havre, where a typical programme was described as consisting of the playing of all the Allies' national anthems, a scenic on Seville, a four-reel French drama, *The World of the Enigma*, an intermission, war newsreels, an episode of *The Exploits of Elaine* – 'It is extremely popular here' – and a French short with the comic Rigadin. One consul summarised the situation:

Prior to the war the weekly production in France of new films was estimated at 25,000 meters (82,020 feet) to 30,000 meters (98,425 feet), while at present probably it does not exceed one-third of that amount. In consequence, French firms are importing films in larger quantities, particularly from Italy and the United States.

Table X shows the amounts of film from various countries shown in France in late 1916 and early 1917.

TABLE X

Sources of films shown in France, December 1916 and January 1917

| Source | December 1916 | | January 1917 | |
	Metres	Percentage	Metres	Percentage
France	28,879	33.3	29,348	37.0
Italy	21,980	25.4	16,454	20.7
USA	24,136	27.8	24,099	30.4
Britain	11,677	13.5	9,374	11.8
Denmark	–		125	0.2
Total	86,672		79,400	

Sadoul has estimated that before the war French films made up about 80% of those shown in its domestic market; Italy and the USA had made considerable inroads by this point.[58]

The American film's success in France, and elsewhere as well, was due in part to fundamental changes that were going on in Hollywood film-making. Elsewhere Janet Staiger and I have described the mid-teens as a period during which the classical Hollywood cinema had nearly completed the formulation of its basic systems, both in terms of its mode of production and its stylistic approach. The feature film was becoming the standard of virtually all programming in America. Popular stars were under contract to studios and made a succession of films quickly, while in Europe film companies still borrowed their actors from the stage on an irregular basis. A systematic division of labour, based on careful planning through a scenario, was making Hollywood's studio system highly efficient. Stylistically, the familiar continuity editing devices were fast becoming standard guidelines for constructing a narrative film and increasing attention to art direction, artificial lighting and canons of beautiful cinematography gave the finished films a polished look unknown in the pre-war period.[59]

To French audiences, who had seen relatively few American films and had not watched these changes emerge gradually, the revelations of the mid-teens American films were stunning. Some commentators became defensive, asserting that French films still could compare favourably with the American product. Others sought ways to improve the domestic product so that it could once more compete at home and abroad. *Le Film* ran editorials in the latter vein during 1916. Henri Diamant-Berger claimed that the war had simply accelerated a decline already in progress:

> What have our producers done? Nothing over the long months. Then, when they timidly wanted to get back up a little to normal, they have been content to imitate that which came to them from elsewhere. They have thus acknowledged the weakness which already overtook them before the war. It is no longer a question of engaging in a ferocious struggle against foreign production; it is simply a question of doing better.

The average French film, he argued, was still good, but the producers did not make an effort to publicise and sell it well. (Ironically, this was the same argument American trade papers had used against American companies in the early months of the war.) And, he declared, there were few great French films at all. Diamant-Berger's colleague, Camille Bardou, followed up this editorial in mid-1916, by claiming that French production had become routine: 'Our art, modernised, well understood, well conducted, will save our cinematographic industry better than will protectionist laws. Let us organise.'[60]

By 1917 the American dominance was apparent. The French could only hope to regain their original place once the war ended; one trade paper editorialised in early 1917:

> At this moment we are rapidly losing our grip on the world markets. In the scramble for the place we held abroad, a new producing centre has appeared in competition and is forging ahead of all others. Powerful in money and other material resources, its success

seems assured for the time being. Will it be able to retain the international trade when conditions become normal?

We do not think so; in fact, we are sure it will not. France will come again into her own, as a river follows its even course after the storm.[61]

At the same time, Pathé's *Iron Claw* serial and *Tillie's Punctured Romance* were among the hits of the Parisian theatres. The French companies were aiding the USA, since they had to distribute American films in order to fulfil their contracts to theatres. Indeed, French distributors and theatres were to become so dependent on the American product that they subsequently resisted the producers' efforts to limit imports after the war. Paris was even beginning to follow London's pattern, gaining part of its film income by distributing the films of other countries: 'Paris is the center of the Latin market and many American and English brands deal through Paris with their Swiss, Italian, Spanish, and even Oriental and South American markets.' In early 1918, some French producers were adopting the star system in imitation of American methods. By July, *Le Film* reported that French export had virtually ceased because the films simply were not available; foreign branches of French distributors were becoming more independent of their parent firms, distributing and even producing non-French films.[62]

In the smaller or less prosperous markets of southern Europe, the higher-priced American films encountered some resistance. Spanish exhibitors were still using mostly Nordisk, French and Italian dramas, only investing in American films for the comic-short section of their programmes. Hence Keystone was one of the few brands shown regularly. Used prints were still undercutting the newer product. By late 1916 Italian brands, Pathé and Gaumont, the London Film Company, and Universal's European branch, Trans-Atlantic, dominated imports; Triangle films were just becoming known. But even by early 1918 Frank J. Marion, head of Kalem, found Triangle films made two years earlier still circulating, with no Fairbanks or Fox films to be seen. The Sociedad General Cinematografica Argentina met with resistance in trying to distribute Famous Players, Lasky, Fox, Vitagraph and World films, because the prices were still high; it succeeded only by renting theatres and showing the films itself. Yet according to trade-paper statistics, the American share of the market appears to have been the largest – although much of the footage involved may have been used prints (see Table XI).[63]

Russia and eastern Europe were among the few areas where American films actually lost ground during the war. This was due in part to currency problems. In 1915, the rouble was down in terms of buying power; the pre-war rate had been 9.5 to the British

90

TABLE XI

Spanish imports in December 1916 and April/May 1918

| Source | December 1916 | | April/May 1918 | |
	Metres	Percentage	Metres	Percentage
France	17,918	13.4	15,000	10.0
Italy	38,620	28.8	50,000	33.3
USA	53,607	40.0	70,000	46.7
Spain	10,121	7.5	15,000	10.0
Scandinavia	13,900	10.4	–	
Total	134,166		150,000	

pound, but the rouble had now fallen to 13 or 14 to the pound. This made obtaining British or American films difficult. But lack of transport into Russia was the primary cause of the decline in imports and the bolstering of the isolated domestic industry. In late 1916, the *Moving Picture World* reported that an American traveller had taken *The Fall of a Nation*, the first American spectacle film to be shown in wartime Russia, to Petrograd on an ocean liner via Finland; the film was to première in November and ten prints would circulate. The main distribution companies in Moscow were Pathé, Gaumont, and Khadjankov; they had trouble obtaining any American films. Because of the depressed rouble, the cost had risen from 8 to 9 cents per metre to about 18 cents. As a result, theatres were increasingly dependent on Russian films. Given that even before the war, only 10 to 15% of films shown in Russia came from the USA, the decline must have meant that few new American films were entering Russia by the time of the Revolution. After the war, films continued to circulate in old prints until channels of exchange were set up through Berlin in the early 20s. Transportation difficulties also virtually eliminated American films from other eastern European markets, many of which were still part of the Central Powers.[64]

Summary

The key to the USA's continued hegemony after the war lies in the fact that the film industry ceased to focus so exclusively on Europe, both as a market and as a point of world distribution. As Table A.III (in Appendix II) shows, in the fiscal year 1913, Europe received over one-half the exported films; sales to Europe and North America (primarily Canada) accounted for nearly nine-tenths of all exported footage. Just before the war (fiscal year 1914), Canada's share was rising, as was

91

Oceania's (Australia/New Zealand), but areas like South America and Asia remained negligible.

This trend continued during the early part of the war. But in the fiscal year 1916, the period of large increases in the USA's exports, the USA sent nearly 80% of its footage to Europe. After mid-1916, however, as we have seen, American exporters turned increasingly away from London as a distribution centre and set up more direct means of selling to world markets. This shows up in Table A.III, beginning in the fiscal year 1917 with a more even spread of shares among the areas of the world. South America took more exported American footage, for example; its purchases quadrupled between 1915–16 and 1916–17, then doubled the next year. Similar jumps upward occur in exports to Asia; even Africa, which had had virtually no direct dealings with the USA, increased its percentage of American exports several times over.

After the war ended a great percentage of American exports once more went to Europe, but never at the pre-1917 levels. Throughout the 20s, proportions of exports remained distributed more evenly across the world than they had been before the changes in distribution methods during the late war period. By the war's end, American exports had reached a point of stability which would aid in maintaining a long-range hegemony.

EFFECTS OF THE AMERICAN ENTRY INTO THE WAR

As Chart 2 (in Appendix III) shows, the total footage exported from the USA fell in July 1917, shortly after the USA's April entry into the war. Although exports rose again later that year, the totals remained somewhat low until the end of the war, when they rose to approximately their pre-entry level. There were two reasons for the decline. First, the American entry caused a slight slowdown in general film production. The National Board of Review, which passed on 99% of the films made in the USA at that time, examined 4,113 films totalling 9,180 reels in 1916; this dropped to 3,114 films, or 8,436 reels, during 1917. The main decline came in the month before the declaration of war and lasted for about two months. Assuming some lapse of time between production and export, this decline in production would help to account for the low level of exports from July to October 1917.[65]

Secondly, and more importantly, government regulation increased at this point, hindering the process of sending films abroad. In July, President Wilson issued a list of items which required a licence to be exported; film was among them. He stated: 'The purpose and effect of this proclamation is not export prohibition but merely export control.' The provision went into effect 30 August and covered exports to virtually every country. American troop transports to Europe had begun in June and the provision gave the government the power to control shipping space. As with the comparable British regulation, another purpose was probably to assure that films did not go through neutral countries into Germany. For the next several months, export was delayed for individual films, but there was little interference by the government to stop any films from going out. On 16 February 1918, a new set of regulations went into effect, more strict than the original ones; again the purpose was to license imports and exports so as to control shipping space for troops and materials. Initially this provision seems to have had little impact, since film negatives took up so little space in comparison with other types of goods.

Then, on 15 July, all types of exposed and unexposed films were added to the Export Conservation list, making film an essential good for war purposes. The new restriction caused film exports to drop to their lowest level since 1915. Exports to South America were embargoed during July and August. During August, the film industry persuaded the government to agree to less stringent regulations; as we shall see, this loosening may have been due to the industry's co-operation with the government's propaganda efforts. During the last months of the war, exports showed signs of a recovery, but there were shortages of American films in some countries. And, because the USA did not declare peace with Germany and the other opposing countries immediately, the regulations were left in force for some weeks after the war ended. The *Moving Picture World* warned in late November that South American orders were already showing signs of shifting back to London. Its Australian correspondent reported that a shortage of American films was resulting in revivals of older films. In December, the War Trade Board announced it was removing restrictions on the export of American films (except to Germany), although it seems to have taken over a month to clear the various films that were being held for censorship and licensing by various agencies. By February of 1919, exports were clearly on the increase.[66]

But if government regulation held down exports for a short time, another government activity may have aided the film industry's long-range prospects abroad. On 25 September 1916, the Committee on Public Information (widely known as the Creel Committee, after its chairperson, George Creel) formed its Division of Films. During the last year of the war, the Division of Films worked closely with the American commercial film industry, both domestically and abroad; by taking educational and commercial American films into markets around the world, the Division probably helped establish the American film more firmly in some areas.

Wilson took the occasion of the Division of Films' formation to give the government's blessing to the film industry:

It is in my mind not only to bring the motion-picture industry into the fullest and most effective contact with the nation's needs, but to give some measure of official recognition to this increasingly important factor in the development of our national life. The film has come to rank as the very highest medium for the dissemination of public intelligence, and since it speaks a universal language, it lends itself importantly to the presentation of America's plans and purposes.[67]

This was hardly the equivalent of Lenin's famous 'most important art' dictum, but it indicated that the government was prepared to co-operate with the industry in order to tap its propaganda potential.

The beginning of government–industry co-operation came when, at a request from the Secretary of the Treasury in May 1917, William A. Brady, president of the National Association of the Motion Picture Industry of America (NAMPI), called a meeting of important film figures. They appointed a committee to help co-ordinate the industry's co-operation with the First Liberty Loan Drive. This was a specific task, but there was need for more generalised co-operation. In early July, at the time of the formation of the War Industries Board and other government agencies designed to co-ordinate the war effort, Wilson requested Brady to call another meeting of NAMPI. By late July, Brady had helped form the War Co-operation Committee, with himself as president and D. W. Griffith as chairperson. The board was to be the liaison between the film industry and the Creel Committee, the various government departments, the Red Cross and the Council of National Defense, in arranging films on wartime goals. The board contained many prominent film figures, each assigned to a specific government department or national organisation. (Adolph Zukor and Marcus Loew were assigned to the Treasury Department!)[68]

These measures initially affected domestic matters only. But in October, Wilson asked Brady to set up methods for distributing American and Allied countries' films in France, Italy and Russia. NAMPI's War Co-operation Committee then set up a special group, the American Cinema Commission, to distribute films in Europe. Jules E. Brulatour, NAMPI's treasurer and an employee of Eastman Kodak, was to control which films the main office sent out. Volunteers would go to each country abroad and set up distribution and exhibition there. P. A. Powers (president of Universal) was appointed for France, Walter W. Irwin (general manager of VLSE) for Russia, and J. A. Berst (president of the Pathé Exchange) for Italy. Brulatour's advisory board in picking the films included Zukor, Goldfish, S. L. Rothapfel, Carl Laemmle and other prominent people in the commercial film industry. Eastman offered its full co-operation; the main office was in the Eastman building in New York City and the company volunteered its facilities in Paris, Moscow, Petrograd and Milan as well. All this work went on under the control of the Creel Committee. As one Division of Films representative declared in a mid-1918 interview:

It may be true to say that the Government has gone into partnership with the moving-picture industry to the end that the unique and tremendous power of the moving picture as an instrument of propaganda may be utilised to the fullest possible extent for the nation's needs.

(This was typical of the War Industries Board and other government groups as well; they used volunteers recruited from the highest levels of private industry and finance.)[69]

To be sure, at the very beginning, when the Division of Films was first formed in September 1917, the emphasis was to be on educational shorts and documentary material. Brulatour solicited donations from various manufacturers, with the idea of showing the American way of life to foreign audiences; he received industrial films from, among others, the Beechnut Packing Co., Edison, Eastman, General Electric, Heinz, Remington Typewriter and, above all, Ford (Ford films included *Ford Tractor*, *Ford Factory*). He also combed government agencies, such as the Public Health Service, for shorts and obtained access to the files of the newsreel companies for scenes of Americana. Programmes sent abroad were to kick off with this footage and lead up to scenes of Americans in combat. But, as Creel explained in his account of the Committee's activities, 'What the war-weary foreigners liked and demanded was American comedy and dramatic film. They had to have their Mary Pickford and Douglas Fairbanks and Charlie Chaplin and Norma Talmadge.' Creel perhaps purposefully leaves the timing of this realisation vague, implying that the Division of Films was only responding to a demand from abroad in its use of commercial films as well as educational ones. But, in fact, by November 1917 (two months after the Division's formation and shortly before the representatives went abroad), the *Moving Picture World* was reporting: 'It is the intention of the commission to send abroad at first pictures of an educational and topical description. When a goodly supply of these are on the way, they will be followed by comedies and five-part [that is, five-reel] dramatic subjects.'

Creel described how he obtained the co-operation of the film industry to acquire these commercial films. Since all films leaving the USA had to have a War Trade Board licence, Creel contacted the Board chairperson and got a ruling that every application had to be endorsed by the Creel Committee: 'the rest was simple'. Creel then called a meeting of the concerned film interests. The Committee promised to expedite film shipments, by dealing with red tape and obtaining shipping space. In turn, the industry officials agreed to three conditions: all export shipments would contain 20% 'educational matter' (this became part of the July 1918 regulations on film export); no American films would be rented to an exhibitor who refused to show Creel-sponsored films; and no American films would be rented to a theatre that showed German films. All this gave the Creel Committee considerable control over films leaving the country; eventually such measures were to be instrumental in combating German films in neutral countries.[70]

The American Cinema Commission seems never to have actually functioned abroad. Instead, the Creel Committee began operating its Foreign Section in October; this section had its own Foreign Film Division, which seems to have taken over the work of the ACC fairly soon. But Brulatour continued his work in the same way, still based in New York. Powers, Irwin and Berst apparently did not go abroad after all, but Frank J. Marion, president of Kalem, went to Spain to set up distribution for Committee films; soon, in fact, Marion became the general Committee commissioner for that country. Marion had trouble getting government-sponsored showings, due to Spain's neutrality; he ended up selling his educational films to a regular distributor, thus covering the films' costs and getting them disseminated. Aside from doing his job in arranging distribution, Marion cabled back to Creel concerning the commercial potential of the Spanish market; a system of American-owned exchanges there 'would greatly enhance my work', he declared, and he volunteered to assist any company wishing to open such exchanges. He also provided information on Spain to the American trade papers, which they duly printed. Pathé's Spanish branch helped with the duplication and titling of the films Marion had brought and as of early 1918 all was reported to be going well.[71]

The Creel Committee also controlled the American combat footage being filmed in France by the Signal Corps. (In mid-1918 the rate was estimated as 30,000 feet per week.) Some of this footage went into the Committee's weekly newsreel, the *Allied Nations' Official War Review*, which was put together by an international committee in New York; representatives of the USA, Britain and France could each include 250 feet of film relating to their respective country. This newsreel was initially distributed by the Pathé Exchange in the USA. Indeed, so close were the ties between the Creel Committee and the industry that Congress held an inquiry into the newsreel situation in July of 1918; the House of Representatives questioned Creel on whether an exclusive contract with Pathé defeated the purpose of wide distribution of the films. Creel replied that in all the Allied countries, official newsreels went through established distribution channels; the Committee series had been offered to the four American newsreel companies (Pathé, Universal, Mutual, and Gaumont), with Pathé the highest bidder. Of the proceeds from a minimum of 2,500 theatres, 80% went to the Creel Committee, to finance the making and distribution of films abroad. Creel declared: 'The funds received from these sources do not represent profit in any sense of the word.' All but one of the American film companies had agreed to this policy. Later, due to pressure either from within the industry or from Congress or both, Creel changed his policy, selling 2,000 feet weekly to each of the four newsreels for a flat $5,000.[72]

The Creel Committee dealings abroad were carried on in much the same way and ultimately benefited commercial film exporting. In countries with established exchange systems, the Creel films were premièred in a rented theatre in the main city, then turned over to a commercial distributor. When no distribution methods existed, representatives worked with the Red Cross, the YMCA, or set up travelling projection systems in areas without theatres (for example, in Siberia and parts of South America). Films went to Japan, Russia, South America, Mexico and, most successfully, to Europe. The Division of Films representatives visited various countries and established distribution during late 1917 and much of 1918.[73]

One of the Committee's first successes came when Guy Croswell Smith (who had sold *Birth of a Nation* and *Intolerance* in South America) went to Scandinavia in March 1918. At that point, he said, about half the films being shown were German. Because of the American film industry's co-operation in not renting to theatres that showed German films, Smith was able to reduce the German share considerably; just after the war he estimated it at only 3%, with films of the Allied nations (mostly the USA) making up 90%.

Llewellyn R. Thomas soon went to The Hague and used similar tactics successfully to combat German films in Holland. Significantly, most of the film used was not the educational material that was supposedly the Creel Committee's main tool. Thomas' footage consisted of 306,000 feet of dramatic films, 52,000 feet of comedies, 12,000 feet of Committee films and 92 reels of news material; of this he fashioned fifty eight-reel programmes – which probably were similar to those one would have seen in an American theatre. According to Creel's official *Report*, all the footage sent to Holland, 'Was sold, not given, to the Dutch exhibitors, for the total sum of $57,340.80 [$365,262 in 1982 terms], with a very considerable profit to the American producers, for whose future benefit, moreover, an American market was thus established.' The same procedure was less successful in Switzerland, where the German film was particularly firm, but there were signs by the time of the Armistice that Committee films were making some inroads. In December, Division head Charles S. Hart visited Switzerland and surveyed the Swiss distributors who wished to acquire the commercial American films used by the Committee. He chose Louis Ador (son of the Swiss president) and gave him a five-year contract on the films: 'Financial arrangements of this sale,' Creel reported, 'were such that we were able to satisfy the producers.' Thus the Creel Committee, in at least this one case, became a selling agent for the American industry.[74]

In Russia, two Committee representatives circulated films from headquarters in Moscow and Petrograd until the October Revolution. At that point they began working through the YMCA to distribute the films, but there proved to be no way of getting new footage to them. The representatives shifted operations to Archangel and Vladivostock, arriving there in September 1918; they received new material through Japan. They sent films all over Siberia through the Red Cross, YMCA, and military groups; again, the programmes included commercial features and comedy shorts. There were 1,500 reels in circulation, both rented to theatres and shown on portable machines; the population proved particularly interested in films on American agricultural methods. (Even though the Division of Films stopped operating in February 1919, the YMCA continued to circulate portable film theatres and American films from Vladivostock until at least late 1919.) A few Committee films were shown in Peking and Shanghai in rented theatres; in Japan they were circulated by existing distributors. Either through distributors, American embassies or the Red Cross, the films made their way throughout South America.[75]

Another indication of the Creel Committee's ties with commercial film-making comes in its production of three money-making features in 1918. These were distributed by commercial concerns and were very successful: as of 1920, *Pershing's Crusaders,* distributed by First National, had 4,189 bookings; *America's Answer,* distributed by World, had 4,548; and *Under Four Flags,* also distributed by World, had 1,820. Out of an estimated 12,000 theatres in the USA, this was considered an extraordinarily high booking rate. This happened in part because the Committee was able to work outside the usual barring clauses in contracts, which give theatres exclusive rights within a certain district. This, the head of the Division estimated, boosted the films' distribution by 75%. On 26 June, *America's Answer to the Hun* (called *America's Answer* in the USA) premièred in Paris; it was distributed by Gaumont and Pathé. In July, the British Ministry of Information and Sir William Jury, head of one of the biggest distributing firms (later MGM's British distributor), co-operated in arranging the London première; Jury put the film into general release in August. The third feature, *Under Four Flags,* was handled in Britain by Pathé Frères Ltd – the reason being, a Division of Films representative explained, 'to get the film into the largest possible number of picture theatres and with the greatest possible expedition, and at the same time on a basis that will be fair and just to every exhibitor.' A regular commercial distributor

98

could have said no more. The features were shown commercially in other European countries as well.[76]

Charles S. Hart, director of the Division of Films, arrived in London in early December 1918, to close down the organisation in Europe. He pointed out that 'The U.S. Government now possesses a perfect moving picture organisation covering all the States and with exchanges in all the exchange cities.' The Division put out its own weekly paper, *The Official Film News*. And no doubt the Division had aided export, in part by becoming a sort of commercial distributor. Indeed, through the Division, the government had virtually gone into competition with the film industry. In late 1918, NAMPI representatives resolved 'that the National Government should forthwith discontinue its commercial competition with the motion picture industry by the rental of films for profits.' The Division of Films responded that it had not made profits, but only money to finance its operations abroad. Yet it had begun with a budget of only $10,000; at war's end it turned over a $580,000 ($3,694,600 in 1982) surplus to the Treasury. Clearly the volunteer labour, donations of educational films and the distribution through commercial distributors had made the government a very successful film producer and exporter; even leaving aside profits, the amount of screen time lost˙ to Committee films represented unwelcome competition.

The Division of Films finally closed down in February 1919. At that time Hart summed up what had probably been the government's most significant contribution to the commercial industry: 'The elimination of the German films was made possible by the patriotic service of the motion picture producers of the United States. They furnished such elaborate programs for our use in the foreign countries that the exhibitors there clamored for them.'[77] Thus, although government regulations caused a temporary decline in American exports during the war, the Creel Committee's activities aided in establishing films more firmly in some foreign markets, especially Scandinavia. The fight against German films was particularly significant, since the German industry emerged from the war in a relatively strong position and would be the only foreign industry to present a potential challenge to American hegemony during the post-war decade.

4 Maintaining the Lead, 1919-28

'We're getting a throttle-hold on the old world; it's all to the jazz and
the celluloid right now.'
Photoplay, 1923[1]

POST-WAR PROBLEMS

Events during the second half of the war had put the American film
industry in a strong position abroad. The move from London to New
York as a distribution centre for non-European markets reduced agent
selling and blanket contracts for world rights; most big American firms
now controlled sales in each major market. Moreover, American
shipping and financial facilities were improving, making New York the
logical permanent replacement for London. American films were
longer and had popular stars, lavish *mise en scène* and skilful
cinematography; during the war these changes in the Hollywood film
gained for it a definite following and other national industries would
have difficulty in creating films as attractive. Finally, the American
government supported the film industry actively – a thing most foreign
governments were initially unwilling to do.

Chart 2 (in Appendix III) shows that exports rose significantly after
the American government eliminated its wartime restrictions. In
general, export figures through the 20s reflect trends in the national
and world economies. During 1919 and 1920, most of the western
Allies and many other countries outside central and eastern Europe
experienced a brief, sharp business boom. With the abandonment of
wartime restrictions, demand rose quickly, driving prices up. Men
being demobilised got jobs making goods to satisfy this demand, and
high employment bolstered the inflationary trend. In the USA, this
boom lasted from about April 1919 to January 1920. Through 1920,
prices fell and unemployment rose, with 1921 bringing in a severe
depression; recovery began in 1922. Later, following reconstruction in
Europe and the stabilisation of most currencies in that region during
the mid 20s, a more sustained economic upswing began. The latter half
of the decade was again a boom period, leading up to the 1929
American stock-market crash and the decline of the world's economy

into the depths of the crisis in 1931. These business cycles are reflected in Chart 2, with a rise in exports in the years after the war, a downward trend throughout 1921 and gradual reversal late in 1922. During late 1924, as stabilisation began occurring on a widespread basis in Europe, exports rose more abruptly and remained at a high level until 1930. There is little evidence that the USA was in danger of any long-term loss of film business abroad.

In the months following the Armistice, American exporters and the trade press were cautiously optimistic. They assumed that European film industries would revive and offer competition abroad; yet they also expressed confidence that the large lead the USA enjoyed would allow it to stay ahead indefinitely. The Americans also welcomed the prospect of getting into markets previously shut off by the fighting. Lewis J. Selznick expressed the universal sentiment of the industry: 'The reopening of the European market is the big opportunity we have been awaiting for four years.'[2]

The export figures for the immediate post-war period show sales nearly equal to those of the best war year, 1916. Table XII shows monthly averages for footage and value for 1919 to 1921, compared with 1916.

TABLE XII

Average monthly American film exports by footage and value

	1916	1919	1920	1921
Average monthly footage	15,732,991 ft	13,582,025 ft	14,599,045 ft	11,740,362 ft
Average monthly value	$588,137	$679,787	$657,392	$542,797
Average price per foot	$0.037	$0.05	$0.045	$0.046

One noticeable aspect of these figures is that, while the post-war footage averages are lower, the prices are proportionately higher. (These figures reflect only the cost of the actual prints sent abroad; their earning power through rights and rentals would be much higher.) Inflation had occurred in the USA during the war and the post-war boom. Yet for the British buyer, the problem was exacerbated by the falling exchange rate of the pound against the dollar: $4.86 to the pound in 1916, hitting a low of $3.50 to the pound in late 1920, for a loss of 28% of British buying power. Thus, while the price rise in American currency was only 0.008 cents between these two years, the price in pounds for the British buyer rose about 64% between 1916 and 1920.[3] In fact, the American price hikes did not keep pace with

101

domestic inflation, but the distributors had to maintain low prices or risk losing European customers who simply could not afford to buy in dollars.

Until the mid-20s there was a lengthy struggle for currency stabilisation. Almost every currency except the dollar had depreciated, primarily as a result of the abandonment of the gold standard early in the war, the skewed balance of trade caused by war demands and the inflationary means most belligerents used to finance the fighting. The USA was in the strongest position, going back on the gold standard in 1919; the dollar became the currency against which others were gauged. Some of the countries that emerged from the war in a fairly strong condition managed to stabilise at pre-war parity (for example, Britain, Switzerland, Holland, Scandinavia and Japan); Britain went back on a gold standard in April of 1925. Others could only stabilise their currencies at levels significantly below those of 1913. This was the most common circumstance; in late 1928, for example, France returned to a gold standard with the franc at only 20% of its pre-war value. Those few countries that suffered hyperinflation during the early 20s (Germany, Hungary, Austria, Poland and Russia) could stabilise only by introducing a new currency.[4]

The dollar's strength in relation to all these other currencies created a trade barrier to exports. It became increasingly expensive for foreign distributors to purchase films priced in dollars. Conversely, currency depression tends to give a boost to a country's exports and a few producing nations of Europe took advantage of this fact to sell films abroad at prices below those of the American pictures. The central export issue in the trade papers from 1919 to 1922 was the dollar's all-too-favourable rate of exchange. Some began to fear that unless stabilisation were achieved, the USA would lose its dominance.

Exporters travelling in Europe in 1919 returned with hints of trouble to come. The president of the Export and Import Film Co. saw a German historical epic, Joe May's *Veritas Vincit*, in Copenhagen and compared it favourably with the pre-war Italian version of *Quo Vadis?* that had done well in the USA. David Howells found production up in France, Italy, Scandinavia, Germany and Britain: there 'the American film is beginning to lose ground, not because of any deterioration in quality, but because of the ruinous rate of exchange and the exorbitant demands of the American producer'. He advised exporters to lower prices, an idea which would become widespread in the next couple of years. By the end of 1919, the problem was obvious. William Vogel, another exporter, reported on a three-month tour of Europe:

> The most alarming situation confronting the American trade is the acute decline in the rate of exchange ... while the Yankee film manufacturer most inopportunely increases his arbitrary price for

exclusive rights to foreign markets, instead of trying to graduate them down to a practical basis and thus protect his own export future, the Briton, the Frenchman, the Italian, the German, and the Scandinavian are finding native film manufacture fostered for them in a way that they had never dreamed possible.

Yet another exporter, Chester Beecroft, circulated a message urging the film industry to lobby for the passage of a peace treaty between the USA and the Central Powers; the lack of such a treaty, he believed, was causing the currency fluctuations, since the USA was unable to make Germany the necessary loans to stabilise its currency. (Loans were indeed to play a vital role in the mark's stabilisation, but a three-year time lag would follow between the treaty and the Dawes Plan.)[5]

On all sides there was news of foreign markets opting for the cheaper European films. Max Glucksmann, one of the biggest South American importers, pointed out that French, Italian, British and German films were coming back into that market; he advised Americans to lower prices and follow the European practice of extending credit. The director of the Scandinavian Film Agency declared that, although Scandinavian audiences preferred American films, the buyers were were being forced toward German imports by the exchange rate. The krona, which had been 230 to $100, was now 570 for the same amount; but while 60 kroner had previously equalled 100 German marks, now only 10 kroner did so.[6]

Why did not the American exporters simply lower their costs to a competitive level as soon as the problem became apparent? One exporter estimated at about this time that 20 to 40% of a film's revenues were typically expected from foreign sales. Before and during the early years of the war the domestic market was enough to amortise a film, with revenues from abroad, beyond the cost of exporting, being profit. But according to Goldwyn's foreign representative, foreign sales had not been reckoned into the original budgeting of a film's negative cost before 1917; around that point, the revenues from abroad became a predictable, fixed portion of the negative cost. At the end of 1919, the *Moving Picture World* pointed out:

The foreign market, by enlarging the scope of the manufacturer, makes it possible for American pictures to be produced on a scale that warrants investments above $50,000.
If the foreign market becomes barren because foreign money is not stabilized the American producer cannot continue the sumptuous production of pictures the American public has learned to expect.

Lowering prices abroad would necessitate cutbacks in production values or reductions in profits.[7]

Some American exporters were complacent about the situation. On 1 January 1920, the *Bioscope* published an ingenuous letter from Carl Laemmle in which he explained that American film costs had risen in the last few years:

Hitherto, the foreign markets have had an easy time of it. They have not had to share their proportionate burden of the cost of production. The new conditions and the new costs, however, have forced an entire change in this respect. Pictures now cost so much that the markets of the whole world must assume their just share of the burden.

The next issue of the *Bioscope* carried a scathing reply, blaming the higher costs on the extravagance of the American studios. Pat Powers, writing in the *Moving Picture World*, reached the same conclusion; because films' costs were now based on worldwide revenues, he argued, the result was exorbitant fees paid to actors and for script rights. He urged producers to go back to basing costs on domestic revenues, thus enabling them to charge lower prices abroad. He also proposed that American exporters accept foreign currencies in payment, taking a temporary loss in order to protect their long-term hold on markets abroad.[8]

Presumably American firms did adjust their rates somewhat to meet the situation, for the debate died down by 1922. Certainly as each country stabilised its currency, it lost its barrier against American imports and its export advantage. In early 1923, when the Allies helped Austria with its currency situation, 90% of its films were reportedly coming from Germany. After stabilisation, there were forty American films to every five German; Fox quickly opened a Vienna office. By 1927, when most European currencies had been stabilised, Paramount's head of distribution reported:

They have this disadvantage in producing, that as money becomes stabilized on the other side their negative costs approach the basis that we are operating on here, but their revenue is limited, compared with ours. If they make a motion picture that costs $150,000, they have only one-fifth of the market in which to get their negative cost back.

Thus the post-war currency situation on the whole failed seriously to damage American prospects abroad.[9]

EUROPE IN THE 20S

The post-war currency problems in Europe presented a potential aid to

104

national film industries there. Currency depreciation, as we have seen, provides a trade barrier, making imported goods more expensive to buy, but allowing firms to export and undersell competition in markets with stronger monetary situations. In practice, this principle aided only those countries which were already in a position by the end of the war to take advantage of it. Germany, with its established companies and facilities, did profit considerably from its inflationary period by exporting films in the late teens and early 20s. Indeed, when Ernst Lubitsch's *Madame Dubarry*, retitled *Passion*, was released with great success by First National in the USA in late 1920, it seemed to start a trend. A few other German films – *Deception* (Lubitsch's *Anna Boleyn*), *The Cabinet of Dr Caligari* – were quickly brought out in early 1921 and some factions within the American industry were convinced that a 'German invasion' was underway. They lobbied for a high protective duty in the 1922 McCumber–Fordney Tariff. But it soon became apparent that few German films could compete in the USA and the ferment died down. Germany's currency situation did, however, make it a threat in many foreign markets.[10]

Members of the trade in the USA also feared that Britain, France and Italy would go into high gear in production. But they were in no condition to do so in more than a weak and sporadic fashion. Britain had fallen so thoroughly under American control that little capital was forthcoming for production; until the British quota of 1927, the USA continued to supply close to 90% of that country's film consumption. France, with the additional problem of the destruction of many theatres, had to face the long and difficult period of reconstruction; theatres were not high-priority items for the country's resources at that time. The Italian industry had a brief recovery, then declined during the 20s.

By 1924 it became apparent that the American hold on the European market was not going to decline under the influence of recovering production in various countries. Rather, the huge American market gave Hollywood film-makers an extensive financial base which most producing countries could not hope to match. In inflationary conditions Germany was briefly able to turn out epics like Lubitsch's *Loves of Pharaoh* and sell them cheaply abroad; yet with the beginnings of stabilisation in late 1923, this advantage disappeared. No one European market could sustain lavish film-making on the basis of domestic receipts alone. But in 1924 producers in a number of countries began to try and co-operate internationally within Europe to create a Continental market which could perhaps rival that of the USA. The result was a concept which had some impact for perhaps five years – until the introduction of sound changed the situation for the worldwide circulation of films. This concept was frequently known at the time as 'Film Europe', and its linchpin was the German industry.

105

Germany was crucial not only because it had emerged from the war
with a relatively strong industry, but because it resisted an American
takeover of its market for years after the war. The German
government's protective measures later became models for similar
legislation in other countries. As we have seen, in early 1916 the
German government had placed an embargo on inessential imports.
The American War Trade Board allowed films to be sent to Germany
as of 14 July 1919, but the permission did not mean the opening of free
trade. Apparently some films did make their way into Germany via the
nearby neutral countries; a salesman for one major export company
described having seen American films regularly in Berlin theatres
during 1919. But on the whole dealers were forced to wait to get large
quantities of film. Also in 1919, a saleswoman told of films 'all over
there at the gates, waiting for the German embargo to be lifted, not
over on this side, mind you, waiting to be shipped'. The embargo was
extended until May 1920 and some German companies were reported
to have block-booked their product into theatres for 1920 and 1921, in
order to prevent American films from flooding in.[11]

On 1 January 1921, Germany put into effect the first of the post-war
European quotas on imports. Its terms allowed in a set amount of film
each year, equal to 15% of the negative footage produced in Germany
in 1919; the foreign portion came to 180,000 metres.[12] In practice this
figure seems to have proven too low; films were apparently granted
import licences to suit market needs. American films led imports and,
according to *Lichtbildbühne* figures, were allowed in to the following
extent (in metres of negative):

1921 – 131,000	1924 – 248,000
1922 – 151,000	1925 – 591,000
1923 – 189,000	

Since other foreign films were coming in as well, the 1921 quota was
not functioning efficiently, although it did probably keep films from
exceeding the level of demand. Famous Players-Lasky, for example,
produced 61 features in 1923, but only released 21 in Germany;
Universal made 49 that same year, with only 10 releases in
Germany.[13]

Up to the end of the hyperinflation period, the currency problem
kept German films at over half the total consumption. But once the
Rentenmark was introduced in November 1923, the German industry
underwent a crisis, due to its declining exports and losses of other
inflation-period advantages. Also, the new currency allowed importers
to buy foreign films at a more reasonable cost and imports took over a
larger share of the market. Table XIII shows the number of features

censored from 1923 to 1929, with the American and German shares of the market.[14]

TABLE XIII

Number of features censored in Germany 1923–9

Year	Total number of features	German Number	%	American Number	%	Other Number	%
1923	417	253	60.6	102	24.5	62	14.9
1924	560	220	39.3	186	33.2	154	24.5
1925	518	212	40.9	216	41.7	90	17.4
1926	515	202	35.9	229	44.5	84	16.3
1927	521	241	46.3	192	36.9	87	16.7
1928	520	221	42.5	205	39.4	94	18.1
1929	426	192	45.1	142	33.3	92	21.6

The rise in the USA's share after 1924 reflects in part a change in the quota law. As of 1 January 1925, the regulation changed to a proportional basis; rather than stipulating a set amount of footage to enter the country, the rule provided that one import licence would be granted to each distributor for each German feature it had handled in the previous year.[15] Theoretically foreign features could never constitute more than 50% of the market on the average. As Table XIII shows, this quota was not entirely successful either. It did, however, discourage American firms from establishing their own distribution offices in Germany, since in order to get import licences, they would have to distribute an equal number of German films. As Chronology 2 (in Appendix I) shows, most American firms moving into this market before 1927 signed agent companies, simply opening Berlin offices to handle their affairs rather than to distribute films. For example, in December 1924, Paramount was distributing in Germany through National Film; MGM signed with Phoebus in February of the following year and then sold the rights to forty films to UFA in July. Universal contracted Bruckmann as its German agent in October 1925. These firms all distributed German features and were able to obtain import licences.

But the push into the lucrative German market was not proceeding quickly enough for the American exporters' tastes. They were in competition for too few import licences, with no guarantee from one season to the next of their positions. So when Universal's officials discovered in the autumn of 1925 that Germany's largest production/distribution company, UFA, was in financial difficulty and looking for a loan, they began negotiations. Of all companies, Universal was probably the most deeply involved in the German market by this time. Carl Laemmle regularly spent his summers in his home town and kept an eye on the German market. In 1925, Universal had registered 78,218 metres of negative for censorship, while the larger companies, MGM and Paramount, had registered 74,648 and 27,213 respectively. During the summer of 1925 Laemmle had been given a tour of the Neubabelsberg facilities of UFA (supposedly modelled on Universal City itself); there he had purchased the American rights to the Schüfftan Process and laid the groundwork for a distribution accord between the two companies.[16]

By late November the terms of Universal's loan were public knowledge and the deal appeared to be set. UFA was to receive 15,000,000 marks, about $3,600,000 (about $19,692,000 in 1982 dollars), at 8.25% for ten years. In exchange, Universal would receive two votes of the five on the UFA board and would be guaranteed distribution in Germany; it would in turn distribute UFA films in the USA. The loan was necessary to pay off UFA's debts held by the Deutsche Bank, resulting from problems created by the stabilisation crisis. As Laemmle set out for Berlin to settle the contract, a Universal representative pointed out the advantages for the American company; the one-to-one quota was a problem for American films:

> In view of the fact that there are less than 100 pictures made in Germany during a year's time it can readily be seen that the 600 or more features made in America, the hundred or so made in England and the Italian, French and Scandinavian pictures all together stand a very small chance of adequate release in Germany. . . .
> But the most attractive feature of the Ufa arrangement so far as Universal is concerned is the 150 theatres which it owns. These Ufa theatres are the cream of the German amusement world.

The 100-film figure is inadequate; as we have seen, Germany made around 200 features a year in the mid-20s. However, the proportion to the number of foreign features awaiting import was still small.

Universal still had its agency through Bruckmann and in addition signed with the Landlicht exchange system, an UFA subsidiary. Laemmle boasted in interviews that he would thus control 85% of American distribution in Germany. But since about 200 American features went into that country each year, the figure is clearly an exaggeration. Universal was to provide 40 films yearly to UFA, the largest of the three companies; the total Universal share of the number of American imports would probably have been closer to one third. But given the fact that UFA controlled the finest German theatre chain,

108

Universal's share of actual screen time and revenues would probably be higher.[17]

The prize was one which would attract competitors. Officials involved in the Universal–UFA dealings hinted to the trade press of other companies that had been negotiating during the autumn, until UFA chose Universal at the end of November. Laemmle spoke of keen competition for the contract and attributed his success in part to his willingness to take only two votes on the UFA board: 'It is a friendly arrangement,' Mr. Laemmle said, 'a friendly arrangement of mutual value. This is one of the chief reasons why Universal was favored. Ufa had no fear of our attempting to dominate.' UFA officials were similarly cheerful in the announcement of the deal in Berlin: 'The desire of the UFA to find a proper outlet for its production in the United States had resulted in a co-operative agreement with an American firm of the first class – the Universal Pictures Corporation of New York.' In most of the publicity at this stage, the contract was treated as a mutual distribution pact, with little mention of the loan.[18]

At this point the situation began to take on the aspect of a network docudrama. Paramount and MGM were among the other companies interested in securing the UFA contract. Laemmle set out on the *Leviathan* from New York on 3 December, with Paramount's general manager Sidney Kent and Loew's general counsel Leopold Friedman sailing on the *Majestic* that same day. Laemmle's two rivals managed to win the race by flying to Berlin from London, while he crossed the Channel and continued by surface travel. Rumour had it that Paramount and MGM wanted, not just two votes on the UFA board, but control of the German company. Negotiations continued through December. The *New York Times* reported that Paramount and Loew's pressured Universal and UFA by threatening to build a chain of theatres in Germany showing their finest films at low prices. (Nicholas Schenck soon denied this report, but Universal officials generally confirmed the accuracy of the *New York Times'* account.) Whatever the hidden bargaining points, at an all-night meeting on 29 December (held under the deadline of UFA's 30 December general meeting), Laemmle agreed to back down, allowing the larger American companies to make the UFA loan.[19]

Universal received generous terms for stepping aside. Under a five-year contract, UFA would distribute ten of its films a year, giving Laemmle a cash advance on the percentage payments immediately. Paramount and MGM also gave Universal a guarantee of preferential treatment of its films, especially in their New York first-run houses; such an agreement from two powerful, vertically integrated firms meant a good deal to Universal, which owned few theatres. With Universal taken care of, Paramount and MGM provided a slightly larger loan to UFA: $4,000,000 (about 22 million in 1982 dollars – this loan was up from the original $3,600,000) for ten years at 7.5% (down from the planned Universal loan at 8.25). UFA put up its main building on the Potsdamer Platz in Berlin as security, later moving into less luxurious quarters as an economy measure. Paramount and MGM were to release 10 UFA films annually in the USA while the three firms set up a joint company for distribution in Germany: Parufamet. UFA had 50% ownership of Parufamet, while the two American firms split the remainder. Parufamet would distribute 20 Paramount, 20 MGM and an unspecified number of UFA films. (UFA's planned production for 1926 was 22 films.)[20]

The deal with UFA was considered a plum for the companies that obtained it, since they now had a guaranteed outlet in Germany. Marcus Loew said in an interview on the negotiations: 'We had been doing business [in Germany], but thought that UFA wanted our pictures more than the money, but apparently they did not, and when we found out about the offer of Universal to loan them money, we were afraid of being frozen out.' The distribution in Germany, rather than the loan, was the main point. Laemmle, who came back with the original $3,600,000, plus the cash advance, professed himself well pleased. Universal announced to the press that Laemmle was 'assured a fine representation in the UFA theatres for Universal pictures, without any loan feature or without taking any chances on releasing UFA pictures in American theatres, on his part'.[21] The loan was in fact not a way of gaining control over German production; Paramount and MGM did not end up with any votes on the UFA board, but with a half-share in a distribution company. For the Americans, the Parufamet deal was a means of gaining import certificates and a secure place in the German market.

For UFA, the loan came at a crucial moment. The stabilisation crisis, plus overly large investments in production, had led to large debts to the Deutsche Bank, which owned a reported 87% of the company's stock at the time of the negotiations with the American companies. The loan did allow it to survive this crucial period. But in late 1926 and early 1927, UFA was reported to be in worse shape than at the time of the loan; its debts to the Deutsche Bank were about 40,000,000 marks (nearly $10,000,000, about $55,000,000 in 1982 terms) and it needed 20,000,000 marks to keep it from going under. In March 1927, UFA sold the building that had been collateral for the loan and paid off Paramount and MGM early. But it was left with little capital for future production. On 21 April 1927, Alfred Hugenberg gained control of UFA, buying the stock of the Deutsche Bank. From that point on, UFA's future had little to do with financial deals with American firms; it had been taken over by the right-wing elements which would steer it into a leading position in the coming Nazi régime. The UFA loan, then, is an issue whose implications ultimately lie more within the German

110

film industry than with any American control of the German situation.[22]

For the American companies, Parufamet was a convenience. Paramount and MGM continued to release in Germany through this company throughout the 20s and into the early 30s. Universal opened its own distribution company, Universal-Matador, in December of 1926 and dropped its distribution contract with UFA in the autumn of 1927. In September 1931 came the announcement of Parufamet's dissolution (UFA had already stopped distributing its films through Parufamet as of 1928); on 15 September the Paramount Film A-G was registered in Berlin, followed by the Metro-Goldwyn-Mayer Film A-G on 22 September. In general, the major American studios were venturing into direct distribution by 1927. For example, First National opened its German branch, Defina (DEutsch FIrst NAtional) in August 1927.[23] But throughout the 20s and 30s, Germany remained one of the most difficult of major markets to subdue.

The Hays Office, 'Film Europe' and the Department of Commerce
In 1924, three events occurred which help indicate how the struggle in Europe against American hegemony would take shape. One was the first intervention by the Hays Office in a matter of restrictive import legislation by a foreign country. The second was an early attempt at reciprocal distribution agreements between European countries in order to build a larger market in which to amortise their productions. Lastly, the League of Nations adopted the cinema as one of its concerns in promoting international understanding.

In early 1922, the American film companies as a group hired Will H. Hays, the Postmaster General, to head their newly formed trade association, the Motion Picture Producers and Distributors of America (MPPDA). The most prominent reason for the formation of this group was to counter the adverse image of Hollywood which a series of recent scandals (for example, the Arbuckle case, the William Desmond Taylor murder) had created. But the MPPDA's original by-laws also charged it to represent the industry's interests abroad. Hays appointed Major Frederick L. Herron (an old friend from his Wabash College days) to handle foreign markets; Herron served in that capacity from 1922 to 1941. In 1923, Hays and Herron went to London to study the most important single market abroad; Herron spent his first three years in office building up relations with the foreign managers and representatives of member companies and with officials of the Departments of State and Commerce.[24]

These links would prove handy in later negotiations with foreign governments over quota legislation. The standard Hays procedure abroad, as described by a sympathetic 1945 history of the organisation, was 'Direct, amicable representation of the American interests, coupled

111

with personal consultation with the foreign interests and government officials concerned.'[25] And, as we shall see, in extreme cases the industry would also use boycotts of the markets of the countries involved. But the first quota legislation after the formation of the Hays Office received milder treatment. In late 1924, when Germany created its one-to-one import law (effective 1 January 1925), Hays sent a protest via the State and Commerce Departments; he declared the proposal unfair to the USA, since it was sending many films into Germany, but only importing a few. The argument was thoroughly naïve, since that was the precise reason for the legislation in the first place. Perhaps Hays had not yet grasped what the Europeans were trying to do, or perhaps he was deliberately obtuse. At any rate, his strategies in moving against later quotas would be more practical.[26]

The second event of 1924 had more immediate impact. During the summer, UFA signed a mutual distribution agreement with the Etablissements Aubert, one of the major French companies. The deal attracted considerable attention. For one thing, just a few years before, the French industry had been adamantly opposed to allowing any German films in at all. French papers expressed this sentiment plainly after the war; an account of a 31 January 1920 meeting of the renters' section of the Chambre Syndicale Française de la Cinématographie reveals the paranoia that existed in the French industry:

> M. Brezillon [president of the Syndicat des Directeurs de Cinémas] indicated that he was informed by many sources that big German and Austrian firms are plotting and manoeuvring to penetrate the French market by circuitous routes. . . . A clandestine sales office is operating in a large establishment in central Paris, where every evening agents and messengers meet and discuss the best moment to make a return, openly or covertly, favourable to their interests.
>
> He recalled the decision taken by the Syndicat Française des Directeurs to boycott our enemies' films for a fifteen-year period. He declared that, for his part, he was completely disposed to honour this decision, and he added that most, if not all, of the French managers were of the same mind.
>
> M. Aubert confirmed that, as far as he knew, none of the Parisian renters had bought German or Austrian films.[27]

The attempt to import *Madame Dubarry* in 1921 had resulted in a ban, due to the perceived anti-French propaganda in the piece. But *The Cabinet of Dr Caligari*, the first German film to play in Paris after the war (opening in February of 1922), helped change French opinion; soon a small, but steady, trickle of German films was coming into France, winning mostly favourable reactions.[28] By 1924, public opinion had changed enough that the French could hail the UFA-

112

Aubert deal as signalling a new era in European co-operation against American domination.

There were many distribution contracts signed between companies of different countries during the decade after the war. But most simply appointed one firm as the foreign distribution agent for another, usually stronger, one. The mutual distribution pact was different, in that it signalled a willingness to open markets for a two-way exchange. French reporters repeatedly interviewed the initiator of the pact, Erich Pommer. As head of UFA, the single strongest firm in Europe, Pommer was seen as a potential leader in a new pan-European industry. He summed up the new approach which many industry members hoped would guide the European film in the future:

> I think, said M. Pommer, that European producers must at last think of establishing a certain co-operation among themselves. It is imperative to create a system of regular trade which will enable the producers to amortise their films rapidly. It is necessary to create 'European films', which will no longer be French, English, Italian, or German films; entirely 'continental' films, expanding out into all Europe and amortising their enormous costs, can be produced easily.[29]

These same opinions were expressed repeatedly in the trade and popular papers of Europe for the rest of the silent period.[30]

The general idea of 'Film Europe' took some time to bear fruit. It came into being shortly before the German industry entered its post-stabilisation crisis.

Financial problems cut short one ambitious European co-operative project. In the autumn of 1924, shortly after the UFA-Aubert deal, the Wengeroff and Stinnes interests in Germany formed Westi, a production and distribution company with subsidiaries in the major producing countries. Wengeroff intended to sponsor production in all these countries (his most famous undertaking being the aborted production of Gance's *Napoleon*, later completed by another company), then to circulate the results throughout Europe. In December, Westi and Pathé formed Pathé-Westi, a mutual production and distribution firm. Again, the move attracted great attention and was seen as a big step forward in the creation of a European film to compete successfully in world markets. A major expansion programme went on in early 1925. But the project's scope went beyond what the current German situation could support; Westi went out of business less than a year later, in July of 1925. Aside from the Westi project, during 1924 and 1925 there was no real follow-up to the hopeful beginning made by Pommer and Aubert. The big international contracts were mostly one-sided, as when Gaumont signed as the agent of the recently-formed MGM in mid-1925.[31] There was no co-ordinated plan for setting up the necessary distribution network and no formal means of communication. The attempt to set these up leads us to the third event of 1924.

On 28 July the International Committee on Intellectual Co-operation of the League of Nations heard a report on the relationship of the cinema to intellectual life. As a result, the League agreed to make the cinema one of its areas of concern and suggested that an international conference on the subject be held. In April 1925, the International Film Congress was announced as scheduled to take place from 22 to 24 June, under the auspices of the Comité National Français de Co-opération Intellectuelle. Invitations went out to a number of prominent Hollywood directors, including Griffith, Rex Ingram, Chaplin, Lubitsch, Cecil B. De Mille and Maurice Tourneur. Most apparently professed to be too busy, and, indeed, it was very short notice. The Congress was postponed until August, then October and finally put off until 1926.[32]

The Congress eventually took place in Paris from 27 September to 3 October 1926, hosted by the League of Nations and organised by the French branch of that group's International Committee on Intellectual Co-operation and by the Chambre Syndicale Française de la Cinématographie. The stated objectives of the gathering were intellectual rather than economic. Aside from industry representatives, there were delegates from educational associations, the Red Cross, children's and women's groups and others interested in the cinema's non-commercial uses. It was an idealistic venture, although there is no doubt that many of the industry officials attending the Congress looked upon it as a way of forging a union against the American film. But during the planning stages, organisers still hoped that American delegates would attend.[33]

Members of the American trade, however, were worried about the 'Film Europe' movement. The trade and popular press expressed scepticism about the Congress, assuming it to be an anti-American ploy. In the summer of 1926, the Hays Office refused to attend the Congress, claiming that it had been given too little notice; Hays asked that the Congress be put off a year. Herron explained why and also suggested the real reason behind the refusal:

America undoubtedly leads the world in motion pictures, particularly in such branches as educational pictures, but if we attempted to tell other nations that, they would want our word backed up. And that would take time to prepare. In order to contribute anything to the Congress we would have to offer something out of our large experience. But even leaving that aside, we felt that the Congress at this time might easily develop into an anti-American affair if we took part in it, and as the foreign situation is none too happy at present we did not want to complicate it.[34]

114

The excuse about time was patently absurd. Given that the Congress had already been delayed, Hays and the rest of the industry could hardly have been caught unawares. And certainly Hays proved he could muster facts and cross the Atlantic swiftly when it came to fighting European quota bills.

The Congress itself was an extraordinary event, attended by 532 delegates, including film-makers Marcel L'Herbier, Abel Gance, Jean Renoir, Germaine Dulac, Karl Grune, Karl Freund, Lupu Pick, G. W. Pabst, Carmine Gallone, Carl Dreyer, René Clair, Louis Lumière and other equally prominent people on the financial side of the European industry (including Sovkino). No doubt a great deal of pragmatic negotiations went on outside the Congress sessions, but the official set of resolutions which resulted from the meeting reflected an idealistic, co-operative spirit. For example, one commission recommended film-makers: '(a) to avoid carefully scenarios liable to arouse a spirit of animosity between nations and tending to perpetuate the idea of war; (b) to avoid presenting foreign nations or races in a degrading or ridiculous light on the screen.' Other resolutions dealt with the need for universal copyright protection, the abolition of censorship, the establishment of national archives and numerous other topics.[35]

The Congress was one of the most potentially progressive undertakings in the history of the cinema. Had there been any systematic way of carrying through the resolutions, world cinema would have benefited enormously. But the Congress shared the weakness of its sponsoring agent, the League of Nations. The League, formed by the Treaty of Versailles in 1919 to foster world peace, suffered from the beginning because of the absence of several key countries. Even though Wilson had favoured such a League in his 'Fourteen Points' speech of 1918, the USA ended up not joining. Most of the initial members were the Allied nations and neutrals, with Germany not being admitted until 1926 and the USSR until 1934. Thus Hays' refusal to attend was consistent with American policy. As a result, the Congress ended up with hopeful plans which the League could not really implement.

The Europeans initially considered the Congress a success. There is evidence that film-makers did take seriously the strictures against militarism and racism in films; reviewers sometimes pointed to the Congress resolutions in criticising offending films. The first Congress' resolutions planned for a second, which eventually was held in September 1928, in Berlin. Attendance was lower and in spite of an enthusiastic tone at the meeting, some observers were sceptical:

When between whiles one heard a few reasonable words, one was apt to imagine that reasonable activities were actually afoot. But from the summoning of a congress to its results is a long step.

115

Between its decisions and their operation lies a wide highway that is sometimes also an endless one.

You have heard perhaps what has become of the resolutions passed by the Paris Congress of 1926? Amongst these were some quite useful suggestions, requiring only to be carried into effect. By the national unions, perhaps, or by individual governments, in any case by the then existing associations. In 1926 nothing was done. In 1928, we are assured, it is to be otherwise.[36]

Again little was done, and there was no third Congress.

The significance of the Paris Congress was thus not so much in terms of direct action; rather, it served to publicise the possibility of co-operation just when the idea of 'Film Europe' had a chance to develop. The German industry was recovering from its crisis and in a better position to lead the European industry in a struggle against American domination. Similarly, other European countries were stabilising their currencies and getting past the main period of reconstruction of wartime damage; they were entering into the boom years that would precede the Depression. Over the next two or three years, a few countries did actually manage to chip away at the American hegemony and to increase the circulation of European films. They did this primarily through distribution contracts and quota laws.

Over these years, production companies continued to sign agencies in other European countries. There were investments from one country in companies abroad. One of the most notable of these came when UFA and Svenska formed a jointly controlled distribution firm, involving French investment, in Paris in mid-1926; its name reflected the sentiments of the period – L'Alliance Cinématographique Européenne. The company announced plans to produce in all three countries, but its main purpose was actually to be an outlet for UFA films in France; it functioned very efficiently as such for the next few years. UFA continued to set the pattern, signing a reciprocal distribution agreement with Gaumont-British in December 1927; this was hailed in Britain as the first such major contract for a British firm. In October 1926, a joint Russian–German production and distribution company was formed, called Derufa (DEutsche–RUssische-Film-Allianz; the name was later changed to Derussa). The investors were Sovkino and Phoenix Films and they planned to co-produce films in Germany and distribute a regular programme of both German and Soviet films. Derussa went bankrupt in the autumn of 1929, after having imported a number of important Soviet films, including Room's *Death Bay*, Barnet's *Girl With a Hat Box*, Pudovkin's *The End of St Petersburg*, and Eisenstein's *Old and New*. The year 1928 was probably the most intense period for international reciprocal agreements. In March, another larger German company, Terra, signed a distribution pact with

Cinéromans; in April, British International did the same with Pathé; in June, UFA and the state-run film agency LUCE, of Italy, signed to distribute each other's films. Other agreements between smaller companies occurred throughout this period. The net result was a noticeable increase in the circulation of films within Europe. Ludwig Klitzsch, the new director of UFA installed by Hugenberg, commented at the time of the LUCE deal:

> A European film cartel is actually established now. The German–Italian agreement was only an incidental step in a whole series of general European agreements. A number of leading film enterprises in important European film countries have joined to form a solid front against America in order to be able to negotiate on terms of equality with the greatest film factor in the world.

The effects of sound would complicate the exchange of films – and indeed, as we shall see, intensify this move toward a 'cartelisation' of European film industries.[37]

In response to the 'Film Europe' movement, the American industry took steps to protect its position abroad. Soon after the anti-American tactics became apparent in 1924, Hays began to lobby the Department of Commerce to create a special Motion Picture Section within its Bureau of Foreign and Domestic Commerce. (Films were currently in the 'Specialties' category, one step up from their early teens position in 'Miscellaneous'.) Early in 1925, the annual bill being prepared by the House Appropriations Committee contained a budget of $15,000 for such a section. Hays had spoken to Director Klein, of the Bureau, about the necessity for gathering information on foreign quotas and other legislation on behalf of the film industry. The effort failed at that point, but in early February 1926, the MPPDA's Washington representative testified to a Congressional Committee that 'agitation or legislation against American pictures' was going on in sixteen foreign countries; he emphasised how important foreign markets were to the American industry. This time the argument worked and Congress appropriated the $15,000 for a Motion Picture Section. C. J. North was its chief, assisted by Nathan D. Golden; a special Trade Commissioner, George R. Canty, was appointed in Europe.* The

---

* Canty, one of the leading experts on European markets during this period, was originally based in Paris and later in Berlin. His many articles and pamphlets on the European film industry for the *Trade Information Bulletins, Commerce Reports* and *Motion Pictures Abroad*, were often cited by European trade publications. Thus in a sense, the American hegemony in world film sales extended to information gathering as well, since no other government could afford so extensive a reconnaissance effort. Even the German trade daily *Lichtbildbühne* and its biannual *Jahrbuch der Filmindustrie*, in spite of their detailed coverage of the domestic market, did not deal so thoroughly with the more far-flung areas of the world.

117

Section received information from 44 foreign offices of the Department, as well as from 300 consular offices. As of 1929, E. I. Way, who had been handling world information on educational films since 1926, began keeping tabs on the Latin American and Far Eastern markets for entertainment films as well.[38]

The Motion Picture Section provided a great deal of information to the trade about world film markets. In addition to articles on film in the *Commerce Reports*, which had been appearing since the early teens, the Section now put out special summaries on the motion-picture industry in various areas of the world as part of the *Trade Information Bulletin* series; it issued weekly press releases, abstracted import/export figures for films in a monthly publication and dealt with non-theatrical films and projection equipment. In 1929, when the Section was upgraded to the Motion Picture Division, it added a bi-weekly publication, *Motion Pictures Abroad*. As a result, members of the trade had access to a remarkable amount of material on foreign markets: figures on American import and export by country, details on all legislation abroad, methods of distribution, average rental fees and theatre admissions, the progress of theatre wiring as sound came in and virtually any other topic which might affect American sales. The Department of Commerce made its overseas facilities available for travelling film people. The staff of the Section actively proselytised for American exporting by contributing articles to the popular press; Golden also helped organise and spoke at the spring 1928 meeting of the Society of Motion Picture Engineers. The Section claimed to have been instrumental in inhibiting the widespread duping that had been going on in Central America and the Far East in the early 20s, by aiding in pressing copyright violation complaints.[39]

QUOTA STRUGGLES

Hays had originally argued for the Section as a way of combating adverse film legislation abroad and much of the information the staff gathered related to that topic. Whenever such legislation was introduced, especially in Europe, Hays went into action. Chronology 3 (in Appendix I) outlines quotas from 1921 to 1934. I have mentioned that Hays protested against the 1924 passage of the one-to-one German quota. By the summer of 1926, when the British trade was discussing what type of quota to recommend to the government, the MPPDA intervened more directly. Its representative, Col. Lowry, tried to forestall any such move by making an offer on behalf of the American film industry: for every thirty American films going into Britain, American capital would subsidise 40% of one British film and guarantee its distribution in the USA with 40% of the profits there going to the British producer. This essentially meant that the USA

118

would invest in perhaps twenty British films a year. The British Board of Trade reportedly considered the offer seriously, but when the group adjourned in early August, the matter was left hanging. The following spring a distribution/exhibition percentage quota went into effect, dictating that an increasing portion of British programmes be given over to domestic films each year; the MPPDA plan was ignored.[40]

Hays also had little luck in fighting the German quota. At a banquet for Ludwig Klitzsch in New York during the 1927 renegotiations of the Parufamet contract, Hays pointedly called for an open market, condemning quotas. Klitzsch, who was about to negotiate a far more favourable deal for UFA in the second Parufamet contract, replied coldly that since the German film industry had no worldwide distribution, it needed protection temporarily. In late 1926, Lowry was in Germany trying to forestall the change in quota systems, from a one-to-one basis over to a fixed number of import certificates per year. The new system, however, went into effect 1 January 1928 and remained in effect in slightly altered form into the Nazi régime.[41]

The British quota probably succeeded to the extent it did because its initial requirements for British production were modest and its increases gradual. Hays could not negotiate a milder quota with the Germans because that country's industry was relatively strong, at least in its own market. But in 1928 and 1929 the French industry and government came up with an overly ambitious quota plan which gave Hays his most signal victory abroad. On 19 February 1928, a French film decree was published, to become effective 1 March. The provisions were not yet made public, but the MPPDA apparently had advance notice of them. Lowry arrived in Paris on 20 February for negotiations. He met with the heads of the American branch offices there to formulate a position, then saw American Ambassador Myron T. Herrick (a close friend of Hays) to explain the situation to him. On 12 March, the quota regulations were made public: every company exporting a French film would receive seven import permits, which could then be sold to other companies. But on 4 April, an additional set of regulations specified that not all seven import licences could be sold to a single country; if a French film was released in the USA, only four permits could go to American films – two would go to German titles and one to a British film. Since the USA exported at least 400 features to France a year, this would mean 100 French films would have to come to the USA – more than the entire French output.[42]

Soon after the publication of the decree, Hays had appointed another representative in Paris, Harold L. Smith, a vice-consul at the American Consulate in Paris. Hays then set out for Paris himself; there he used Smith's contacts to arrange meetings with various government officials. On 5 April, just after the new regulations came out, Hays conferred with American branch-office heads; they decided to oppose

119

the proposed four-to-one quota on American films, if necessary by refusing to sell American films in France. There was only enough film on the French market to last five or six months. On 12 April, Hays met with his friend, Ambassador Herrick, to get official backing for the industry's position; the next day Hays spoke to the French official most directly involved, the Minister of Public Education, M. Herriot, proposing that the quota be replaced with a tariff. (The American firms almost invariably preferred tariffs to quotas, since the former meant an unrestricted number of films could enter and the companies could usually make a profit in spite of the additional cost.) Negotiations went on for two weeks. By late April Hays was threatening a boycott to begin 1 May, unless a compromise was reached. He proposed: (a) the quota be suspended for one year; (b) that the American industry promise to make no derogatory films about the French; (c) that American producers fund a French mission to visit Hollywood and study how to make films for the American market; and (d) American companies consider all French films for release in the USA.

On 1 May Herriot gave Hays a counter-proposal; he would not suspend the quota, but would agree that for every French film distributed only in France by American companies, seven import certificates would be awarded. Hays accepted this compromise on 4 May. This gave the American firms three ways to import into France: produce in France (yielding seven licences per production); distribute a French film (also seven); or buy licences from French companies. If an American firm distributed a French film in the USA, it received two extra licences. In addition, French firms received a number of licences equivalent to 60% of the total imports during 1927.[43]

This was a considerably watered-down version of the original regulations. Hays triumphed by threatening a lengthy boycott, since French production was not substantial enough to supply its domestic market if American films were withdrawn. Indeed, since few of the French firms were vertically integrated, the producers were pitted against the distributors and exhibitors in the quota controversy. Producers needed protection, but distributors and exhibitors wanted to rent and show the lucrative American product. The industry as a whole was too weak to make an ambitious quota work.

Hays used similar tactics in 1929, when the Hungarian government proposed a plan to encourage native production. Hungary had instituted a rather feeble quota system at the beginning of 1928, requiring that for every twenty imported films, one must be made in the country *or* that the importer pay a heavy tax on each film. Now the government proposed dropping the payment option. Hays arrived in Budapest on 23 February 1929 to protest, hinting of a boycott similar to the one threatened in France the year before. Apparently he was successful, for no more steps were taken, and the twenty-to-one quota was even dropped the following year in favour of a straight fee for import licences.[44]

In early 1929, the quota controversy between the French and American industries came to a head once more. The terms of the May 1928 agreement had been so generous to imports that there was in fact an oversupply of films on the market, with import certificates having no market value. Negotiations between the Chambre Syndicale and Harold Smith of the MPPDA had begun in December of 1928, with the French asking the American industry voluntarily to cut back imports by 20–25%. In January, the Americans replied that they would cut back 10% if the quota were abolished. Negotiations broke down and in early March the government approved the Chambre's new plan: a three-to-one quota, with distributors being allowed to import, in addition, 20% of their previous year's imports without licences. On 1 April American firms shut down their operations in France and on 12 April, the French government received a note of protest from the US State Department. The State Department sent similar notes to Berlin, Rome, Madrid, Vienna, Prague and Budapest – capitals of all the countries with current or proposed quotas. The *New York Times* reported that the American government did this in part because it was worried that such quotas might set precedents which could then be applied to the many other American products then flooding into European markets. The film companies' boycott in France continued until 19 September, when Smith and Charles Delac, president of the Chambre, reached an agreement. The American offices re-opened on 25 September. Capitulating entirely, the French reinstated the 1928 seven-to-one quota until 1 October 1930, to be renewed if no alternative were agreed upon by 1 May of that year. No agreement was, and the same quota continued until 1 July 1931, when it was abolished.[45]

There was another reason for opinion to run against the American film in foreign countries and here the sentiments extended beyond simply the film industries of the various countries fuelling the quota controversies. During the war, the rise in American exports of other goods had paralleled the increasing number of films going abroad. American businessmen quickly realised the advertising potential of films; late in the war *Collier's* outlined the situation:

> After the war is won, as we all know, America's overseas trade must be developed enormously. It is not only an opportunity but a necessity. As stated in this page not long ago, Chairman Hurley of the U.S. Shipping Board says we will have 25 million tons of shipping to be employed.
> Well, consider what the American moving picture is doing in

121

other countries. It is familiarizing South America and Africa, Asia and Europe with American habits and customs. It is educating them up to the American standard of living. It is showing them American clothes and furniture, automobiles and homes. And it is subtly but surely creating a desire for these American-made articles.

The various 'educational' films sent abroad by the Creel Committee were often little more than advertisements for the products of the firms donating the footage. Frank J. Marion, in charge of the Committee's work in Spain, reported: 'Trade follows the film. The projection of industrial pictures, backed by distribution of the product advertised, will create an immediate outlet for goods of American manufacture.'[46]

The cinema was the first mass entertainment form; it could be made comprehensible throughout the world by the simple procedure of translating the intertitles. People in every imaginable social and cultural situation were suddenly seeing vivid demonstrations of American consumer products – especially cars, furniture and fashions. Indeed, during the post-war decades, the general domination by many American industries on world markets occurred precisely because they exploited new products. Inventions which had been made before the war in the highly industrialised nations were now exploited worldwide: electricity and its dependent products, machinery using the internal-combustion engine, chemical products and goods which could be manufactured on the assembly line. The USA, with its newly built factories and efficiency measures, was in a better position to exploit this type of product than was Britain, which depended on less modern industries. By the 20s, 'The benefits of modern consumer technology were even penetrating outside the confines of the western world, into Asia, Africa, and Latin America.'[47]

The film, already widely established in these markets, could introduce their populations to the new products in the most visual, glamorous ways. Government officials and members of foreign cinema industries were well aware of this. According to North, such an awareness was one reason for quota legislation in Europe:

> The film is a silent salesman of great effectiveness, and by that method much trade is being diverted to America. Moreover, through American motion pictures, the ideals, culture, customs, and tradition of the United States are gradually undermining those of other countries. The film industry of these other countries must be built up as a barrier against this subtle Americanization process.[48]

Today we are inured to the idea that the mass media have taken western, and particularly American, culture and consumerism into virtually every nation on earth. But at this point, the process was just

122

beginning in earnest. American film officials patted themselves on the back over the discovery and used it to drum up support for the film industry among government officials and members of other industries in the USA.

It was part of the MPPDA's public-relations duty to deal with the effects of advertising via films. Hays and his staff walked a tightrope on this issue. They wanted to convince American business and government officials that film *did* sell American goods abroad and there are numerous articles and speeches of the period in which they claimed as much. One MPPDA representative addressed the Society of Motion Picture Engineers in 1926, assuring them that films 'are advertising American goods to the world . . . our films are doing more to sell American goods than 100,000 travelling salesmen could do.' In a 1930 talk to the Foreign Trades Council, 'Declaring that motion pictures exert a profound influence upon the buying habits of mankind, Mr. Hays pointed out that 250,000,000 people throughout the world go to picture theatres in the state of mind that a master psychologist would deem ideal if he wanted to make an impression upon them.'[49] Hays and others frequently quoted a Department of Commerce estimate that for every foot of film sent abroad, one dollar in other goods was exported.

But the Hays office had simultaneously to counter this same notion abroad. Universal's director of publicity, after returning from a trip to Europe in 1926, remarked upon the production revival in France and Germany: 'There is terrific national pride in every country in Europe. Just now it centers around their own pictures. Mr. Hays must convince our friends that we are not trying to sell B.V.D.'s to Polynesians nor make foreigners like our cigarettes.'[50] However much Hays' staff might boast of the American film achievements when addressing groups at home, they tried to play them down abroad. Hays found the chauvinism of the American film industry and trade press working against him overseas. The excellent coverage of foreign markets by journals which were then read abroad caused the MPPDA group some anxiety in 1927, during the 'Film Europe' movement:

Complaints are made by executives in the foreign departments of distributing companies that too much export news is appearing in the trade papers. Three different officials have quoted Will H. Hays and Major Herron, chief of foreign relations for Hays, as warning that trade papers print too much 'ammunition' for foreign politicians.

The printed facts, especially figures, it was said, awaken foreign readers to a belief that American films dominate their countries, and stir them onward to renewed propaganda and legislation against the US.

That the Hays organisation has issued any such warnings to distributors was denied by Major Herron. The only suggestion made, he said, has had to do with 'flag waving', an excess of patriotism in ballyhooing themselves as the best producers in the world and in quoting extravagant, and often inflated, salaries and receipts.[51]

At every opportunity when abroad, Hays and his staff would deny the intentional use of American films as ads and would downplay the overwhelming proportion of screen time taken up by American films. Yet the evidence was abundantly apparent and the European industries continued their efforts to combat American encroachment.

THE USA'S POSITION IN EUROPE

As we have seen, Germany, Britain and France were the leading forces in the 'Film Europe' movement. They were the main producing countries there; all tried to fight American dominance with quota systems. A comparison of these markets indicates the slight, but noticeable, success they achieved in the late 20s.

Table XIV gives similar information for the three countries: how many American, German, French and British feature films were censored in each during the second half of the decade and what percentage each country had of the total number.[52]

All three countries indicate a drop in the American share after 1926, when the European economy had recovered enough to make production more feasible. Germany's share climbed steadily in both the French and British markets, paralleling the rise in contracts between countries for distribution. In Britain, sound caused a drop in foreign-language films; but by dint of making French-language versions, Germany built up its share of the French market again in 1932. Germany's relatively strong production and its quota laws enabled it to regain the largest portion of its domestic market by 1927.

Britain, starting from a very low state of production, with American films dominating its market to a considerable extent in 1926, also managed to improve steadily. The effects of the 1927 quota are obvious, with the British share of the market rising. (Undoubtedly, however, some of these films were the notorious 'quota quickies', receiving a limited release and intended primarily to clear the way for the importation of American films.) Partly because of the 'Film-Europe' co-operation of this period, the quota had a restraining effect on American imports, while German ones continued to rise until sound came in.

124

TABLE XIV
Number of features censored in Germany, France and Britain 1926–32

Year	USA Number	%	Germany Number	%	France Number	%	Britain Number	%	Total Number
a) Germany									
1926	229	44.5	202	39.2	22	4.3	2	0.4	515
1927	192	36.9	241	46.3	27	5.2	2	0.4	521
1928	205	39.4	221	42.5	24	4.6	15	2.9	520
1929	142	33.3	192	45.1	16	3.8	17	4.0	426
1930	97	31.8	151	49.5	13	4.3	9	3.0	305
1931	80	28.0	148	51.7	32	11.2	3	1.0	286
b) France									
1924	589	85.0	20	2.9	68	9.8	–	–	693
1925	577	82.0	29	4.1	73	10.4	7	1.0	704
1926	444	78.6	33	5.8	55	9.7	2	0.4	565
1927	368	63.3	91	15.7	74	12.7	8	1.4	581
1928	313	53.7	122	20.9	94	16.1	23	3.9	583
1929	211	48.2	130	29.7	52	11.9	24	5.5	438
1930	237	49.6	111	23.2	94	19.7	16	3.3	478
1931	220	48.5	60	13.2	139	30.7	8	1.8	453
1932	208	43.4	99	20.7	140	29.2	7	1.5	479
c) Britain									
1926	620	83.6	43	5.8	24	3.2	36	4.9	742
1927	723	81.1	71	8.0	34	3.8	40	4.5	892
1928	558	71.7	93	12.0	24	3.1	95	12.2	778
1929	495	74.7	60	9.0	16	2.4	87	13.1	663
1930	519	69.5	49	6.6	22	2.9	142	19.0	747
1931	470	72.6	16	2.5	10	1.5	139	21.5	647
1932	449	70.0	18	2.8	7	1.1	153	23.9	641

France

Of the three, France benefited least from the co-operative move against American hegemony. True, the American share of the French market fell steadily from 1924 to 1929. But France's gains were outstripped by Germany's. For the French industry, the deals with Germany meant mostly that German films were imported, while

125

French exports to Germany remained low. Even British films, though never really significant, increased at a greater rate in the French market than did the native product.

We have already seen in the quota fights some indications of why these trends occurred. It was also the case that the French government was little inclined to support the film industry in general; there were constant complaints through the 20s of high ticket-taxes and government indifference. Also, the French market was not a lucrative one; in 1925, although France was fifth among all foreign markets in terms of the footage imported from the USA, it yielded only 3% of the USA's foreign revenues. Attendance per capita was relatively low; many of France's approximately 2,500 theatres showed films only a few days a week. Films were not blocked-booked, but rented individually, often to only a few theatres. Hence gross rentals were often low; the average films would gross only 50,000 francs (about $2,000 or nearly $11,000 in 1982 terms). A big American special might bring in 200,000 francs, with the record being 500,000 francs. Low theatre admissions, high taxes and stiff competition on the open market meant that American firms often did not make money in the French market. And since they were trying to make back only the costs of importation and distribution, one can imagine the difficulties of a French production company trying to recoup its entire costs of production.[53]

The American companies maintained offices there, however; often these were the head offices from which branches in the smaller surrounding markets were controlled. Of the 313 American features released in France in 1928, 231 (73.8%) were handled directly by American firms. That number fell in 1929, during the quota boycott; of 211 features, 133 were distributed directly (63%). (It is an indication of the French industry's weakness that the vacuum created in 1929 by the reduction in American films was filled by German, rather than French, productions.) In 1930, direct distribution went up once more (170, or 71.7%, of the 237 American features). Thus the American industry, entrenched in France, controlled its own releases and was capable of taking measures to counter French moves against it. The lack of vertical integration within the French industry robbed it of unity in seeking aid from the government.*[54]

Britain
During the 20s, Britain remained the key foreign market for American

* A striking example of the French government's indifference came in 1926. That spring, Marcus Loew had taken over the management of Gaumont's string of theatres through the formation of GMG (Gaumont-Metro-Goldwyn); he directed the introduction of American exhibition methods in these theatres. The government responded that summer by awarding Loew the medal of the Légion d'Honneur. (Martin J. Quigley, 'Our American Letter', *Bio*, 2 Sept. 1926, p. 38.)

126

films. It was first in the quantity of film imported from the USA for most years (falling to fourth in 1922 and 1927, third in 1923 and fifth in 1926), but it paid the highest revenues in all cases; as of 1925, it was bringing in 35% of foreign revenues. British capital went primarily into the lucrative distribution and exhibition wings of the industry, perpetuating the dependence on American imports. Moreover, rather than seeking an alternative to Hollywood-style film-making as Germany had done with some success, British producers were content to copy American films. One producer stated this view in 1920:

> We must acknowledge the supremacy of American production methods and we are willing and anxious to learn from them. . . . We believe that England can supply stories and themes to the American people which will come to them with a fascinating freshness, but we are fully alive to the fact that such stories have got to be presented in the best possible way and must follow to a large extent American ideas and customs.

It was a common attitude, but without the lavish facilities of the Hollywood studios, the results were usually pale imitations.[55]

As we have seen, Britain was a closed market by the end of the war. American firms had introduced long-term block-booking and they continued to keep British theatres' schedules sewn up for one to two years in advance. The average film grossed about £2,000, or $10,000 (about $55,000 in 1982 terms) – five times what it fetched in France; specials might bring in £50,000, or rarely, up to £150,000. But the quota law of April 1927 outlawed block- and blind-booking in Britain. This provision further explains why American films dropped to around 70% of the market after 1927 and why German films were able to enter the newly open market more freely at that point. Thus the government action favoured both British and European films over American.[56]

Germany

We have already seen how consistent German government support kept a reasonably effective series of quotas in force throughout the decade. In addition, capital was far more accessible, since stock in UFA and other large firms was held by powerful groups in Germany's banking, electrical and other businesses; investment in production was especially high during the inflationary period. As Table XIII shows, the only years when more American features than German were registered for censorship were 1925 and 1926, during the post-stabilisation crisis. The one-to-one quota was in operation during this period, but obviously was not being rigorously enforced – the number of German features was about 50 below half of the total. At this point the German market was heavily dependent on American films. Using *Lichtbildbühne*

127

figures on features shown in Germany in 1925, one German observer found that of a total of 618, the American share was 218, or 35%; 286 German and 114 other features were shown. (These figures do not tally with the censorship figures for 1925, presumably because some features censored in previous years were still in distribution.) This writer concluded:

> Theoretically speaking, if Germany really wanted to do entirely without American films, European production would have to increase by 50 per cent., in order to cover the demands of the market. In other words, German home production would have to be increased by about 430, and imports from other European quarters to about 170. In order to accomplish such an increase of production, the German industry would have to be raised by more than a million pounds.

Such an increase was not possible at that point, he concluded.[57]

By that point, American firms were well-established in Berlin; ten had their own offices and the majority of smaller producers had contracted with a German agency. The market was a lucrative one; as of 1926, American films were grossing an average of $20,000 (about $136,000 in 1982 terms), with specials getting $100,000 and the occasional highly successful film going as high as $750,000. This was even higher than the British average – but not necessarily because the overall market was better. With the new 1928 quota limitations, fewer American films could enter the market. One expert estimated that only 40% of American films could get into Germany: 'This market would be as profitable as the British market were it not for the heavy quota imposed. The gross business would certainly be as good.' But with the quota, American firms tended to send only their most successful, prestigious films; this helps account for the high average grosses. On the whole, however, the German market was a constant source of frustration for the American industry.[58]

Other European Markets
Elsewhere in Europe, the American film fared well, easily staying ahead of Germany in most markets. As we saw in the previous chapter, Scandinavia and Finland were switching from German to American films late in the war. These countries became a sizeable, steady market after the war. Neutral countries tended to emerge during this period with healthy monetary systems; Denmark, Sweden and Norway embarked upon ambitious theatre-building immediately. By 1920 there were 1,300 cinemas in the three countries. Estimates during 1923–5 consistently put the American share of the Scandinavian market at 70%, with Germany gradually gaining a place. As of 1926, there were

eighteen distribution companies in Sweden, of which seven were American branches, nine Swedish, one Danish and one German. Two other American companies distributed through Svensk Filmindustri, another through UFA's branch. Four other Swedish firms handled American films. The situation was similar in Copenhagen, with three American and six Danish distribution companies operating. Table XV summarises the American share of these four markets in the late 20s; the figures are percentages of the number of feature films censored during the year. Germany consistently had the second largest share, averaging around 15%.[59]

TABLE XV

American percentage of features in Scandinavian markets in the late 20s

Year	Denmark %	Norway %	Sweden %	Finland %
1925	64.1	?	?	?
1926	59.8	?	?	?
1927	? .	62.8 of total footage	?	?
1928	53.8 of all features 71.1 of total footage	69.9	75.0	65.6
1929	57.7 of all films 67.9 of total footage	64.1	57.0 of total footage 64.1 of all features	61.4 of total footage 61.3 of all films
1930	58.4 of all films	?	53.3 of total footage	59.2 of total footage 64.3 of all features

In Holland, Belgium, Luxembourg and Switzerland, the USA also led the way. But it faced competition because some areas of these countries shared languages with Germany and France. In 1920, the USA had an estimated share of 60% of the Swiss market. Later in the 20s, however, Switzerland, with its German- and French-speaking sections, depended less on American films than did most other European countries. Switzerland kept neither censorship nor customs figures on imports, but estimates based on trade sources are consistent, showing the USA with a 50% share, Germany with 40% and about 8% coming from France. In 1930, as sound was coming in, the American share rose, to 65% of the new silent features and 55% of the sound ones. The Belgian, Dutch and Swiss markets had been largely controlled by German films during the war; the Dutch and Swiss had begun to switch over only in 1918. At the Armistice, German films, predictably, disappeared from Belgium. French companies which purchased the Belgian rights for American films flooded them into the market, where they reportedly were well received. As the resentments from the war receded, however, the market became more balanced. In the late 20s, the USA held a steady share of 70–80%, with Germany a distant second and France third; when sound came in the French share jumped to about 50% with the USA in second place at 40%. Germany gained a similar advantage in Holland in 1930 (see Table XVI: censorship figures).

TABLE XVI

The market in Holland 1928–30

Year	USA %	Germany %	France %
1928	80.9	10.5	4.0
1929	85.7	?	?
1930	57.2	30.5	4.2

As of 1929, Holland had seventeen distribution companies, three of which were American branches and one an office of UFA.[60]

Even Austria, a market traditionally tied by bonds of language and culture to Germany, depended increasingly on American films during the 20s. In 1922, there were two American branch offices there, but 55% of the 1921 imports had come from Germany. The USA brought in only 20%, with the remainder coming from France, Italy, Sweden and Norway. By 1926 there were three American and three German distributors in a total of twenty. The percentages of the feature-film market were as shown in Table XVII for the remainder of the decade (based on censorship figures). Again, the effects of the introduction of sound are evident in the 1930 figures.[61]

We have seen how a few major American firms were gaining a hold on the Italian market in the last years of the war. But the actual move to first place in that market seems not to have occurred until the early 20s. As of 1922, American imports were third, behind French and German. Domestic production made an attempt at a comeback, but a lack of export markets and a use of overly lavish production values caused it to decline steadily and precipitously through the decade: 220 films in 1920, down to 100 in 1921, 50 in 1922, between 20 and 30 in

130

TABLE XVII

The market in Austria, 1926–30

Year	USA %	Germany %	France %
1 January 1926–31 October 1927	48.0	37.0	7.0
1927 (not including Austrian films)	49.8	35.4	7.0
1928	47.4	41.5	2.8
1929	54.3	37.2	2.8
1930	43.4	47.4	3.7

1923, 15 to 20 in 1924, about 15 in 1925–6 and below a dozen in 1927–8. American films filled the gap; they passed French and German films, to make up 30% of the 1923 imports. The *Moving Picture World* insisted that American firms could benefit by opening direct distribution offices; they were still mostly selling to Italian agents. Thereafter the American proportion of films rose as native production fell: an estimated 40% by 1924, to Germany's 20%. By the next year American films occupied an estimated 70% of exhibition time. Of the forty distribution companies in 1926, only twelve were considered major: six were American, six Italian. The Italian rights, when sold to a domestic distributor, brought an average of $1,000 (about $5,500 in 1982 terms), plus the sale of from ten to fourteen positive prints. Italy did not keep import figures by country, so it is rather difficult to get a consistent set of figures from year to year. In 1928, estimates of the number of features in distribution put the American share at 80.1%, followed by Germany at 9.6%, Britain at 3.8%, France at 3.2% and Italy contributing a mere 2.6%. In 1929, the USA's share of the features censored was 54.1%, but American films were reported to be enjoying longer runs than most others. For 1930, imports in metres were: the USA, 58.9%; France, 19.4%; Britain, 11.4%; and Germany, 8.2%. Other 1930 estimates put American films at 75% of the imports. (The lower figures for 1929 and 1930 may be due in part to the inclusion of raw stock – mostly from France – in the import figures and in part to the fact that some films coming from France were actually foreign-language versions produced by Paramount at its studio at Joinville.)[62]

In 1918, American films made up just under half of those used in Spain; Italian films still held one-third of that market. But in mid-1919, the *Moving Picture World* reported, 'Spain and Portugal, at last, have decided to accept American moving pictures. It took a long time and a great deal of effort to convince the Iberians that good photoplays were being produced in the United States.' In 1922, customs figures for film imports reveal the following market shares for Spain: the USA, 50.7%; Germany, 31.2%; Britain, 8.1% – with the remaining 10% coming from various sources. As we might expect, Italy has virtually disappeared from this market. By 1926 there were thirty distributors in Spain, all Spanish except for one French and five American branch offices. The exclusive rights for a film on the Spanish market brought an average of $700 (about $3,800 in 1982). Import and censor's figures were not kept; estimates of the 1926 market found the Americans providing 70%; France, 20%; with Germany and Italy each at about 5%. An American consul estimated that same year that American films occupied closer to 80% of exhibition time. For 1928, the American share of all feature films in distribution was 77.3%; the Germans supplied 12%; the British and French, 3.7% each; Italy, 1.8%; and domestic film, 1.5%. For the season 1929–30, the proportions held fairly steady: the USA, 75%; Germany, 10%; France, 8%; Britain, 3%; and others, 4%. And in 1930, America went up to 80%, with the remainder equally distributed among France, Germany and Britain. Portugal, which obtained many of its films from Spain, followed a similar pattern. In 1928, there were 200 theatres in the country; two American companies had branches in Lisbon, with local distributors handling other American brands. A minor quota meant that one domestically made one-reeler, usually a travalogue, played on each programme. Otherwise American, German and French films shared the market (see Table XVIII for censorship figures).[63]

TABLE XVIII

The market in Portugal, 1929–30

Year	USA %	Germany %	France %	Others %
1929	61.1	17.1	11.5	10.3
1930	74.3	14.3	6.3	5.2

The eastern European and Russian markets had been virtually inaccessible to American films during the war. Russia, which had been developing its own industry, was cut off from the West after the Bolshevik Revolution and screenings were largely dependent on news-reels and old prints. In late 1921, as part of the New Economic Policy, the Soviet government authorised the importation of films from Germany. Thereafter Berlin became the main conduit for film going into, and later coming out of, the USSR. This meant that at first, during the inflationary period, German imports dominated the Soviet market. But as the post-stabilisation crisis set in, from 1924 to 1926, American films surged into first place, even though Berlin remained the distribution point (see Table XIX). But the Soviet government gradually succeeded in building up production and limiting exports.[64]

Eastern Europe was in considerable chaos after the war, due to the shifting of boundaries and creation of new independent states through treaties in 1919 and 1920. Aside from the non-Russian Soviet nations, these new states in Europe were Poland, Finland, Estonia, Latvia, Lithuania (the latter three part of the Baltic States), Czechoslovakia and Yugoslavia. The processes of setting up new currencies, financial and transportation systems and the like were often difficult, delaying the American film's move into the various markets. Even those countries which had existed before the war took few American pictures. In early 1919, Greece was reportedly using almost nothing but Italian and French films. Similarly, the 116 theatres of Bulgaria rented their films from agencies in Germany, Italy and Denmark; they showed such brands as Nordisk, Eiko, Messter, Itala, Torino, Ambrosio and Pathé Frères, many undoubtedly produced years earlier. An observer reported in 1920 that American films were still largely unknown in the Balkan States (Greece, Yugoslavia, Romania, Bulgaria, Albania and European Turkey); a whole country's rights for a feature film typically fetched only a few hundred dollars. Pathé and Gaumont had agencies in Athens, but American firms had not entered these markets seriously.[65]

TABLE XIX

The market in Russia, 1921–31 (features only)

Year	France Number	%	Germany Number	%	USA Number	%	Russia Number	%	Total number
1921	1	14.3	–	–	2	28.6	(est.) 4	57.1	7
1922	15	21.4	41	58.6	7	10.0	7	10.0	70
1923	40	13.7	137	47.1	101	34.7	13	4.5	291
1924	41	10.1	94	23.3	231	57.2	38	9.4	404
1925	53	13.0	53	13.0	241	58.9	62	15.1	409
1926	18	9.1	24	12.1	86	43.4	70	35.4	198
1927	8	4.3	24	12.8	86	45.7	70	37.2	188
1928	4	2.3	26	15.2	32	18.7	109	63.7	171
1929	8	4.6	18	10.3	42	24.1	106	60.9	174
1930	1	0.7	9	6.0	33	22.1	94	63.1	149
1931	1	1.1	1	1.1	4	4.5	83	93.3	89

The areas formerly under German/Austro-Hungarian control had, of course, seen few American films during the war. Before the war, Czechoslovakia had used about 40% American films, 40% Italian and 20% French; during the war, only German, Austrian, Hungarian and Scandinavian films showed there. As of 1919, used prints of French, Italian and American films were coming in from Paris to the country's 350 theatres. That year the shares of imports were: Germany, 60%; France, 14%; the USA, 12%.

Poland, also with 350 theatres, was in a similar situation, with the USA beginning to make a bid for the market in 1921. That same year, Yugoslavia had 400 theatres, with eight importers getting films from France, Italy, Germany and Austria; some of these were undoubtedly American. As of the 1919 to 1921 period, the USA had a negligible hold in the eastern European countries.[66]

Over the next two years, American films crept into these markets; the main competition was usually Germany, geographically nearby and profiting from the inflationary period. There was a demand for the American product, but most of these countries were suffering from depreciated currencies and simply could not afford them. A sale of eleven prints was considered good for virtually the whole territory of eastern Europe, including Austria; Czechoslovakia, in better shape than most, took three of these. In 1923, Yugoslavia was still dominated by German and Italian films. Estonia showed 85% German pictures and only 10% American. Late that year, an American consul in Athens found American films predominating, but with considerable numbers of Italian, French and German pictures being shown. Similarly, a consul in Hungary stated: 'Until recent years Hungary usually imported its films from Germany, Italy, and France, but the place formerly held by Germany is now occupied by the United States.' In the Baltic States, distributors in Riga, Reval and Kovno obtained films from major-export centres – Berlin, London and New York. Imports for 1923 had been 65% German, 30% American and 5% French; but in early 1924, American imports were estimated to be up by one-half, due to the decrease in German production.[67] The German post-stabilisation crisis was beginning to have its effects on exports to this area; from 1924 on, the American takeover would be rapid.

The pattern is a familiar one by now and there is no point in detailing the move into these countries. I shall simply present an abbreviated statistical summary of the American share of each market in the late 20s, comparing it with other countries' portions where possible. Since not all countries kept exact import and/or censorship figures, the data within individual tables may be of different types from year to year.

As of 1926, there were forty-nine distributors in Hungary – three

134

American, the rest local. Three-year exclusive-rights contracts brought from $1,200 to $5,000 (about $6,500 to $27,000 in 1982 terms). The American share of the market was estimated at 65% that year – one of the worst years for German production. By 1928 Germany had recovered as much as it would ever do during this period; censorship figures indicate the shares for the major foreign suppliers (see Table XX). (Hungary itself contributed a large number of short films, helping to account for the large share in the 'other' column.[68])

TABLE XX
The market in Hungary, 1928–30

Year and type	USA	Germany	France	Austria	Other
1928 (percentage of features)	51.7	41.9	2.2	2.3	1.9
1928 (percentage of all films)	50.0	16.6	5.8	1.6	26.0
1929 (percentage of all films)	51.7	19.3	3.4	1.6	24.0
1929 (percentage of total footage)	52.2	27.1	4.9	2.4	13.4
1930 (percentage of all films)	50.7	21.6	1.1	2.0	24.6
1930 (percentage of total footage)	55.2	31.2	1.8	1.6	20.5

By 1927, one American firm had opened a branch in Riga, Latvia, to serve the Baltic States; other companies sent in prints from their Berlin offices. In the late 20s, the USA held 40–50% of the Latvian market, around 60–75% of the Estonian, and an estimated 27% of the Lithuanian. The Polish market went over to American films by 1924 and the lead over Germany increased over the next two years, with the American share settling down in the 60% range for the rest of the 20s. Table XXI is based on the total number of films censored. A ban on German-language films in 1930 accounts for the sudden decrease in that country's share and the accompanying rise in the American share.

As of 1926, most American firms had agents in Czechoslovakia and four had branch offices. With the exception noted, the percentages in Table XXII are based on the total length of films censored in each year.[69]

About 1928, American films rose to about a 50% average share of the entire Balkans market, from 20 to 25% in previous years. Bulgaria

TABLE XXI
The market in Poland, 1924–30

Year	USA %	Germany %	France %	Austria %	Other %
1924	39.4	23.1	19.1	8.9	9.5
1925	52.9	10.9	23.8	6.8	5.6
1926	70.6	9.9	11.8	4.0	3.7
1927	62.2	16.8	13.2	2.8	5.0
1928	62.7	14.6	10.9	3.2	8.7
1929	68.8	11.7	6.3	3.7	9.6
1930					
Silent*	77.9	8.3	?	?	13.8†
Sound	86.4	5.8	?	?	7.8†

* First nine and a half months.
† Including France and Austria.

TABLE XXII
The market in Czechoslovakia, 1925–30

Year	USA %	Germany %	France %	Czechoslovakia %
1925	54.8	21.8	8.8	6.6
1926	52.4	24.3	8.4	9.0
1927	48.3	28.9	8.0	7.9
1928	41.6	34.5	7.0	10.0
1929	42.9	30.0	7.4	8.9
1930*	51.2	24.2	4.3	14.1

* Total number of all films censored.

had 138 theatres as of 1929; no American companies had offices there. The government did not keep censorship or import figures by countries of origin, but contemporary trade estimates put the German share of the market at about 50% with the Americans controlling 10% or less.[70] Yugoslavia obtained most of its films via Germany and Austria. The figures in Table XXIII are based on the total number of films imported.[71]

Greece also kept no import figures by country; contemporary estimates put the American share at about half in the late 20s, jumping

TABLE XXIII

The market in Yugoslavia, 1926–30

Country of origin	1926 %	1927 %	1928 %	1930 %
USA	56.5	64.5	63.9	61.4
Germany	19.6	25.1	22.4	19.6
France	10.1	2.1	1.1	3.7
Austria	5.1	1.4	2.8	11.7

to nearly three-quarters with the introduction of sound.

Romania was a relatively lucrative market. Exclusive-rights contracts might bring as much as $6,000 (about $34,000 in 1982 terms). Of the twenty-six distribution firms, three were American; UFA's local branch handled virtually all the German films coming in. Local firms that handled no American product could 'scarcely compete with the predominating popularity of American pictures'. In Table XXIV, estimates for 1925–9 are based on the total number of films imported, for 1930 on the total length of the films censored.[72]

TABLE XXIV

The market in Romania, 1925–30

Country of origin	1925 %	1926 %	1927 %	1928 %	1929 %	1930 %
USA	20.0	25.0	35.0	45.0	60.0	59.3
Germany	30.0	40.0	35.0	30.0	20.0	22.4
France	30.0	20.0	10.0	5.0	5.0	13.1
Austria	5.0	5.0	10.0	10.0	10.0	0.4
Italy	10.0	5.0	5.0	5.0	–	0.6
Others	5.0	5.0	5.0	5.0	5.0	4.2

THE USA'S POSITION IN NON-EUROPEAN MARKETS

Australia and New Zealand

During the 20s, Australia was consistently among the top five world purchasers of American films in terms of quantity; for 1922, 1923, 1926 and 1927 it was the top market. (In terms of revenue, however, Britain was always the best foreign customer.) Both Australia and New

TABLE XXV
The market in Australia, 1919–21

Country of origin	1919–20		1920–21	
	Footage %	Value %	Footage %	Value %
USA	91.1	89.5	88.3	87.7
Britain	6.7	7.5	8.9	9.4

Zealand had received a boost in both agricultural and industrial production during the war; this relative prosperity meant people had money to spend at cinemas and the markets were lucrative. New Zealand had about 200 theatres directly after the war, with an average seating capacity of 750; consuls estimated in the post-war years that from 90 to 95% of screening time there was given over to American films. Import figures for Australia show a similar trend in the post-war years (see Table XXV). Most of the British imports were newsreels.[73]

TABLE XXVI

The market in Australia, 1927–31

	1927 %	1928 %	1929 %	1930 %	1931 %
American share of all films	78.1	69.3	79.2	86.5	78.0
American share of features	86.9	89.4	86.3	90.5	79.0
British share of all films	12.6	12.9	9.1	5.3	16.7
British share of features	5.5	11.6	7.4	8.6	19.5

There were sporadic attempts to promote a domestic industry in Australia, but these failed to make headway against the flood of American films. As of 1926, the latter made up 93% of imports to Australia and were still estimated to take up 95% of screen time in New Zealand. As in Britain and elsewhere, the American firms' practice of block-booking helped maintain this situation. The figures in Table XXVI are based on import records. The increases in the British share reflect the larger percentages of British films required under that country's 1927 quota as the years went on.[74]

Central and South America

After the war South America continued to grow into one of the key non-European markets for the USA. By 1922 both Argentina and Brazil had entered the ranks of the top five markets in terms of quantity and by 1926 Argentina was number two after Australia; Brazil was number three. In 1920, Jacobo Glucksmann, the New York buyer for his brother's big import firm of Max Glucksmann, estimated that 95% of screening time in South America was occupied by American films. By 1921 of ten distributors in Rio de Janeiro, three were branches of American firms and four others acted primarily as importers.[75]

The post-war currency problems in Europe led to a brief period when Italian, French and especially German films were increasingly returning to South America. One observer in Santiago, Chile, estimated that American films dropped from a 95% share in 1921 to 65% a year later. But American stars had become popular and most American films still had more lavish production values; in later 1922, a consul reported 'a reaction in the Brazilian film market has taken place and American motion pictures are once more being displayed in theatres that were almost exclusively showing German and French films.' During 1923, American officials scattered around the continent estimated that American pictures made up 90% of the Bolivian market, 80% of the Brazilian and 'the great majority' of the films shown in Venezuela. Since most of the smaller countries received their films from either Rio de Janeiro or Buenos Aires, the pattern would tend to be the same throughout the area. Shares based on Brazilian figures for the total number of films censored in the late 20s show the same situation continuing, with the Germans regaining some ground after the post-stabilisation crisis ended (see Table XXVII).

Similarly, in Argentina, where five American firms had branches as of 1929, American films made up 80% of these years' imports by weight.[76]

TABLE XXVII

The market in Brazil, 1927–9

Source	1927 %	1928 %	1929 %
USA	88.3	84.2	85.9
Germany	3.0	6.4	7.7
Brazil	4.3	2.4	2.6
France	2.7	5.1	2.0
Others	1.7	1.9	1.9

In Mexico, Central America and the Caribbean, a similar pattern emerges. Some of the smaller, poorer markets, however, did not draw the American firms to make any great selling efforts. Again, the European price advantage after the war created a brief competition. In 1922 an American consul found European films being shown in Guatemala, 'because the cost is very much lower than the American product'. Cuba, a more lucrative market, attracted American investment; in 1923, American firms were running two large Havana theatres and had investments in the area; only small numbers of German, Italian and French films appeared. In 1924, American films were reported dominant in Puerto Rico.[77]

Interestingly, Mexico was virtually the only country in the world to offer opposition to the American hegemony on ideological rather than economic grounds. Various foreign nationals had provided Hollywood with some of its enduring stereotypical images, of course, and Mexicans were consistently used in villainous roles, especially in Westerns. In 1921, the Mexican market was finally becoming stable enough to be attractive to American firms, which began opening offices in Mexico City. But in early 1922, the government there placed a ban on films coming from any company that made movies portraying Mexicans in an offensive way – a ban which applied even if the offending films were not themselves sent into Mexico. Some American companies promised to comply with the Mexican demands. By the summer of the next year, an American official in Yucatan reported American films as 'by far the most popular'. Import figures for the first five months of 1925 show the American share at a level comparable to those in South American markets (see Table XXVIII).

The ideological problem was not completely solved, however, for in mid-1927, the Mexican government again instituted a brief embargo, this time only banning those films with racist depictions of Mexicans.[78]

TABLE XXVIII

The market in Mexico, January–May 1925

Source	Share by weight %	Share by value %
USA	86.6	88.4
Germany	5.1	4.2
Spain	1.1	1.4
France	2.6	2.0
Britain	0.5	0.4
Others	4.1	3.6

Japan was the most developed of Oriental film markets after the war, but it presented some problems for importers. Since duping was widespread there, firms wanted direct representation. Also, a few large Japanese firms still controlled many of the theatres. In 1921, the largest company, Nippon Katsudoshashin Kabushiki Kaisha, owned 350 of the 600 regular theatres. The regular theatres were the only ones showing imported films; another 2,000 theatres playing part-time used the domestic product. The Japanese government also instituted various measures to discourage importation: a tax of $15 a reel on imports in the early 20s and various local censorship codes. These were relatively ineffectual, however. By 1923 all the main American companies had representation in Japan; Universal, United Artists and Famous Players-Lasky had branch offices. The president of Shochiku, Henry Kotani, declared in a 1922 interview, 'We receive large amounts of the Gaumont films, or German or Italian productions, but spectators particularly love American films.'[79]

The great earthquake of September 1923 damaged some of the American branch-office facilities, but it virtually devastated domestic production for a short time, giving the American firms a temporary advantage. After the disaster, the Japanese government requested the film companies' aid in keeping up public morale; open-air theatres were hastily set up to give free showings and makeshift theatres were also built. American firms sent large shipments of film at once to replace inventories lost and exports took a jump for about eight months. Japanese production also recovered quickly, however. Indeed, the reconstruction of the Japanese industry was carried through so effectively that domestic production regained and kept a considerable share of the market.

In June of 1924, a few Japanese film companies took advantage of anti-American sentiment in the country to attempt a boycott. The strict limitations instituted in the USA by the Immigration Act of 1924 had discriminated against Japanese by forbidding them to settle in the USA at all (other nationalities were simply assigned very small immigration quotas). The boycott lasted about a month and American firms cancelled their orders to the USA; exports to Japan fell to a fraction of their typical levels. But the public still demanded American films and the boycott broke down. Initially a few independent theatres returned to showing American films and by mid-July the four companies that had organised the attempt cancelled their agreement and returned to distributing and showing the American pictures.[80]

Nevertheless, the USA's overall share of the Japanese market shrank in the late 20s. By 1927 the main Japanese buyer in New York, U. Ono, returned from a trip home to report that the number of theatres showing American films was in decline: where formerly 200 to 250 had shown them extensively, now there were only 20 to 30 showing American films exclusively. An economic crisis had led to lowered admissions at theatres which then could not always afford the high prices for American films. In addition, an increasing number of successful Japanese films had lured more production companies into existence and production was up to around 400 films in 1926. The five biggest Japanese firms were vertically integrated to a degree that existed in no other major producing nation outside the USA, and the result was that the native firms controlled theatre time. For the period 1926 to 1934, a growing number of the country's theatres were closed to imported films (see Table XXIX).[81]

TABLE XXIX

Proportions of Japanese theatres showing imported films 1926–34

Year	Theatres showing only domestic films Number	%	Theatres showing only imported films Number	%	Theatres showing both Number	%	Total Number
1926	414	39.2	39	3.7	604	57.1	1,057
1927	577	49.2	39	3.3	556	47.4	1,172
1928	714	56.3	46	3.6	509	40.1	1,269
1929	807	63.5	53	4.2	410	32.3	1,270
1930	925	66.5	53	3.8	410	29.5	1,392
1931	1,029	71.0	53	3.7	367	25.3	1,449
1932	1,025	70.2	49	3.4	386	26.4	1,460
1933	1,065	71.1	47	3.1	386	25.8	1,498
1934	1,076	70.0	46	3.0	416	27.0	1,538

By 1928 seven American companies had branch offices in Japan. It is extremely difficult to get a definite sense of the Japanese market at this time. Most records are based on censorship figures, but since censorship was done by more than one board, there are conflicting figures available. These are not broken down by source and import statistics are not compared with domestic production. In calculating the American share of the market, I have added Department of Commerce totals for both negative and positive footage together for each year from 1926 to 1934 and compared those with the amount of footage censored in Japan in those same years. These two sets of figures are compatible, in that they both reflect all the prints released, rather than simply one print of each film. The results are approximate at best, however; films registered late in one year in American customs would not appear in censorship records until the following year. The American totals also contain negative footage, which would have been used for striking multiple prints; these percentages are thus somewhat low. (Negative footage was, however, a small fraction of the whole.) But, given these provisos, these figures may yield some sense of the USA's share of the Japanese film market (see Table XXX).

TABLE XXX

The USA's share of the Japanese market, 1926–34

	1926 %	1927 %	1928 %	1929 %	1930 %	1931 %	1932 %	1933 %	1934 %
American share of silent films	10.9	11.4	10.6	11.2	3.0	0.9	0.5	0.2	0.2
American share of sound films					90.7	62.8	45.5	42.1	18.6
Sound films' share of total market					5.7	8.4	17.3	23.0	40.3

Determining the relative share of European films is even more difficult; another source with a different set of censorship figures, however, shows American films to have been about 80% of total imports.[82]

Judgments on the American position in other Far Eastern markets must usually be based on American consular reports or opinions of exporters' representatives who travelled in the area. In late 1919, the Oriental representative for the New York exporter David P. Howells declared that in the past year the market for junk films had declined considerably in the Orient: 'the responsible renters now require new prints of leading brands.' This was less the case for China, where political unrest kept the theatres limited mostly to the treaty ports; it had recently taken new prints of a few specials, but still relied mostly on second-hand. As a result, American firms made little attempt to court Chinese customers; in 1920, films were still shown in China with English intertitles, necessitating a translator in the theatre. Nevertheless, with only a small amount of native production going on sporadically, the Americans had a considerable hold on the field. A 1921 consular report from Hong Kong found that 'practically all the pictures shown are of American manufacture'.

In spite of China's huge population, the market was relatively small. In 1922, an American trade official found that there were fewer than 100 theatres, with only forty showing new American films. By 1923, another official found that the used-film trade had further declined, with most prints shown now being new; he estimated that American films made up 80% of those shown in the Peking and Tientsin areas. At the same time, American films were reported as 90% of those shown in Hong Kong; as this port was the distribution point for the southern part of the country, that proportion presumably held good for the whole area. This figure was confirmed in 1926 by Luther M. Jee, a Chinese distributor and film-maker – he estimated that about 450 foreign films had been shown in China during 1926, with 90% being American; the Chinese had made 57 films that year.[83]

Siam continued to get its films from Singapore, where Universal and Pathé controlled distribution. Java's 250 theatres used a majority of American films. Some figures are available for the Philippines, showing a predictably high share for American imports: 91.7% of the total footage imported in 1921, 83.2% for 1928. The Islands had 275 theatres as of 1929 and were a distribution point for other parts of the area.[84]

India and the Middle East
During the war the Indian film market fell almost completely under American control. By 1919 wartime building restrictions were lifted, theatre-building resumed and the business became more lucrative. The Department of Commerce estimated that American films made up 95% of all imports. The *Bioscope*'s Indian correspondent reported in 1922 that there were about 200 theatres in the country, with 90% of the films shown being of American origin; the rest came from Britain, Italy, France, Sweden and Germany.[85]

During the mid-20s indigenous Indian film-making slowly increased. It had an uphill battle, since American films had been amortised already before reaching this market and could be offered at prices that undercut the native product. An Indian film would cost an average of 20,000 rupees and could not be exported; yet the rights to an inexpensive American feature might cost as little as 2,000 rupees. In addition, the powerful Madan Theatres Ltd chain bought groups of American films under a block-booking scheme and based the bulk of its programming on these imports. Indian films were popular when shown, however, and by 1926–7 they comprised 15% of releases, the imports still being mostly American.

In later 1927, after the British quota had gone into effect, the Indian Cinematograph Committee was formed to study the situation in India and make recommendations. It included three Indian and three British members. One of the British purposes in making the investigation seems to have been to establish a quota in India for 'Empire films' – those produced in Britain and throughout its colonies. Nominally such a quota would have encouraged the production of Indian films, but the effect probably would have been minimal. A Madras newspaper

144

editorialised in 1927: 'There is widespread suspicion that the real object of the inquiry is to check [the USA's] supremacy and bolster up the inefficient British industry.' Ultimately the Indian half of the Committee jettisoned the 'Empire' notion and recommended measures to support the native industry. The government failed to act on the Committee's recommendations and sound soon changed the conditions upon which the Committee had based its report. During the mid-30s, with the development of a unique native version of the musical genre, the Indian film industry was to begin its growth into one of the world's largest; India would eventually become, along with Japan, one of the few non-socialist countries where the domestic film could compete on equal terms with American imports.[86]

Like eastern Europe, the Middle East in the post-war years consisted of a number of new or altered countries, carved from the old Turkish Empire; several were occupied or under the protection of various Allied victors. Films for these areas tended to come from companies in the occupying country or simply from the nearest distribution point. For example, the British occupation of Iraq began in 1919 and immediately a few theatres were built to entertain the troops; films came mainly from London exporters, with some from Bombay. The market developed slowly thereafter, however; in 1923 there were still only seven theatres in the country and no exchanges, films being sent in by parcel post to the theatres.

Initially, after the war, Constantinople's eleven theatres were getting mostly Italian, French and Danish films, presumably in old copies. But by 1923 the city was up to thirty theatres and American films were the most popular; these came from distributors in Paris or London.[87]

The Middle East remained a series of small markets, most of which were not lucrative enough to attract any direct American sales efforts. If American films were shown to any extent, it was because they were what the European agencies sent out. Arabia in 1927 was a very small market, due to Moslem opposition to the cinema; four theatres in Aden formed the only regular outlet. About 70% of the films were American, but most came from an agency in London; one theatre obtained its prints from Bombay. Only 50% of the films shown in Persia were American and these were old prints rented from Baghdad, London and Paris; German and Russian films came in as well. The Persian market went from nine theatres in 1928 to twenty-six in 1929, to thirty-three in 1930. Import statistics were not kept; on the basis of a distributor's estimates, the shares of the main suppliers for Persia in the late 20s are shown in Table XXXI.

The American films continued to be old prints. A favourable exchange rate with France encouraged the use of French films; the German industry, however, waged a vigorous campaign during these years, selling at even lower prices than did the French. One American

145

TABLE XXXI

Main suppliers for Persia, 1928–30

Source	1928 %	1929 %	1930 %
USA	43.6	49.3	41.8
France	32.8	23.9	27.1
Germany	9.8	10.2	17.3
Russia	10.5	12.4	12.1

consul summed up the situation in Persia in 1930 and the same might apply to other markets in the region: 'Producers and distributors in the United States are not prepared to exploit a territory where the returns are comparatively small, with the result that only the cheapest and oldest films reach this country.' Most films had to be taken in by camel or lorry; only Germany and Russia had direct rail lines into Persia, giving their films an extra advantage.

American films did make headway in Turkey, however, with its proximity to Europe; they constituted about 80% of the 210 silent films released in 1929; in addition, twelve sound features came in from the USA.[88]

Africa
Africa remained a minor market for American films and all selling was done indirectly. After the war, the African Film Trust still controlled South Africa; it was a vertically integrated company, allied with the African Theatres Trust and African Film Productions (for scenics and newsreels). The company, still owned by I. W. Schlesinger, bought its films new in London or New York, showed them in its own first-run houses and then rented them to independent, peripheral theatres. The company's entire yearly schedule was planned in New York each September; other theatres had to take the programmes exactly as dictated. Of the 3,400,874 feet of film imported in 1920, 71.2% was from the USA (or 77.1% in terms of value); Britain contributed 20.7% (in value), with less than 3% coming from other countries. In 1922, an American consul estimated that American films made up 85% of programmes in South Africa. The same conditions continued for the next few years; when the British quota law became inevitable in 1926, Schlesinger joined the board of British International and agreed to make up 12.5% of the programmes of British films.[89]

Because it was a relatively poor market where the predominant language in use in film titles was French, Egypt came rather late under

146

American control. By 1920 the films in use were mainly French and Italian; American films were popular, but usually badly worn by the time they reached Cairo. Later in the 20s, the balance had shifted. Exact figures are impossible to determine, since import figures showed only where the shipments originated, not where the films were made. France supplied about half the imports, but many of the films coming from there were American; a sale to a French agent usually included rights for Egypt, Palestine and Syria as well. In 1929, an American official estimated the actual American share of screen time at 70%. There were other, smaller African markets, but these typically were unable to take new prints. In 1923, Portuguese East Africa had only four or five theatres; American films predominated, followed by British, French and Italian; the prints came in about two years after their original release, being distributed from South Africa. In 1928, American films were estimated to make up 80% of those shown in the Canary Islands.[90]

SUMMARY

During the post-war era the USA had firmly established itself in nearly all world markets. There were a few exceptions, however. The USSR had, by dint of government regulation and support, regained its own market to a large extent by this point. Germany had not only driven American films into second place, but had managed to compete to a small degree in markets abroad. Japan, depending upon several strong, vertically integrated companies, was unique in keeping a large portion of its domestic market for native productions without extensive regulation. A few small markets, like Persia, depended on films from the nearest, cheapest sources and American firms were content largely to ignore them. There is also some evidence that the various distribution agreements and general co-operation among European countries were slowly easing the American stranglehold. Yet extreme right-wing elements were gaining increasing influence over the German industry and the Fascists had been involved in Italian film-making for several years. In general the spirit of pacifism and co-operation that had fostered the brief 'Film Europe' movement was soon to disappear.

However, at the end of the 20s, the relative stability of the USA's considerable lead in world film markets seemed to be threatened by the introduction of a new factor – sound.

5 Surviving Talkies and the Depression, 1929-34

'Now, indeed, is Hollywood become the modern Babel.'
Clifford Howard, 1931[1]

By the early 20s, the American film industry had virtually taken over world markets. I end this study in 1934, however, in order to include an assessment of how sound and the Depression affected exports. The period of the introduction of sound abroad, from 1929 to about 1932, was the last time when there was widespread hope of breaking the USA's hold on foreign markets. On the one hand, the hundreds of European patents seemed to offer a means of forcing the American firms out of Europe or at least of curbing their power. On the other hand, the problem of translating English dialogue into a variety of foreign tongues suggested that trade barriers might automatically appear and that American films might be confined to markets like Britain and Australia. Eventually both these hopes proved misleading; the Depression had more adverse impact on American exports than did problems relating to sound. And once the recovery began in 1934, American film exports continued in a steady flow for decades, only slightly affected even by such major events as World War II.

THE EUROPEAN SOUND-PATENTS STRUGGLE

Sound offered the first situation since the Latham-Loop decision of 1912 in which patents could be used to control large areas of film-industry activity. As during the MPPC period, companies holding basic sound patents could go to court and possibly keep products out of an entire country. A number of powerful European companies, centring around the two patent-holding German sound firms, Tobis and Klangfilm, combined to present a solid front against the American sound film. And for a period of about a year, from mid-1929 to mid-1930, they managed to hold most of the American industry at a stand-off. In effect what the patents offered was a way of enforcing systematically the notion of 'Film Europe'. From the mid-20s on,

148

occasional reciprocal distribution arrangements between firms aided the circulation of films within Europe. But if firms in different countries could combine and pool patents, they could litigate to limit their competitors' activities. This is in part what the Tobis-Klangfilm group initially tried to do. In another sense, their activities in the 1929–30 period are somewhat similar to what the MPPC had tried in the USA against foreign firms years earlier; this time, companies in several producing countries attempted to band together and use patents to protect a pan-European market. There were literally hundreds of sound patents issued in Europe in the 20s and 30s, most of which came to nothing and had no impact on American export. The most significant group of patent-holders is that which grew up around the German Tri-ergon sound system, for this is the one which successfully used patents to force the American sound interests into a deal on worldwide sound rights in 1930.

The history of the invention, innovation and diffusion of sound in the USA has been analysed thoroughly elsewhere and there is no need to deal with it here.[2] Suffice it to say that the innovation process began with Warner Bros.' Vitaphone shorts and *Don Juan* in August of 1926 and was well under way by the time of *The Jazz Singer*'s première in October of 1927. The situation was quite different in Europe. The most important sound system had been invented as early as 1918 by three Germans, who named it Tri-ergon ('the work of three'). They tried to innovate it in film-making between 1922 and 1928; but although UFA optioned it in 1924, Tri-ergon was not put to use during this period. Thus the innovation of sound in Europe began in 1928, two years behind the American industry. On 27 September, *The Jazz Singer* opened at London's Piccadilly Theatre, leased by Warner Bros. to show its own films; it ran a month and was followed by *The Terror* and *The Home Towners*. Universal showed sound films at the Rialto in late November and the New Empire had talking shorts at that same time. There were a number of British sound systems being used during this same period; near the end of 1928, the Capital was running films recorded by British Acoustic, the British version of the Danish Petersen-Poulsen system, which used a separate strip of 35 mm film for the soundtrack. (This system would later be the basis of partially successful litigation to force the USA to pay licensing fees in Scandinavia.)[3] The American sound film seemed on the verge of a peaceful move into the European market.

At the same time, however, opposing forces were building up. Douglas Gomery has suggested that in this period the central economic strategy among countries was cartelisation and other forms of combination: 'After World War I a monopolist corporation rarely operated in a single nation-state.' The American film industry had become a group of multinational corporations through their creation of

149

distribution networks abroad: 'European corporations, the former imperialist powers, had to retreat and develop methods by which to respond to aggressive United States competition.'⁴ The German sound companies formed the core of a multinational group.

By July 1928 news from the USA had made it clear that sound was a viable technology for the future. That month, representatives of two major sound systems formed the Tonbild-Syndikat A-G (Tobis). (Fig. 2 lays out this series of events in schematic form.) The two sound systems were the German Tri-ergon, a method using a wider filmstrip with the track outside the sprocket holes, and the Dutch Küchenmeister, a similar system of recording on the outside margin. Tobis, registered on 19 September with a capital of 12 million marks ($2,859,600, or $16,013,760 in 1982 terms), invested in by German, Swiss and Dutch interests, also controlled the Petersen-Paulsen double-strip system and the Messter synchronised-disc system. Indeed, it owned all the significant German sound methods except the Breuning disc system, owned by the Lignose-Hörfilm GmbH. British Phototone Ltd gained control of this company in July. This latter transaction was reported by Canty as creating 'the first organization in Europe by which distribution of international sound films is assured in Great Britain, France, Germany, and Belgium'. (British Phototone would later come under the control of the Tobis-related interests.)⁵

Tobis brought together smaller companies which held over 500 sound patents. The idea was to control the market so thoroughly that competition would be eliminated. But a month after Tobis' registration, a second major company was formed. In October, two extremely powerful German electrical firms, Siemens & Halske and Allgemeine Elektrizitäts Gesellschaft (AEG), and a phonograph company, Polyphon Werke, registered the Klangfilm GmbH. (The electrical firms each held 45% interests, with Polyphon taking the remaining 10%.) Klangfilm's sound system was based on research done within the founding companies; aside from the Polyphon patents, the group controlled the patents of Telefunken, a branch of AEG and Siemens & Halske. They also had international patent affiliations with General Electric in the USA. Thus Klangfilm constituted a serious threat to Tobis; they competed in wiring German theatres, and Tobis immediately brought a suit against Klangfilm. The struggle continued for less than six months. As the American firm Electrical Research Products Inc. (ERPI, a subsidiary of Western Electric) began wiring German theatres with its equipment, the two German firms combined to oppose it. On 13 March 1929, they closed an arrangement whereby the sound-film business was divided among the participating groups: Klangfilm took over the wiring of theatres, Tobis the production of sound films and Siemens & Halske the manufacture of the equipment. On 8 April Tobis-Klangfilm signed a major contract with UFA, to wire

150

four large studios being built at Neubabelsberg; twenty-two sound films were planned for the 1929–30 season. This promised to be the beginning of large-scale sound production in Germany.[6]

These were the relations of the firms within Germany. But at the time of its formation, Tobis had raised money by selling its foreign rights to an international finance syndicate controlled by the Dutch

FIG. 2

Formation of the German-Dutch sound syndicate

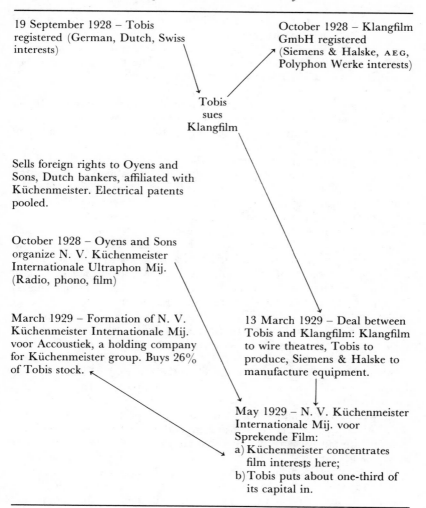

19 September 1928 – Tobis registered (German, Dutch, Swiss interests)

October 1928 – Klangfilm GmbH registered (Siemens & Halske, AEG, Polyphon Werke interests)

Tobis
sues
Klangfilm

Sells foreign rights to Oyens and Sons, Dutch bankers, affiliated with Küchenmeister. Electrical patents pooled.

October 1928 – Oyens and Sons organize N. V. Küchenmeister Internationale Ultraphon Mij. (Radio, phono, film)

March 1929 – Formation of N. V. Küchenmeister Internationale Mij. voor Accoustiek, a holding company for Küchenmeister group. Buys 26% of Tobis stock.

13 March 1929 – Deal between Tobis and Klangfilm: Klangfilm to wire theatres, Tobis to produce, Siemens & Halske to manufacture equipment.

May 1929 – N. V. Küchenmeister Internationale Mij. voor Sprekende Film:
a) Küchenmeister concentrates film interests here;
b) Tobis puts about one-third of its capital in.

banking house of Oyens and Sons. The bank, affiliated with the Küchenmeister group, put Tobis in with a whole variety of electro-acoustical processes. In October 1928, Oyens and Sons organised the N. V. Küchenmeister Internationale Ultraphon Mij., a loose company embracing interests in radio, phonographs, records and sound films. The following spring the Küchenmeister group reorganised; in March it created a holding company, the N. V. Küchenmeister Internationale Mij. voor Acoustiek. This company bought 26% of Tobis' stock. In May, Küchenmeister Internationale Ultraphon Mij. concentrated its film interests in a separate company, the N. V. Küchenmeister Internationale Mij. voor Sprekende Film; Tobis put about one-third of its capital stock into this company. Thus the Küchenmeister group owned a total of about 68% of Tobis, making the latter a foreign subsidiary of the Dutch holding company. (The remainder of Tobis' stock was owned by a syndicate of the Commerz and Privatbank in Germany.)[7]

There were other patents and companies involved besides these German and Dutch interests. (See Fig. 3 showing the group's connections in Britain.) Tobis itself set up subsidiaries in a number of countries. But perhaps equally importantly, the members of the Küchenmeister group were forming alliances which brought additional patents under its control. Shortly after its formation, in November 1928, Klangfilm had bought a majority interest in Lignose Hörfilm Ltd, the British company which controlled the Breuning disc patent and which was in turn under the control of British Phototone; this brought British Phototone and its sister French company, French Phototone, into the Tobis-Klangfilm group. The Phototone deal did not, however, result in the anticipated use of the Klangfilm system for actual production, so in May 1929, Klangfilm Ltd formed in Britain and licensed First International Sound Pictures (a producing wing of British International) to use the Tobis-Klangfilm system. Another important deal was made with the British Talking Pictures Corp. This company was owned by a group headed by I. W. Schlesinger (our old acquaintance, the American who had since 1913 owned that very effective South African monopoly, the African Film Trust). His brother, M. A. Schlesinger, controlled the General Talking Picture Corp. in the USA – owner of the DeForest sound patents. In July of 1929 an agreement was reached whereby British Talking Pictures and Tobis-Klangfilm would merge and pool their patents. In November, they formed the Associated Sound Film Industries Ltd (ASFI), with £1 million capital; it was to be a holding company for the Küchenmeister group and General Talking Pictures. Thus one large, complex organisation had concentrated virtually all the major sound patents in the European market. As in the later Paris agreement with the American sound firms, the ASFI contract allotted specific geographic

152

divisions to its various subsidiaries. ASFI also had Italian connections, since British Talking Pictures later formed SA Films Sonori in Rome, in conjunction with the Italian government; British Talking had 40% of the company, which gained the exclusive rights to the DeForest patents for Italy. SA Films affiliated with the Ente Nazionale per la Cinematografica and LUCE.[8]

FIG. 3

The Küchenmeister group's links in Britain

November 1928 – Klangfilm gets majority holding in Lignose-Hörfilm Ltd, which owns the Breuning disc system and controls the British Phototone Co. (This comes to little ←————→ Linked to French Phototone in terms of production.)

May 1929 – Klangfilm Ltd formed in Britain.

First International Sound Pictures Ltd, film production wing of British International, acquires Tobis-Klangfilm licences for Britain, produces sound films.

British Talking Pictures Corp. (owned by group headed by I. W. Schlesinger), linked to General Talking Pictures Corp., USA (controlled by M. A. Schlessinger), which owns DeForest patents for Britain and USA.

November 1929 – Associated Sound Film Industries Ltd (ASFI) formed. Holding company for Küchenmeister group and General Talking Pictures Corp.

Later also forms SA Films Sonori Rome, with aid of Italian government. 40% of stock to British Talking Films. Sonori has DeForest rights for Italy.

Affiliations with Ente Nazionale per la Cinematografica, LUCE and music publishing houses.

153

In France, the main aim was to control production and wiring, since no French company controlled an important patent. Indeed, the French industry was in a crisis in 1929; production had fallen to 52 films (as opposed to 94 in both 1928 and 1930). The major companies were in retreat, merging and changing control. In February, Charles Pathé had retired and Pathé-Cinéma was sold to a financial group run by banks; it became Pathé-Natan-Ciné-Romans. Similarly, a major theatre chain, Etablissements Aubert, had merged with Société Franco Film, a production company. In January of 1930, Gaumont raised its capital and took over Aubert-Franco to form Gaumont-Franco-Film-Aubert (GFFA), controlled by a large bank and by Swiss electrical interests. At the same time the GFFA acquired the Etablissements Continsousa, a manufacturer of theatre-sound equipment. Tobis' French subsidiary, Société des Films Sonores Tobis (formed February 1929, for production), closed a deal with the GFFA in April of 1930 for the reciprocal sale of equipment and the distribution of films.[9]

This complex series of transactions established Tobis-Klangfilm as the most powerful European sound company; it was producing abroad or licensing other companies to produce. If it could control American competition, it could also dominate the wiring of European theatres. Aside from the links with British Talking Pictures and the GFFA in France, these deals were all made before any American talkie had entered the German market. Tobis-Klangfilm was in a powerful position to challenge the American industry. In April 1929 (less than a month after Tobis and Klangfilm joined forces), Warner Bros. announced that *The Singing Fool* would soon première in Berlin. Tobis-Klangfilm immediately brought a patents suit against Western Electric. In mid-May, Siemens & Halske obtained a temporary injunction to stop the première, but it soon ran out. Telefunken got another injunction to halt the press screening of the film; again it ran out and the companies were unable to get a third before 3 June, when three screenings of the film, showing in English without any translation, won applause from Berlin audiences. On the basis of this success, Western Electric began wiring a few Berlin theatres. But on 20 July, the court decision in the patents case upheld Tobis' exclusive rights and the sound equipment had to be removed. Tobis-Klangfilm brought similar suits in Britain, Switzerland and Czechoslovakia, hoping to force American firms to pay to show their talkies on German equipment all over Europe.[10]

At first there was hope of an amicable solution; representatives of the two major American sound firms, RCA and ERPI, began negotiations in New York with representatives of Siemens & Halske, AEG, Tobis, International Tobis and Küchenmeister. Their purpose was to standardise technology and arrange for the international use of the different companies' equipment. There seemed to be tentative

154

agreement, and ERPI sent John Otterson to Germany in August to finalise the deal; but Tobis-Klangfilm held out for higher royalties and Otterson contacted Will Hays to boycott the German market. While the boycott went forward that autumn, litigation intensified. Tobis-Klangfilm got final injunctions in Czechoslovakia, Holland, Hungary, Switzerland and Austria, and won appeals in Germany. ERPI retaliated, attempting to break the German ban by suing United Picture Theatres Ltd and Klangfilm's subsidiary in Britain and Klangfilm and UFA in Germany.[11]

The effectiveness of the American boycott in Germany is difficult to judge. The patents dispute left the German market in an unsettled state; the total number of feature films censored in 1929 was down by nearly a hundred from the previous year (see Table XIV). Over half of this drop came in the American share, yet export figures show record amounts of footage going to Germany from the USA up until November; monthly totals for 1929 and early 1930 were as shown in Table XXXII.[12]

TABLE XXXII

Monthly American film exports to Germany 1929–30 (in feet)

Month	1929	1930
January	1,231,432	1,984,192
February	931,994	1,377,521
March	1,486,011	832,853
April	546,136	1,762,587
May	409,509	
June	2,033,003	
July	1,842,994	
August	1,542,571	
September	1,509,055	
October	1,902,570	
November	919,434	
December	832,386	

NOTE: By way of contrast, the average monthly exports to Germany during 1928 were 934,939 feet.

Of course, it is possible that this footage was being stockpiled and not released, but this is unlikely, given that the American contribution to the German market in 1930 was lower than in 1929. There was reported to be a shortage of product in the German market, but this

155

was also due to a drop in domestic production as firms awaited the outcome of the dispute. This delayed the widespread introduction of sound in Germany. Western Electric had retaliated against the German court decision by arranging a boycott to keep German films out of the American market. As a result, by March of 1930, UFA suspended sound-film production for three months, having six films near completion; it found it could not amortise them on the home market. In addition, audiences in other countries were quickly accepting sound films as the standard. Hence it became difficult to sell silent German films abroad; these, too, had a hard time making back their costs within Germany.[13]

The American boycott lasted through the autumn of 1929. But dealings were under way which would weaken it. In July 1929, General Electric purchased part interest in AEG, enabling GE's subsidiary, RCA, to make an agreement with Tobis-Klangfilm; RKO, the film company formed to produce with the RCA system, began releasing in areas controlled by Tobis in March 1930. In September 1929, Warner Bros. had begun negotiations with the Küchenmeister group (including the Internationale Mij. voor Sprekende Film, Tobis itself, the English holding company ASFI and Tobis' French subsidiary); the American company received a temporary licence and began releasing in the areas controlled by the European trust. In April 1930, a delegation came to New York to conclude the deal, including Heinrich J. Küchenmeister, the manager of the Commerz und Privatbank (holding the German share of Tobis which Warners obtained), a partner in the Oyens and Sons bank and other representatives. On 8 April, Warners acquired 20% of Tobis-Klangfilm for $10,000,000, to be paid in instalments; thus it gained the right to distribute its sound films all over Europe.[14]

All this left Western Electric and the majority of the Hollywood firms out in the cold. In May, Adolph Zukor went to Berlin and conferred with the directors of Siemens & Halske and the representatives of Tobis. He proposed a meeting to organise the sound-film industry of the world. The meeting began 19 June in Paris; Will Hays chaired it and handled the public-relations end. About thirty delegates did the negotiating, including representatives for Western Electric, RCA Photophone, the American production companies contracted to Western Electric, Siemens & Halske, AEG, and Warner Bros. By 12 July an agreement had been reached and a committee was appointed to draft a memorandum embodying its provisions. On 22 July the agreement was ready. According to Gomery, the Hollywood production firms never signed the memorandum; the sound companies – Tobis-Klangfilm, RCA and ERPI – did sign, however. The sound-patents agreement made its members into an international cartel, dividing up the entire world into territories. The Dutch–German

156

interests received exclusive rights for sound equipment sales in Germany, Danzig, the Saar Basin, Memel (a territory of East Prussia), Austria, Hungary, Switzerland, Czechoslovakia, Holland, the Dutch East Indies, Denmark, Sweden, Norway, Finland, Yugoslavia, Romania and Bulgaria. The American manufacturers were to control the USA, Canada, Newfoundland, Australia, New Zealand, the Straits Settlements, India and the USSR. (The latter developed its own sound systems and declined to import American equipment.) The rest of the world was open to either type of equipment. The agreement opened the USA to German films and vice versa.[15]

The Paris agreement hardly settled the sound-patents disputes, however. On 15 July 1930, as the sound memorandum was being drawn up, the German government issued new quota regulations effective until the end of 1931. The provisions were hard on American films. Two-thirds of the import licences were reserved for silent films; import licences could be bought, but only at a high price. The Department of Commerce's resident expert pointed out: 'The American prospects are hardly good enough to warrant the payment of 25,000 marks for a transferable import permit . . . when the high cost of printing, distribution and license fees to the Tobis is taken into account.' He estimated that the new regulations would make only 35 permits available for American sound films for the 1931–2 season. In response, Hays advised the Hollywood production/distribution companies not to sign the Paris memorandum. They agreed but went ahead with imports into Germany, paying the royalty fees under the agreed-upon schedule. The first American films to reach Germany as a result of the accord were some Fox Movietone newsreels in September.[16]

Over the next year and a half, American and German interests negotiated informally to iron out the differences. They held a second, ten-day conference in Paris, beginning 8 February 1932. There French representatives complained of having to pay inordinately high royalties, both on the equipment they rented and for the right to distribute their own films in their own market. The Americans accused the Germans of reducing their prices in France by up to 50% below those agreed upon at the 1930 meeting. A compromise was reached, with the royalties for France being lowered; in return, Switzerland was taken out of Germany's exclusive territory and became part of the area open to both countries. According to Gomery, other quarrels emerged and in effect the cartel was breaking up. As a result, other patents disputes began. For example, the Danish firm of Nordisk had acquired the rights for the Petersen-Paulsen system in 1929; the Küchenmeister group had later taken over the patent. But with the 1930 cartel in disarray, Nordisk went to court against the Hollywood firms to claim exclusive rights for Denmark, thus allowing it to collect royalties on imported sound films; it won its case in October 1933 and began suits in Norway, Sweden and Finland, eventually winning only the Swedish one. As a result, in November 1934, the American companies agreed to Nordisk's terms and signed a contract for Denmark and, later, one for Sweden.[17]

In the meantime high royalties in Germany led the American companies to withhold payments, beginning 1 January 1933. There followed two more years of negotiations; in March 1935, the American firms paid a substantial portion of their accumulated royalty debts to the Germans. This opened the way for more negotiations and another Paris meeting. On 18 March 1936, the parties signed a new agreement, reorganising the cartel, with lower royalty rates for the future. This had little effect on American films in Germany, since most firms by this point had responded to the severe quota and Nazi restrictions by withdrawing from direct distribution. The new royalty schedule did, however, save the USA money in other Tobis-controlled areas. The cartel operated until the outbreak of World War II, when ERPI's licensees ceased paying royalties to Tobis-Klangfilm.[18]

LANGUAGE AND QUOTA BARRIERS

The successful introduction of sound in the USA caused the trade much anxiety about the possible loss of world markets. Trade barriers had made only slight inroads in the USA's total exports, but language barriers might cut off all but the English-speaking markets. Producers and distributors tried a number of different translation methods over the next few years and it was not until 1931–2 that they settled upon the most successful solutions.

In early 1928, Louis B. Mayer declared that he was not worried; he assumed that the popularity of American films would lead to the use of English as a universal language. Indeed, editorials and politicians in various countries decried this as a real danger. There were reports during 1929 from both Brazil and Scandinavia that learning English had become a fad as a result of American talkies; a South American film critic described spectators of the first talkie shown in Rio de Janeiro, *Broadway Melody,* reciting the dialogue to friends to practice their new skill.[19]

This was hardly a basis for the whole sound industry, but no one best translation method was apparent to the exporters of the first sound films. Dubbing was virtually impossible in the very early period, since mixing was not yet in use; all sound had to be recorded simultaneously. The first films shown abroad were usually presented in English. When talkies made their way to Britain there was no problem, of course. When *Le Chanteur de jazz* showed in Paris in early 1929, the intertitles were in French, with printed translations for the few moments of dialogue projected on to an adjacent screen. Later that year, *The Singing Fool* screenings in Berlin used no translation. In such screenings abroad, the novelty value attracted audiences even if they could not understand the language. This worked primarily because Hollywood had a head start in sound-film production; as one American producer pointed out in late 1929:

> While it is true that right now many of these countries are tolerating pictures with English dialogue, this is due to the scarcity of suitable sound pictures in their native language and talkies of the revue type are more or less adaptable on account of the magnificent settings and musical reproduction. The novelty is rapidly wearing off, however, and already in many countries the agitation is growing keener against the invasion of the English language.

As this analysis suggests, the revue musicals of the early talkie era were among the most successful exports. Even with no translation they proved attractive; when subtitled they required a minimum of writing to keep the audience up with the action. It seems likely that the vogue among the studios for this genre had partly to do with the desire to maintain exports. In mid-1930, Canty reported that in central Europe American films 'that combine song and dance with occasional sequences of the English language have found satisfactory appeal', unlike straight dialogue films. Similarly, the decline in the production of revue musicals may have been due not so much to the passing of a fad among American audiences as to the development of satisfactory translation procedures by 1931.[20]

By late 1929 the novelty value of English-language films was wearing off. During the year, various means of translation had been tried. In Poland, sound films were shown with the dialogue passages cut out completely and replaced with intertitles; the effect was of a clumsily paced silent film with music and effects. This was among the cheapest ways of translating a film and it was used mainly in the less lucrative markets. In 1930, First National showed *Sally* in Berlin this way, but it did not prove an adequate solution there. But in early 1931, it was still reported to be in use in Egypt, with French intertitles replacing dialogue and Arabic captions projected on a second screen. Three other, more promising means of translation were also tried during 1929. Superimposed subtitles were employed in several moderate-sized markets, including Holland and Sweden. Observers found they worked best when there was a limited amount of dialogue, for audiences found them distracting otherwise; the Department of Commerce deemed them primarily useful for smaller countries like Portugal, Greece and Bulgaria. At the end of 1929, C. J. North commented on the high export levels: 'During the past year our sound pictures have reaped a harvest even though presented in English before non-English speaking audiences with such super-imposed titles in the appropriate language as would enable the action to be followed.' But there were objections to subtitles, especially in the dialogue-filled early talkies; other solutions seemed desirable. The Department of Commerce suggested in early 1930 that there were three types of market in Europe:

a) markets which could be supplied with versions in the main language – Britain, Germany, France, Belgium (French), Switzerland (French and German), Spain and Austria (German);
b) countries too small to warrant separate versions in the local language and where versions in one of the four main languages would not be acceptable – Sweden, Norway, Denmark, Italy, Czechoslovakia, Hungary and Poland;
c) small countries where one of the four main languages was in use as a second language; these versions could be released with subtitles in the main local language: Holland (second language, German), Portugal (Spanish), Turkey, Greece, Romania (French), Bulgaria (French or German), Yugoslavia, the Baltic States and Finland (German).[21]

Two methods of translating the soundtracks themselves into spoken foreign dialogue came into use in 1929. By October the Hollywood studios were beginning to dub soundtracks. RKO dubbed *Rio Rita* that month and United Artists, Paramount, Fox and MGM initiated this procedure as well. But there were still technical problems that made the results sound crude; sound could not be mixed and there were no Moviolas that allowed accurate synchronisation of non-direct dialogue. One 1931 account recalled that such early dubbing attempts as Universal's 1929 *Broadway* and *Showboat* 'were all but laughed off the screen at the time'. By the end of 1929 Sidney Kent, Paramount's general manager, declared that dubbed versions had failed to produce satisfactory results.[22]

The second translation method seemed more promising – making the same film over with the actors speaking a different language. In mid-November, MGM announced a $2 million programme of multiple-language films; foreign versions would be made in French, German and Spanish, with other languages to be added if the method worked. This was the most costly way of translating a film; while subtitling a silent film had cost only about $2,500, a foreign version of a talkie would require $30,000–40,000 above the cost of the original English production – an average 30% extra per version. The other big studios followed MGM's lead; Fox set up French and Spanish units in August of 1930 and Warner Bros. had made fourteen foreign versions by the end of 1930. Paramount varied the procedure by setting up a studio at

160

Joinville, outside Paris, in the winter of 1929–30. Paramount's programme was the most ambitious, with a $10,000,000 budget and a 60-film-a-year schedule in six languages; only English and Spanish versions would be done in Hollywood and at Astoria. (For the 1930–1 season, 72 films were planned.)[23]

The foreign-language versions made in the USA were typically done using *émigré* directors and casts in place of the original ones from the English version. Some actors could do one or two foreign versions themselves; Jacques Feyder, who had directed Garbo in *The Kiss*, a silent MGM film of 1929, also made the German version of *Anna Christie*, with Garbo redoing her role. (Clarence Brown had directed her in the original, with an entirely different supporting cast.) But Norma Shearer did only the English version of *The Trial of Mary Dugan*, directed by Bayard Veiller in 1929 for MGM. Arthur Robinson then made the German version with Nora Gregor in the lead. At Warners, William (né Wilhelm) Dieterle got his start by taking such roles as Ahab in *Dämon des Meeres*, directed by Michael Curtiz. (The original was *Moby Dick*, with John Barrymore.) Dita Parlo, Gustav Fröhlich and others found work briefly in Hollywood during this period. The foreign colonies which had grown up during the silent era were swelled even further.[24]

The year 1930 was a key date in the worldwide introduction of sound. A great deal of theatre-wiring went on, especially after the July Paris agreement clarified the patents situation. North summarised the situation late in the year:

The year 1930 witnessed the final domination of sound over silent films in our foreign trade. Out of approximately 210,000,000 feet of motion pictures exported during the first nine months of 1930 no less than about 138,000,000 feet were synchronised for sound, showing a percentage of 67 for sound as against 33 for silent.

Wiring spread in South America, and in March, Chile heard its first talkie, a subtitled musical; this type of film did well in South America throughout the year. Subtitles continued to be used in European markets as well. Experimentation also continued with dubbing methods. The first dubbed film to play in Berlin, Columbia's *Fliers*, showed at the UFA Palast with some degree of success, followed by a dubbed version of *The Great Gabbo*. By late in the year, dubbing technology had improved; a new multiple-track Moviola had made synchronisation easier and it was possible to mix several tracks. Thus the music and effects could be recorded separately and mixed separately with any number of different vocal tracks to create dubbed versions in many languages.[25]

For most of the big studios, 1930 was also the high point for the

161

production of foreign-language versions. RKO was the only major to hold back on this method, waiting to gauge its success; as of November 1930, it had only one French version, of a film called *The Queen's Husband*, in production. Possibly this delay had been due to the studio's work on a method which it announced in August – the Dunning process. This was a process whereby the backgrounds and extras were filmed in American studios, with these shots being sent abroad; foreign producers could then film local artists in their native language against the Hollywood scenes in back projection. It was a cheaper, but obviously less acceptable, system. By late 1930, one observer in Europe found foreign-language versions unpopular: 'It is financial suicide for Hollywood studios, even with native players, to make foreign versions, for there is no market big enough to assure profit over cost.' Even Spanish, theoretically the most widely used foreign language, had so many dialects as to render versions acted or dubbed in classical Castilian useless in many areas. In addition, foreign-language versions usually jettisoned the popular Hollywood stars for lesser-known actors; for the most part, only those foreign versions which retained the original stars (for example, Dietrich, Garbo, Navarro) did well. Conversely, foreign audiences would put up with a considerable amount of incomprehension to see their favourites. French fans, for example, were keen on the Marx Brothers in spite of the language barrier (as they are to this day). They preferred the German version of *The Blue Angel* to *Morocco* dubbed into French and made Sternberg's *An American Tragedy,* in English, one of the biggest hits of late 1931.[26]

During 1931 the production of foreign-language versions declined. In April, MGM shut down its foreign units and dismissed most of their personnel. By May Fox's Spanish unit was described as the main foreign-language producer in Hollywood; it operated until 1935. American companies continued to produce original films in Europe during the 30s. This was a practice some of them had initiated in the 20s; such production had little to do with the translation of American films. More often it was a way of getting around local quotas or gaining a share of the better European films' earnings. (Warner Bros., for example, co-produced Pabst's *Die Dreigroschenoper,* and Fox Europa co-produced Lang's French film, *Liliom*.)[27]

At the same time, dubbing and subtitling were improving and gaining wide acceptance. During 1931 South American audiences preferred 'English sound pictures done by first-class actors with titles in Spanish to a Spanish talkie done by poor actors'. In mid-1932, the Society of Motion Picture Engineers reported on dubbing: 'The increase in the number of synchronised foreign sound versions has been phenomenal during the past six months, these versions entirely replacing those using separate foreign casts for each version. Recently, pictures have been synchronised in the oriental languages.' Techniques

162

of lip synchronisation had improved hugely since 1929. Originally German audiences had rejected dubbing; by 1933 an observer found that:

> Audiences have gotten used to German conversation dubbed to American lip movements. The critics do not even mention it in their reviews unless it happens to be particularly ineffective, which is seldom the case today. Despite the campaign against dubbing which filled the German press when the first synchronised pictures appeared here, there is no doubt that it has come to stay and that the average public accepts it without worrying about who owns the voice that comes out of the loudspeaker.

By the end of 1931, then, the language problem was largely a thing of the past; subtitles and dubbing provided the two standard solutions.[28]

In general, dubbing was used only for the markets dependent on German, French and Italian. In the cases of German and French, this was probably because those countries had domestic production and audiences could have rejected subtitled versions in favour of locally made films. In 1929, Italy instituted a regulation banning the use of non-Italian dialogue and it was strictly enforced; all films had to be dubbed. In other markets, where less common languages were in use and where native production was less a threat, American films were shown with subtitles. This would have been the procedure in eastern Europe and Scandinavia, South and Central America, and so on.

Some countries adjusted their quota laws to deal with sound. France had abolished its quota in 1931 (except against Germany, which was the only country which had a quota affecting French films). On 29 July 1932, however, it issued new restrictions: films in their original foreign languages could only be shown in a limited number of theatres (five in Paris and five in the provinces) and all dubbing had to be done in Paris. On 22 July 1933, the French quota was altered to limit the number of dubbed foreign films to 140 for the next year; the number of provincial theatres showing original versions was raised to ten. (These restrictions continued in similar form through the 30s.) Germany retained its quota, specifying a different number of licences each year; on 1 July 1932, it also began requiring all dubbing to be done in Germany. This latter provision was dropped, however, in the Nazi reorganisation of film regulations in 1933. In the smaller producing countries, sound tended to loosen the quota restrictions, since native firms had a harder time amortising talkies in the local languages. In 1929, both Austria and Italy had to let in more films than their modest quotas permitted; during 1930 the Austrian and Hungarian quotas were barely enforced.[29]

163

What effect did the introduction of sound have on American film exports? As Chart 2 (in Appendix III) shows, 1929 was a very good year for the American film industry, peaking in September and October; 1930 levels remained higher than those of the pre-1929 period, with a gradual decline into 1931 and 1932. A slight recovery becomes apparent beginning in late 1933.

As Gomery has pointed out, we cannot treat sound as an isolated element. The introduction of sound coincided with changes in government regulations and with the worldwide Depression and we must weigh the relative impact of all three sets of factors in explaining the changes in exports during these years.

First, in spite of the film-industry executives' fears about language barriers, talkies did not cause a decrease in exports. Quite the contrary: early sound exports, beginning in late 1928 and accelerating in 1929, coincide with a sharp rise. According to C. J. North, the acceptance of talkies in English-speaking countries during 1929 resulted in a rise in revenues as well as footage:

> American revenues from such countries shared by the end of the year an increase far exceeding that of any preceding year. This increase out-weighed any incidental losses from certain continental European countries where legislative difficulties and other factors curtailed somewhat the distribution of films from the United States.[30]

North refers here primarily to the French quota boycott and the patents struggle in Germany. France had brought in less than 3% of the USA's revenues in 1925; assuming that figure still held, a half-year's boycott would cut only a little over 1% into American foreign income. Germany had brought in nearly 10%. A boycott of a few months could have reduced revenues by two or three percentage points. (However, the German share had probably declined since its high point in the mid-20s.) But these situations were soon resolved. Higher rentals from the lucrative British and Australasian markets might well have counterbalanced them. Similarly, the novelty value of sound made even non-English-speaking audiences accept talkies in 1929.

During 1930, however, foreign sales declined slightly, revenues more precipitously. North and Golden found that, while the silent film had typically brought in 30–40% of its revenues from abroad, during 1930 the share had dropped to 25%; they attributed this to the end of the novelty-value period. This was not to be a long-term problem; by 1931–2 the translation quandary had been largely solved. But, as we shall see, it is also probable that the drop in revenue had to do with the deepening world Depression, which would reach its trough in 1931.[31] Sound, then, initially boosted American exports; possibly the failure of multiple-language versions and early dubbing had a depressing effect during 1930 and 1931. It seems more likely, however, that the other two factors, government regulation and the Depression, had equal or greater impact.

We have seen that several countries used quotas to erode the American domination. In Britain, the 1927 quota, with its yearly increases of 2.5% up to 1936, did regain about one-fifth of the market for domestic films; some of these were 'quota quickies', produced by British or American firms cheaply to fill up the required screen time in order to import a more lucrative film. But by 1932, the British industry was building up its foundations and putting out larger-budget films; in 1933, *The Private Life of Henry VIII* was released in the USA through United Artists and was a great success. This prompted more willingness by British and American firms to invest in and distribute British films. But Robert Murphy has argued that the British industry overextended itself; other films did not do so well in the USA and by 1936–7, the British firms were cutting back. The British quota did aid the industry there, but without exports to the USA, there remained a limit to what it could do; American films remained at close to 80% of the market.[32]

The German quota was the most effective, keeping American films at one-third or less of the feature market in the early 30s (see Table A.IV, Appendix II). France, despite its economic problems, benefited from the coming of sound, in that there were quite a few foreign markets which could use French-language films; by 1930 when the government dropped the quota against all nations but Germany, the American share was at about half (see Table A.IV, Appendix II). Yet by limiting the number of dubbed films that could be imported and the number of theatres in which original-language versions could be shown, the French quota of 1932 put a lid on the American domination: the American share of features in Table A.IV for 1932–3 remained relatively high, but the share of screening time would be lower. In contrast, the Hungarian and Austrian quotas were at least temporarily rendered inoperative by the introduction of sound.

Quotas were, in a sense, a means of stimulating the post-war recoveries that had not been able to occur (or, in Germany's case, had been thrown off balance by the sudden stabilisation). The European film industries ideally needed access to the large American market to amortise their films. Failing that, they needed protection so that they could find their equilibrium: what level of domestic production could be amortised at home and on a few limited foreign markets? The British industry temporarily overexpanded, then contracted; yet this did set up the conditions for the relatively successful wartime and post-war production by Rank and Ealing. French production also increased in the early 30s, from the low of 52 in 1929 to 247 films in 1932. (The most successful of these were not always French-financed; Clair's three exported sound features, *Sous les toits de Paris, Le Million* and *À nous la liberté*, were all made by Tobis' French subsidiary.) But again, without substantial exports, there was a limit to what the industry could do. The quotas did reduce the American share of these markets slightly and also allowed the French, German and British films to compete in some other markets – thereby reducing the American share. A glance through Table A.IV shows some decreases in American percentages (for example, in New Zealand) and a few cases where the USA at least temporarily lost its dominant share (for example, in Denmark, Romania, Syria, Belgium, Bulgaria). (Most of these seem to be temporary problems with translation methods rather than the results of legislation; the British quota did, however, enable it to nibble away at the American hold in Australia and New Zealand.) Overall, though, the averages remain overwhelmingly in the USA's favour.

The quotas may have had the most lasting impact on American competition with other producers abroad, but there can be little doubt that the Depression was the main cause of the 1930–3 decline and slump. In the general American economy, domestic industrial production fell off by 16% between 1930 and 1931 (the worst year internationally of the Depression). Exports declined by 35% in volume between late 1929 and the end of 1931; given the depreciation of the dollar, export prices fell even further – about 67%. The net result was a decline in revenues of just over 50%.[33]

The close link between film exports and overall exports is apparent from a comparison of Figs. 4 and 5, measuring respectively the value of finished manufactures and of motion-picture film (positive and negative footage) exported from 1928 to 1934. (As always, this is the value of the prints, not of revenues from rentals and sales abroad.)[34]

The peaks for films are not of exactly the same height as the general exports, but they tend to coincide temporally: late summer and late autumn highs in 1928, three peaks in each chart for 1929, a similar decline with four low peaks in 1930 and so on. The main anomaly is the extraordinary slump in film exports in March and April 1931. I can find no explanation for this given by observers at the time. (The explanation must lie within the film industry, rather than in some external factor – for example, a dock strike – since there is no corresponding slump in other exports.) The pattern of the exports for those two months is suggestive. Virtually no silent films were sent out in March and very few in April. Argentina, Chile, China, Germany, Spain, Britain, Sweden and others, received only sound films in March. The slump also comes after various studios had decided in late January to stop multiple-language production. In addition, one local Hollywood trade paper announced in late February that the studios were resuming the production of silent versions for distribution abroad. We should remember that the exports of March and April would be of

FIG. 4

Value of finished manufactures exported from USA 1928–35

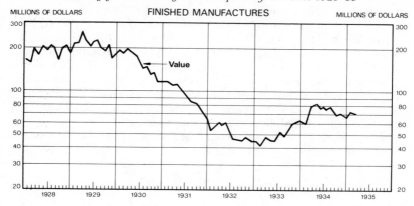

FIG. 5

Monthly value of American film exports 1928–34

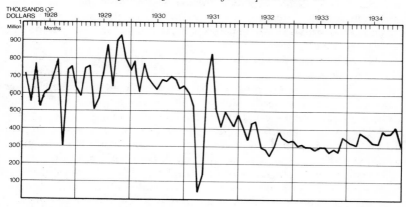

films planned and produced months earlier. The evidence is slim, but the timing suggests that the slump reflects the failure of the 1930 policies of: a) eliminating silent versions; and b) depending on foreign-language versions. The decline would thus represent a period when the studios were switching over to other ways of coping with the language problem and had little product, especially silent, to send abroad.[35]

I end this study in 1934, because by that point the recovery from the Depression had begun. There were many small factors – local legislation, increasing production in countries like India and so on – that would subsequently affect the American hegemony. But a final glance at Chart 2 (in Appendix III) shows that after late 1935, the exports remain remarkably stable, at about the same level as during the 1927–8 boom. Exports fall off, predictably enough, in 1940, to a low in 1942. But even then the effects of World War II are surprisingly limited; from 1943 to mid 1945, exports are scarcely below the late 30s' levels. After the war, exports go steeply up and remain very high through the 50s. Again, predictably, the widespread dissemination of television in Europe at the end of that decade coincides with a sudden decline in the 1960–1 monthly averages. (Thereafter the American customs' system for reporting exports changed completely and comparisons become difficult.) Thus whatever changes there have been on a local level, the overall American hegemony on world film markets has remained solid since the early 20s.

CONCLUSIONS

One major implication of this study is that we should be careful when we formulate film history in terms of 'national cinemas'. The idea of a national cinema remains a useful one for some purposes. After all, a national film industry will tend to take shape following practices in operation within the larger business community in that country and government regulation will encourage certain tendencies which may be peculiar to that country.

Yet while recognizing the necessity for studying these factors, historians should also be aware that few national cinema industries operate in isolation; through foreign investment, competition and other types of influence, outside factors will almost invariably affect any given national cinema. Such effects have implications for most types of historical study – whether of film style, industry workings, government policy, technological change or social implications. For example, Siegfried Kracauer's famous social study of German film in the 1918 to 1933 period, *From Caligari to Hitler* (Princeton, 1947) seeks to interpret evidence of the German public's collective state of mind by looking at the films they saw. Yet Kracauer looks only at German films, ignoring the fact that, as we have seen, German audiences attended many American films during this period – especially in the mid-20s, when the gradual political shift toward the right was intensifying. Similarly, it is virtually impossible to assess a national industry in any given period without dealing with its attempts to counter American competition at home and abroad. Richard Abel's *French Cinema: The First Wave 1915–1929* (Princeton, 1984) provides an example of an historical examination which does take that competition into account.

The current study has shown that American influence on film markets has been far-ranging on a long-term basis. Indeed, the struggle for world markets began, as we have seen, much earlier than World

168

War I, with the patent and licensing battles of 1907. We must conclude that the American film industry did not simply grow up and then take over world markets at an opportune time during the war. Rather, the beginning of the industry's move toward its eventual oligopoly structure, with the formation of the MPPC, coincided with the first serious moves toward blocking imports, and slightly later, toward expanding distribution abroad. Export considerations thus helped shape the formation of the American industry. Without these considerations, American distributors probably would not have been in a position to seize their opportunity when the war caused production cutbacks in France and Italy.

We have also seen that the wartime takeover was not just a matter of American films flooding into a void created by the slowing of European production. The American position on going into the war, of selling abroad largely through London offices, reflected the relatively undeveloped state of the industry in the early teens. The expansion of the American film companies into a more sophisticated and successful oligopoly was occurring in the mid-teens – the very years during which the war presented them with the opportunity to seize markets abroad. As firms moved toward a strategy of direct-sales networks around the world, they were simultaneously becoming more powerful at home. Thus by the end of the war, the sales advantage abroad had grown so great that other countries' film industries found it difficult to retain a place on their domestic markets, let alone compete extensively abroad.

The post-war inflation years, though potentially offering European countries a trade barrier against the increasingly expensive American imports, actually benefited only Germany to any degree – and that only because the government there backed this advantage up with quota legislation. Indeed, the 20s were a period when the other producing countries tried various tactics to combat American competition, both through legislation and, increasingly, through co-operation among firms of various nationalities. Some of these efforts were at least partially successful and by the late silent period there was a slight, but distinct, downward trend in the degree of American control in several European countries; Germany was the spearhead of the struggle and benefited most from it, being able to send more of its own films abroad.

The factors that ultimately defeated this co-operative move during the early 20s were complex and it is difficult to assess their relative impacts. The coming of sound chipped away at the co-operative spirit, reinstilling a sense of keen competition as national firms used the new technology to try and gain advantages over each other. The Depression weakened many markets and firms and, as political and artistic control tightened in Germany and the USSR, their films became less exportable. Although these two markets became less accessible to

American films, the remaining foreign industries lost any particular coherence in resisting American competition and American dominance became a permanent condition.

I mentioned in the Preface that my main concern here is the fact that one basic style of film-making – the classical Hollywood cinema – has been dominant through much of the world for nearly six decades. This study has shown that in fact film-makers and film viewers in most countries of the world have had the opportunity to become familiar with the norms of classical practice. Some commercial cinemas have imitated the basic conventions, both narrative and stylistic, of the classical cinema. Most British feature films have done so, giving rise to the common view that Britain's main claims to fame in cinema have been in the area of documentary film-making; distinctive studios (for example, Ealing) or directors (for example, Powell and Pressburger) tend to stand out as exceptionally skilful or popular practitioners of the norm – in much the same way that Hollywood directors came to be considered as auteurs because they worked skilfully within the dominant system. The post-war French 'cinema of quality' was also basically an attempt to conform to Hollywood's norms of excellence in its most 'high-art', studio-made literary adaptations (for example, MGM's 1936 *Romeo and Juliet*, Goldwyn's 1939 *Wuthering Heights*); the French New Wave emerged as a reaction against the cinema of quality. Indeed, virtually any avant-garde style in the cinema can be studied as a direct or indirect reaction against the dominant norm of Hollywood-style film-making. As we continue to re-examine the conventional wisdom of traditional film histories, we should keep that idea in mind. Alternative cinemas gain their significance and force partly because they seek to undermine the common equation of 'the movies' with 'Hollywood'.

Notes

KEY TO NOTE ABBREVIATIONS

Bio   *Bioscope*
CR   *Commerce Reports* (US Department of Commerce)
DC & TR   *Daily Consular and Trade Reports* (US Department of Commerce)
ENHS   Edison National Historic Site
FYB/FDYB   *Film Year Book/Film Daily Year Book*
JdF   *Jahrbuch der Filmindustrie* (Berlin: Verlag der Lichtbildbühne), Vol 1 – 1923; Vol 2 – 1926; Vol 3 – 1928; Vol 4 – 1930; Vol 5 – 1933.
LBB   *Lichtbildbühne*
Mot   *Motography*
MPA   *Motion Pictures Abroad* (US Department of Commerce)
MPN   *Motion Picture News*
MPW   *Moving Picture World*
NYT   *New York Times*
TIB   *Trade Information Bulletin* (US Department of Commerce)
    no. 499 – George R. Canty, 'Market for Motion Pictures in Central Europe, Italy and Spain' (1927)
    no. 542 – George R. Canty, 'The European Motion-Picture Industry in 1927' (1928)
    no. 553 – George R. Canty *et al.*, 'Market for Motion Pictures in Scandinavia and the Baltic States' (1928)
    no. 608 – 'Motion Pictures in Australia and New Zealand' (1929)
    no. 617 – George R. Canty, 'The European Motion-Picture Industry in 1928' (1929)
    no. 630 – 'Motion Pictures in Argentina and Brazil' (1929)
    no. 694 – 'European Motion-Picture Industry in 1929' (1930)
    no. 752 – 'European Motion-Picture Industry in 1930' (1931)
    no. 797 – 'The Motion-Picture Industry in Continental Europe in 1931' (1932)
    no. 801 – James Summerville Jr., 'The Motion-Picture Industry in the United Kingdom in 1931' (1932)
    no. 815 – George R. Canty *et al.*, 'European Motion-Picture Industry in 1932' (1933)
TSMPE/JSMPE   *Transactions* [later *Journal*] *of the Society of Motion Picture Engineers*

Preface

1. C. J. North, 'Our Foreign Trade in Motion Pictures', *Annals of the American Academy of Political and Social Sciences*, Nov. 1926, p. 107.
2. Peter Morris, *Embattled Shadows* (Montreal: McGill-Queen's University Press, 1978).

1 Regaining the American Market, 1907–13

1. Robert C. Allen, *Vaudeville and Film 1895–1915: a Study in Media Interaction* (New York: Arno Press, 1980).
2. Frank A. Southard Jr., *American Industry in Europe* (Boston: Houghton Mifflin Company, 1931), p. 3.
3. Letters: F. Z. Maguire to Thomas A. Edison, 9 Nov. 1894, File D, 'Motion Picture, 1894'; Maguire to Edison, 24 Mar. 1897, File D, 'Motion Picture, 1897'; J. H. White (National Phonograph Company Ltd, European Sales Manager), to W. H. Mark Graf (Kinetograph Department Manager, Orange plant), 3 Dec. 1903, File D, 'Motion Picture – Sales, 1903', all ENHS.
4. Letter, W. E. Gilmore to J. R. Schermerhorn, 31 May 1904, File D, 'Motion Picture – Film, 1904', ENHS.
5. 'Vitagraph Buys British Exchange', *MPW*, 16 Aug. 1919, p. 975; 'Vitagraph Co. to Print in Paris', *MPW*, 7 Mar. 1908, p. 186; W. Wallace Clendenin, 'Cameras of Yesteryear', Pt 3, *International Photographer*, Feb. 1949, p. 13; Joseph V. Mascelli, 'Those Were the Days – ', *International Photographer*, May 1947, p. 7.
6. W. Stephen Bush, 'The Film in France', *MPW*, 12 July 1913, p. 179.
7. Paul Hammond, *Marvellous Méliès* (New York: St Martin's Press, 1974), p. 49.
8. 'Pathé Announces Work of Six Months', *MPW*, 28 July 1917, p. 622; *United States of America vs. Motion Picture Patents Co. and others*, District Court of the United States for the Eastern District of Pennsylvania, no. 889 (Sept. Session, 1912), vol. 3, pp. 1765, 1968.
9. Georges Sadoul, *Histoire générale du cinéma* (Paris: Les Éditions Denoël, 1947), vol. 2, pp. 243–6; Letter, Horace M. Wilson to Thomas A. Edison, 18 Mar. 1908, File D, 'Motion Pictures, General Correspondence, 1908', ENHS.
10. Sadoul, op. cit., pp. 248–54; 'The Moving Picture in Australia', *MPW*, 14 Aug. 1909, p. 223; 'Australia and the Bioscope', *Bio*, 22 July 1909. p. 31; 'The Bioscope in Cape Town', *Bio*, 14 Mar. 1912, p. 761; Ad, Pathé, *MPW*, 25 Apr. 1914, pp. 480–1.
11. Quoted in Sadoul, op. cit. p. 51.
12. Letter and attached translation, Charles Pathé to Edison Import House, 1 July 1904, File D, 'Motion Picture – Film, 1904'; letter, Frank L. Dyer to W. E. Gilmore, 21 July 1904, File D, 'Motion Picture – Film, 1904'; letters, Gilmore to George Kleine, 15 Aug. 1904, File D, 'Motion Picture, 1904'; Kleine's reply to Gilmore, clipped to previous letter; letter, J. H. White to Gilmore, 7 Oct. 1904, File D, 'Motion Picture – Film, 1904', all ENHS.
13. Letter, W. E. Gilmore to G. Croydon Marks (Edison's British patents consultant), 10 Apr. 1907, File D, 'Motion Picture – Film, 1907', ENHS; 'What Does It Mean?', *MPW*, 26 Oct. 1907, p. 536; letters, Thomas Graf (Managing Director, National Phonograph Co. Ltd and Edison-Gesellschaft mbH) to

Gilmore, 21 June 1907, and letter, Gilmore to Graf, 16 Dec. 1907, both File D, 'Motion Picture – Sales, 1907', ENHS.

14. 'The Outlook – What of It?', *MPW*, 24 Aug. 1907, p. 388.

15. Copy of cablegram, W. E. Gilmore to G. Croydon Marks, 15 Mar. 1907; letter, Marks to Gilmore, 19 Mar. 1907; copy of cablegram, Marks to [Gilmore], undated [*c.* 20 to 27 Mar.], all File D, 'Motion Picture – Pathé, 1907', ENHS.

16. Copy of cablegram, Thomas A. Edison to W. E. Gilmore, 2 Apr. 1907, File D, 'Motion Picture – Pathé, 1907'; letter, Gilmore to G. Croydon Marks, 10 Apr. 1907, File D, 'Motion Picture – Film, 1907', both ENHS.

17. Letter, G. Croydon Marks to W. E. Gilmore, 22 Apr. 1907, File D, 'Motion Picture – Pathé, 1907', ENHS. All foreign currency exchange rates from R. L. Bidwell, *Currency Conversion Tables* (London: Rex Collings, 1970); modern equivalents are given for May 1982 dollars, using Consumer Price Index tables from *Historical Statistics of the United States, Colonial Times to 1970* (US Department of Commerce, Bureau of the Census, 1975), pp. 210–11, and *Statistical Abstract of the United States 1982–1983*, vol. 103, (US Department of Commerce, Bureau of the Census), p. 461.

18. Letter, G. Croydon Marks to Pathé Frères, 21 May 1907; copy of translation of letter, Pathé Frères to Marks, 22 May 1907, both File D, 'Motion Picture – Pathé, 1907', ENHS; 'Trade Notes', *MPW*, 22 June 1907, p. 249.

19. Letters, W. E. Gilmore to Thomas A. Edison, Gilmore to W. Pelzer, both 28 May 1907, File D, Edison letter in 'Motion Picture – Films, 1907', Pelzer in 'Motion Picture – Pathé, 1907', ENHS.

20. 'What Does It Mean?', op. cit., p. 536; *USA* vs. *MPPC*, op. cit., vol. 3, pp. 1,763–71.

21. Sadoul, op. cit., pp. 490–6, has a more detailed account of the FSA's formation.

22. Sadoul, op. cit., pp. 499–500; *USA* vs. *MPPC*, op. cit., vol. 1, pp. 140–5; Ad, *MPW*, 22 Feb. 1908, p. 130; 'Trade Directory', *MPW*, 28 Mar. 1908, p. 274.

23. 'American Mutoscope and Biograph Co. and the Recent Manufacturers' Combine', *MPW*, 22 Feb. 1908, p. 139; 'Interview with F.S.A. Members and Others', *MPW*, 28 Mar. 1908, p. 261; 'Chats With the Interviewer: George Kleine', *MPW*, 4 Apr. 1908, p. 288.

24. 'Interview with F.S.A. Members and Others', op. cit., p. 260.

25. 'Chats With the Interviewer: I. W. Ullmann', *MPW*, 4 Apr. 1908, p. 288.

26. Report, Joseph F. McCoy to Frank L. Dyer, cover letter dated 3 July 1908, File D, 'Motion Picture – General Correspondence, 1908', ENHS. (The totals have corrected a mistake in the original addition.)

27. 'Edison Company's Statement', *MPW*, 29 Feb. 1908, pp. 158–60; Briefs and other material, Legal Box 115, Folder 7, ENHS; 'The Film Service Situation', *MPW*, 4 Apr. 1908, p. 287; 'The Great Northern Film Company', *MPW*, 14 Mar. 1908, p. 207; Ad, Great Northern, *MPW*, 21 Mar. 1908, p. 226; Sadoul, op. cit., p. 510.

28. Glenn Porter, *The Rise of Big Business 1860–1910* (Arlington Heights, Illinois: AHM Publishing Corp., 1973), pp. 51, 71–9.

29. ibid., pp. 83–4.

30. Ibid., p. 81.

31. Harry N. Scheiber, Harold G. Vatter and Harold Underwood Faulkner,

American Economic History (New York: Harper & Row, 1976) pp. 313–15; *USA vs. MPPC*, op. cit., vol. 7, p. 3,912; see Ralph Cassady Jr., 'Monopoly in Motion Picture Production and Distribution', *Southern California Law Review*, summer 1959, for a longer account of the MPPC and General Film Co.'s structures and for the details of the MPPC case.

32. Manuscript, 'Proposed Scheme', File D, 'Motion Picture – Biograph and Armat, 1908', ENHS.

33. 'Trade Directory', *MPW*, 28 Mar. 1908, p. 274; 'Pathe Will Not Invade Rental Field', *MPW*, 12 Sept. 1908, p. 192.

34. Copy of agreement, 29 July 1908, File D, 'Motion Picture – Agreements, 1908', ENHS; Cassady, op. cit., p. 329; *USA vs. MPPC*, op. cit., vol. 7, p. 3,456.

35. *USA vs. MPPC*, op. cit., vol. 2, pp. 1,260–74; vol. 7, pp. 3,833, 3,835.

36. Hammond, op. cit., pp. 147, 149, 72; John Frazer, *Artificially Arranged Scenes* (Boston: G. K. Hall, 1979), pp. 48–9.

37. T[homas] B[eddings], 'News From America', *Bio*, 24 June 1909, p. 25.

38. 'Pathé Frères and the Motion Picture Patents Company: an Important Interview With J. A. Berst', *MPW*, 8 May 1909, p. 590; 'Pathé's to Produce in America, Germany, and Italy', *Bio*, 14 Apr. 1910, p. 59; Sadoul, op. cit., vol. 3, p. 67; 'Pathé's American Film', *MPW*, 14 May 1910, p. 777; *USA vs. MPPC*, op. cit., vol. 1, bet. pp. 547–8.

39. 'The Moving Picture Outlook in America: Important Interview with Ingvald C. Oes', *MPW*, 1 May 1909, p. 550.

40. 'Trade Notes', *MPW*, 28 Mar. 1908, p. 262; 'Important Meeting in Paris', *MPW*, 21 Mar. 1908, p. 232; Sadoul, op. cit., vol. 2, pp. 509–27.

41. 'Foreign News – America', *Bio*, 25 Feb. 1909, p. 19; Cassady, op. cit., p. 364; 'Will G. Barker in America', *MPW*, 10 Apr. 1909, p. 440.

42. Cassady, op. cit., p. 364; 'American Notes', *Bio*, 29 Apr. 1909, p. 11; 'News From America', *Bio*, 13 May 1909, p. 13.

43. Tariff averages from Scheiber, *et al.*, op. cit., p. 286.

44. 'Europe Pitted Against America', *MPW*, 5 Feb. 1910, p. 163; table compiled from Scheiber, *et al.*, op. cit., pp. 286–7; letter, W. E. Gilmore to G. Croydon Marks, 29 Mar. 1907, File D, 'Motion Picture – Pathé, 1907', ENHS; W. Stephen Bush, 'The New American Tariff. US Censorship', *Bio*, 23 Oct. 1913, p. 287; Clarence L. Linz, 'Film Industry to Express Views on Proposed Tariff Revisions', *MPW*, 18 Dec. 1920, p. 837; 'Senate's Tariff Ideas Prevail in Bill Reported by Committee', *MPW*, 23 Sept. 1922, p. 257.

45. For a summary of the MPPC's forty suits, 1909–11, see Cassady, op. cit., p. 365; 'Europe Pitted Against America', op. cit., p. 163.

46. T[homas] B[eddings], 'News From America', *Bio*, 14 Oct. 1909, p. 19.

47. Cassady, op. cit., pp. 370–1; T[homas] B[eddings], 'News From America', *Bio*, 21 Oct. 1909, p. 21; for a summary of the IPPC's operations as they relate to the domestic market, see Allen, op. cit., pp. 254–9.

48. 'An Open Market', *MPW*, 31 Dec. 1909, pp. 952–3; 'News From America', *Bio*, 14 Apr. 1910, p. 21; 'The World's Press: Passing of Murdock', *Bio*, 10 Feb. 1910, p. 27.

49. Cassady, op. cit., pp. 342–3; 'Foreign News: America', *Bio*, 6 Jan. 1910, p. 27; W. Stephen Bush, 'Film Conditions in the United States', *Bio*, 17 Oct. 1912, p. 177.

50. 'Montagu Talks Early Days', *MPW*, 7 Apr. 1917, p. 101.

51. Cassady, op. cit., p. 371; 'The Situation in America', *Bio*, 16 June 1910,

174

p. 89; 'Cines of Rome', *MPW*, 1 Apr. 1911, p. 694.

52. Cassady, op. cit., pp. 37–72; 'The Situation in America', op. cit., p. 89; Paul H. Cromelin, 'Motion Pictures Under the Open Market', *MPW*, 11 July 1914, p. 213.

53. 'The Open Market – II', *MPW*, 11 Mar. 1911, p. 517.

54. Cassady, op. cit., pp. 373–4; 'The American Trade', *Bio*, 30 May 1912, p. 611; 'Ambrosio in America', *MPW*, 28 Sept. 1912, pp. 1,260–1.

55. 'The American Trade', *Bio*, 2 Jan. 1913, p. 3.

56. 'Visit of a Royal Film Maker', *MPW*, 7 Oct. 1911, p. 48; Cassady, op. cit., p. 380.

57. *USA* vs. *MPPC*, op. cit., vol. 7, p. 3,446.

58. W. Stephen Bush, 'Our American Letter', *Bio*, 16 Apr. 1914, p. 287.

2   Crossing the Herring Pond, 1909–15

1. For an excellent brief summary of the industry's structure in the late silent period, see J. Douglas Gomery, 'The Coming of Sound to the American Cinema' (Ph.D. diss., University of Wisconsin, Madison, 1975), pp. 78–93.

2. J. D. Whelpley, 'England', *DC & TR*, 29 May 1911, p. 913.

3. Emory R. Johnson, T. W. Van Metre, G. G. Huebner and D. S. Hanchett, *History of Domestic and Foreign Commerce of the United States*, vol. 2 (New York: Burt Franklin, 1915), pp. 84–5; C. Ernest Fayle, *The War and the Shipping Industry* (London: Oxford University Press, 1927), p. 6.

4. 'Items of Interest', *Bio*, 2 June 1910, p. 13; John Griffiths, 'Cinematograph Films in the United Kingdom', *DC & TR*, 28 Apr. 1911, p. 423; 'B. Nichols, of London', *MPW*, 14 Sept. 1912, p. 1060.

5. 'We Sacrifice Markets in East, Says Howells', *MPW*, 5 May 1917, p. 769.

6. 'London's Comeback as Trade Center Discussed From Practical Viewpoints', *MPW*, 21 June 1919, p. 1,838.

7. Edwin N. Gunsaulus, 'South Africa', *DC & TR*, 13 Jan. 1912, p. 224; 'Items of Interest', *Bio*, 30 Oct. 1913, p. 355.

8. 'The Bioscope in India', *Bio*, 26 May 1910, p. 49; 'The Bioscope in India', *Bio*, 16 June 1910, p. 85; W. Stanley Hollis and Jesse B. Jackson, 'Syria', *DC & TR*, 13 Jan. 1912, p. 222; C. L. L. Williams, 'The Cinematograph in China', *DC & TR*, 14 Oct. 1911, p. 244.

9. Harold Z. Levine, 'An Analysis of the English Market', *MPW*, 5 Sept. 1914, p. 1,350.

10. Ad, *Bio*, 8 Sept. 1910, pp. 33–43; 'Items of Interest', *Bio*, 22 Feb. 1912, p. 501.

11. '1913 – A Year of Progress', *Bio*, 1 Jan. 1914, p. 5; Rice K. Evans, *et al.*, 'United Kingdom', *DC & TR*, 15 Apr. 1914, p. 257.

12. Ernest A. Dench, 'The American Product in Britain', *MPW*, 11 July 1914, p. 192.

13. Levine, op. cit., p. 1,350.

14. 'Foreign Trade Opportunities', *DC & TR*, 20 Feb. 1911, p. 688; Robert P. Skinner and Frank Dillingham, 'Germany', *DC & TR*, 29 May 1911, p. 915; Alexander M. Thackara, *et al.*, 'Germany', *DC & TR*, 13 Jan. 1912, pp. 213–18; Frank D. Hill, 'Germany', *DC & TR*, 13 Jan. 1912, p. 215; W. Stephen Bush, 'Conditions in Germany', *MPW*, 31 May 1913, p. 899. Table

computed from 'German News', *Bio*, 28 Nov. 1912, p. 636; 'News in Germany', *Bio*, 19 Dec. 1912, p. 907; 'German News', *Bio*, 9 Jan. 1913, p. 127; 'German News', *Bio*, 6 Feb. 1913, p. 407.

15. John Cher, 'Parisian Notes', *Bio*, 29 Nov. 1911, p. 649; 'Parisian Notes', *Bio*, 21 Mar. 1912, p. 843; also 19 Sept. 1912, p. 853; 26 Sept. 1912, p. 957; 21 Nov. 1912, p. 581; 23 Oct. 1913, p. 279; 6 Nov. 1913, p. 505; John Cher, 'Paris Letter', *MPW*, 14 Mar. 1914, p. 1,374.

16. 'News in Brief', *The Cinema News and Property Gazette*, 12 Mar. 1913, p. 7; W. Stephen Bush, 'Notes from Italy', *MPW*, 21 June 1913, p. 1,229; Charles B. Perry and Leon Böhm de Sauvanne, 'Italy', *DC & TR*, 20 July 1914, p. 369; 'Changes in Italian Market', *Mot*, 22 Aug. 1914, p. 260.

17. W. Stephen Bush, 'Notes from Italy', op. cit., p. 1,229; 'A Review of the Cinematograph Industry Through Belgium, Switzerland, and France', *Bio*, 11 Dec. 1913, p. 1,101; 'The Cinematograph in Denmark', *Bio*, 22 Sept. 1910, p. 50; Henry Bordewich, 'Norway', *DC & TR*, 13 Jan. 1912, p. 220; B. M. Rasmussen, 'Norway', *DC & TR*, 15 Apr. 1914, p. 263.

18. 'Trade Notes', *MPW*, 17 Aug. 1907, p. 375; Harry H. Morgan, 'Spain', *DC & TR*, 29 May 1911, p. 916; Editor of *La cinematografica española*, 'Some Reflections on the State of the Cinematograph Market in Spain', *Bio*, 26 Oct. 1911, p. 269; John Cher, 'Parisian Notes', *Bio*, 16 May 1912, p. 511; Charles S. Winans, 'Trade of Southwestern Provinces of Spain', *DC & TR*, 2 July 1913, p. 23; Charles S. Winans, 'Spain', *DC & TR*, 15 Apr. 1914, pp. 263–4.

19. 'The Cinematograph in Serbia', *Bio*, 28 Dec. 1911, p. 925; Samuel H. Shank, 'Cinematograph Business in Hungary', *DC & TR*, 20 Oct. 1913, p. 364; 'The Cinematograph in Greece', *Bio*, 4 Dec. 1913, p. 978; A. Petrescu, 'Roumanian Notes', *Bio*, 20 Nov. 1913, p. 739.

20. John H. Snodgrass, 'Russia', *DC & TR*, 14 Jan. 1911, p. 163; John H. Grout, 'Russia', *DC & TR*, 13 Jan. 1912, p. 221; John H. Snodgrass, 'Russia', *DC & TR*, 29 July 1914, p. 373; Richard Taylor, *The Politics of the Soviet Cinema 1917–1929* (Cambridge: Cambridge University Press, 1979), p. 9.

21. William W. Canada, 'Travelling Picture Shows in Mexico', *DC & TR*, 7 Oct. 1911, p. 124; Alban G. Snyder, 'Panama', *DC & TR*, 15 Apr. 1914, p. 264; T. C. Hamm, 'Mexico', *DC & TR*, 17 June 1912, p. 1,158.

22. James C. Kellogg, 'Panama Trade Notes', *DC & TR*, 2 Jan. 1914, p. 15.

23. 'Moving Picture Conditions in Porto Rico', *MPW*, 25 Jan. 1913, p. 345; Wilbur T. Grace and Gaston Schmutz, 'Mexico', *DC & TR*, 10 May 1913, p. 725.

24. Charles H. Small, 'Columbia', *DC & TR*, 14 Jan. 1911, p. 165; F. Langdon Goding, 'Uruguay', *DC & TR*, 14 Jan. 1911, p. 163; 'Items of Interest', *Bio*, 12 Dec. 1912, p. 785; 'A Cameraman's Experiences', *MPW*, 28 Mar. 1914, p. 1,666.

25. 'Trade Conditions in the Antipodes', *MPW*, 7 Mar. 1908, p. 187; W. H. H. Lane, 'The Moving Picture in Australia', *MPW*, 13 Feb. 1909, p. 174; W. H. H. Lane, 'The Moving Picture in Australia', *MPW*, 31 Dec. 1909, p. 965; Henry D. Baker, 'Photographic Goods in Australia', *DC & TR*, 6 Aug. 1910, p. 390; 'Australia', *Bio*, 8 Sept. 1910, p. 55; 'Topics of the Week', *Bio*, 8 Sept. 1910, p. 4.

26. W. H. H. Lane, 'From the Other Side of the World: Australian Letter', *MPW*, 4 Feb. 1911, p. 237; Jason S. McQuade, 'Chicago Letter', *MPW*, 23 Sept. 1911, p. 880.

27. Jason S. McQuade, 'Chicago Letter', *MPW*, 27 Jan. 1912, p. 290; William A. Prickitt, 'New Zealand', *DC & TR*, 13 Jan. 1912, p. 224.

28. 'Spenser Control in Australia', *MPW*, 8 Mar. 1913, p. 1,003.

29. Edwin S. Cunningham, 'India', *DC & TR*, 17 June 1912, p. 1,159; W. Exley, 'The Bioscope in India', *Bio*, 17 Apr. 1913, p. 191; Edward J. Norton and Maxwell K. Moorhead, 'India', *DC & TR*, 10 May 1913, p. 727.

30. George Horton, 'Moving Pictures in Turkey', *DC & TR*, 20 Aug. 1910, p. 558; G. Bie Ravndal, 'Turkey', *DC & TR*, 22 Aug. 1911, p. 819; John L. Binda, 'Turkey', *DC & TR*, 13 Jan. 1912, p. 221; I. Montesanto, 'Turkey', *DC & TR*, 17 June 1912, p. 1,157; George Horton, 'Turkey', *DC & TR*, 13 Feb. 1913, p. 787.

31. D. Milton Figart, 'Straits Settlements', *DC & TR*, 13 Jan. 1912, p. 223; also 17 June 1912, p. 1,157; Edwin S. Cunningham, 'Malaya', *DC & TR*, 10 May 1913, p. 728; Casper L. Dreier, 'Cinematograph Popular in Singapore', *DC & TR*, 2 May 1914, p. 637.

32. George E. Anderson, 'China', *DC & TR*, 22 Aug. 1911, p. 820; C. L. L. Williams, 'The Cinematograph in China', *DC & TR*, 14 Oct. 1911, p. 244; 'Pictures for China', *Mot*, Nov. 1911, p. 211; Nelson Trusler Johnson, 'China', *DC & TR*, 10 May 1913, p. 728; F. D. Cheshire, 'China', *DC & TR*, 13 Feb. 1913, p. 788; Samuel S. Knabenshue, 'China', *DC & TR*, 17 June 1912, p. 1,156.

33. S. Kurimoto, 'The Progress of Cinematography in Japan', *Bio*, 26 Oct. 1911, p. 259; Thomas Sammons, 'Japan', *DC & TR*, 13 Jan. 1912, p. 223.

34. J. J. Robinson, 'From the Other Side of the World: Letter From the Philippines', *MPW*, 4 Feb. 1911, p. 236.

35. 'South Africa', *Bio*, 8 Sept. 1910, p. 55; 'Edison Films in Cape Town, South Africa', *Edison Kinetogram*, London ed., 15 Nov. 1911, p. 14; Edwin N. Gunsaulus, 'South Africa', *DC & TR*, 13 Jan. 1912, p. 224; Lionae, 'From South Africa', *MPW*, 4 Oct. 1913, p. 36.

36. Chart from Grace A. Witherow, 'Foreign Trade of the United States in 1931', *TIB*, no. 808, 1932, p. 1.

37. Johnson, *et al.*, op. cit., pp. 86–90.

38. Ibid., pp. 92–7.

39. W. Stephen Bush, 'Opportunity', *MPW*, 26 Sept. 1914, p. 1,751.

40. 'New Fields For American Film', *MPW*, 24 Oct. 1914, p. 468; Arthur J. Lang, 'Cashing in on Europe's War', *MPN*, 28 Nov. 1914, pp. 25–6.

41. John Cher. 'Chaos in France', *Bio*, 6 Aug. 1914, p. 571; John Cher, 'The Sad City', *Bio*, 20 Aug. 1914, p. 749.

42. John Cher, 'No Panic in Paris', *Bio*, 27 Aug. 1914, p. 825; John Cher, 'Paris Letter', *MPW*, 19 Sept. 1914, p. 1,630.

43. Bush, 'Opportunity', op. cit., p. 1,751.

44. Fayle, op. cit., pp. 36, 60; Frank P. Chambers, *The War Behind the War 1914–1918: A History of the Political and Civilian Fronts* (New York: Harcourt, Brace and Company, 1939), p. 8; Fayle, op. cit., pp. 39, 36, 41–2, 67.

45. 'Facing the Future', *Bio*, 6 Aug. 1914, pp. 525, 528; 'Trade Topics', *Bio*, 3 Sept. 1914, p. 861.

46. Evan Strong, 'Optimism and the Future', *Bio*, 22 Oct. 1914, p. 349.

47. 'British Notes', *MPW*, 28 Nov. 1914, p. 1,238; Harry G. Seltzer, 'Germany', *CR*, 3 Apr. 1915, pp. 51–2.

48. Evan Strong, 'War's Black Mark', *MPW*, 12 Sept. 1914, p. 1,515; Jason S. McQuade, 'Chicago Letter', *MPW*, 17 Oct. 1914, p. 317; 'The Industry in Spain and Holland', *Bio*, 7 Jan. 1915, p. 27; Joseph Lamy, 'Markets for American Films', *MPW*, 20 Feb. 1915, p. 1,127; W. Stephen Bush, 'Williams Back From India', *MPW*, 27 Feb. 1915, p. 1,278.

49. A. Gordon Brown, 'Mexico', and C. Donaldson, 'Costa Rica', both *CR*, 3 Apr. 1915, p. 48.

50. 'The War and the Pictures', *MPW*, 15 Aug. 1914, p. 963; 'Business', *Mot*, 19 Sept. 1914, pp. 407–8; 'South American Business', *Variety*, 10 Oct. 1914, p. 24.

51. William Dawson Jr., 'Argentina', and Robert Frazer Jr., 'Brazil', both in *CR*, 3 Apr. 1915, pp. 44–5.

52. Samuel Hamilton Wiley, 'Paraguay', and Herman L. Spahr, 'Uruguay', both in *CR*, 3 Apr. 1915, pp. 47–8; Ross Hazeltine, 'Motion-Picture Opportunities in Cartagena', *CR*, 6 May 1915, p. 611; Isaac A. Manning, 'Columbia', *CR*, 3 July 1915, p. 57.

53. 'The War and the Pictures', op. cit., p. 963; 'Trade News From Abroad', *Bio*, 18 Jan. 1917, p. 227; Jason S. McQuade, 'Chicago Letter', *MPW*, 3 Apr. 1915, p. 46; 'Film Tax Hurts Australia', *MPW*, 24 Apr. 1915, p. 562.

54. 'Williams Back From India', op. cit., p. 1,278; A. E. Carleton, 'China', *DC & TR*, 4 Sept. 1914, p. 1,253.

55. 'Alberto Ramella Returns to Italy', *MPW*, 27 Feb. 1915, p. 1,266; 'Gloria's Representative in Town', *MPW*, 13 Feb. 1915, p. 1,619; 'G. McL. Baynes Visits New York', *MPW*, 25 Dec. 1915, p. 2,334; 'Ambrosio Comes Back', *MPW*, 1 Jan. 1916, p. 88; 'Ambrosio Sails', *MPW*, 5 Feb. 1916, p. 752; 'Great Northern Announcement', *MPW*, 6 Nov. 1915, p. 1,148.

56. 'Sues to Get Back 5 Film Companies', *NYT*, 2 Sept. 1915, p. 9; 'The Truth of the Gaumont Rumors', *MPW*, 25 June 1910, p. 1,094; 'News From America', *Bio*, 16 Nov. 1911, p. 493; 'The War and the Pictures', op. cit., p. 964; Ad, *MPW*, 9 Jan. 1915, p. 288; 'Gaumont Finds Conditions Good', *MPW*, 22 Apr. 1916, p. 597; C. S. Sewell, 'States Rights Department', *MPW*, 30 Mar. 1918, p. 1,837.

57. *Pathé Frères Cinema, Ltd. Weekly Bulletin*, 3 Feb. 1913, p. 5; W. Stephen Bush, 'Charles Pathé's Views', *MPW*, 24 Jan. 1914, p. 390; *USA* vs. *MPPC*, op. cit., vol. 3, p. 1,785; Ads, Pathé Frères, *MPW*, 9 May 1914, p. 835; *MPW*, 16 May 1914, p. 975; and *MPW*, 13 June 1914, p. 1,524.

58. 'Arthur Roussel', *MPW*, 11 Apr. 1914, p. 197; 'Pathé Stock Co. to be Disbanded', *MPW*, 25 July 1914, p. 587; 'Calendar of Licensed Releases', *MPW*, 5 Sept. 1914, p. 1,396; 'Horsley in Licensed Group', *MPW*, 3 Oct. 1914, p. 71; J. B. Sutcliffe, 'British Notes', *MPW*, 10 Oct. 1914, p. 171; 'The King of the Cinema: An Interview with Monsieur Charles Pathé', *Bio*, 15 Oct. 1914, p. 241; 'Film Releases', *Bio*, 27 Feb. 1913, p. xxxvii; *Bio*, 24 Sept. 1914, pp. xxi–xxviii; *Bio*, 6 May 1915, pp. xvii–xxiv.

59. Sadoul, op. cit., vol. 4, pp. 32–3.

60. 'Charles Pathé in New York', *MPW*, 31 Oct. 1914, p. 619; Sadoul, vol. 4, p. 35; Ads, *MPW*, 14 Nov. 1914, pp. 892–3; 'Pathé Sails For Europe', *MPW*, 16 Jan. 1915, p. 342; 'Mr. Charles Pathé's Activities in America and Italy', *Bio*, 4 Mar. 1915, p. 810.

61. 'Present American Stockholders Acquire Control of Pathé; Brunet Returns to Office', *MPW*, 2 July 1921, p. 39.

3 Cashing in on Europe's War, 1916–18

1. W. Stephen Bush, 'Leon Gaumont on a Visit', *MPW*, 8 Apr. 1916, p. 233.
2. Gerd Hardach, *The First World War 1914–1918* (Berkeley: University of California Press, 1977), p. 2; Scheiber, *et al.*, p. 282.
3. Hardach, op. cit., p. 4; Scheiber, *et al.*, op. cit., p. 319; Chambers, op. cit., pp. 197–8.
4. Hardach, op. cit., p. 77; Scheiber, *et al.*, op. cit., p. 318; Hardach, op. cit., pp. 95–6; Fayle, op. cit., pp. 283–4; Hardach, op. cit, p. 49.
5. Fayle, op. cit., p. 284; Hardach, op. cit., pp. 287–8.
6. Chambers, op. cit., pp. 193–4; Hardach, op. cit., p. 46; Chambers, op. cit., p. 443; Fayle, op. cit., p. 332.
7. Hardach, op. cit., pp. 147–8, 290.
8. Ibid., pp. 269–70.
9. Chambers, op. cit., pp. 135, 203, 208; 'Anderson Finds Market Good', *MPW*, 4 Sept. 1915, p. 1,657; Chambers, op. cit., pp. 235, 282, 230, 413, 417, 353.
10. 'U-Boat Sinks Essanay Prints', *Mot*, 10 Mar. 1917, p. 527; 'Submarines Have Sunk No Fox Films', *MPW*, 20 July 1918, p. 380; J. B. Sutcliffe, 'British Notes', *MPW*, 27 July 1918, p. 562; 'Who Cries "Wolf"?', *Bio*, 9 Jan. 1919, p. 7; 'Work of Famous Players Foreign Offices in Films', *MPW*, 31 Jan. 1920, p. 737.
11. 'The Film Tax', *Bio*, 30 Sept. 1915, p. 1,435; Jason S. McQuade, 'Chicago News Letter', *MPW*, 9 Oct. 1915, p. 270; J. B. Sutcliffe, 'British Notes', *MPW*, 13 Nov. 1915, p. 1,300; 'The Budget Duties', *Bio*, 14 Oct. 1915, p. 117; J. B. Sutcliffe, 'British Notes', *MPW*, 1 Jan. 1916, p. 69.
12. 'Facts and Comments', *MPW*, 30 Oct. 1915, p. 759; 'The Revised Duty on Films', *Bio*, 16 Dec. 1915, p. 1,193; J. B. Sutcliffe, 'British Notes', *MPW*, 6 Nov. 1915, p. 1,125; J. B. Sutcliffe, 'British Notes', *MPW*, 27 Nov. 1915, p. 1,631; 'The Revised Duty on Films', op. cit., p. 1,193.
13. Rachael Low, *The History of the British Film 1914–1918* (London: George Allen and Unwin, 1950), pp. 111–12; 'Changes in British Conditions', *MPW*, 25 Dec. 1915, p. 2,347.
14. 'Fox Film Corporation Invades Europe', *Bio*, 6 Jan. 1916, p. 17; 'The Suggested Film Blockade', *Bio*, 10 Feb. 1916, p. 541; J. B. Sutcliffe, 'British Notes', *MPW*, 15 Jan. 1916, p. 433.
15. 'Export of Films Prohibited', *Bio*, 23 Mar. 1916, pp. 1,233–4; Chambers, op. cit., pp. 133–4, 145, 150.
16. J. B. Sutcliffe, 'British Notes', *MPW*, 20 May 1916, p. 1,326; Jason S. McQuade, 'Chicago News Letter', *MPW*, 25 Mar. 1916, pp. 1,986–7.
17. 'Limitations of US Imports', *Bio*, 28 May 1918, p. 8.
18. W. Stephen Bush, 'Our Chances in Europe', *MPW*, 8 Jan. 1916, p. 217.
19. 'Facts and Comments', *MPW*, 9 Dec. 1916, p. 1,467; *MPW*, 10 Mar. 1917, p. 1,539.
20. H. N., 'The World's Film Markets', *Bio*, 11 Jan. 1917, pp. vii, ix; 'New York or London?', *Bio*, 5 Apr. 1917, p. 5; 'London or New York?', *Bio*, 5 July 1917, p. 9; A. E. T., 'Cinemas in Other Lands', *Bio*, 12 July 1917, pp. vi–vii.
21. 'Facts and Comments', *MPW*, 10 Nov. 1917, p. 829; 'Monat Comes to Buy and Sell Films', *MPW*, 24 Nov. 1917, p. 1,152; 'Cromelin Tells What Inter-Ocean Is Doing', *MPW*, 29 Dec. 1917, p. 1,921.

22. 'us Film Exports', *Bio*, 22 Aug. 1918, p. 10; F. G. Ortega, 'London Agent Presents Export Views', *MPW*, 14 Sept. 1918, p. 1,556.

23. Tadao Sato, *Currents in Japanese Cinema*, trans. Gregory Barrett (Tokyo: Kodansha International, 1982), p. 33.

24. 'Paramount's Progress in Australia', *MPW*, 20 Sept. 1919, p. 1,792; 'We Have With Us Today', *MPW*, 1 May 1920, p. 667.

25. E. R. Dickover, 'Foreign Films in Japanese Theaters', *CR*, 2 Nov. 1916, p. 442; 'Kalem's "Hazards", A Japanese Favorite', *MPW*, 4 Nov. 1916, p. 723: William R. Langdon, 'Film Exhibitions and Markets Abroad', *CR*, 12 Dec. 1916, p. 972; P. S. Cawley, 'Picture Conditions in Japan', *MPW*, 21 Apr. 1917, p. 439.

26. Julean Arnold, 'Native Subjects Required For Films in China', *CR*, 29 Aug. 1916, p. 790; P. R. Josselyn, 'China', *CR*, 21 Feb. 1917, pp. 712–3.

27. M. H. Kenyon-Slade, 'Conditions in Singapore', *MPW*, 30 Sept. 1916, p. 2,085.

28. From official statistics given in 'Trade Prospects in the Far East', *Bio*, 25 Oct. 1917, p. 11, and 'The Cinematograph in Malaya', *Bio*, 28 Apr. 1921, p. 23.

29. Table calculated from Carl C. Hansen, 'Siam's Motion Picture and Photographic Goods Trade', *CR*, 17 May 1918, p. 647; these official figures include all photographic materials, but the bulk are probably films. 'The Picture Business in Java', *MPW*, 24 Feb. 1917, p. 1,190; 'We Sacrifice Markets in East, Says Howells', *MPW*, 2 May 1917, p. 769; 'Inter-Ocean Emissary Carries "No Junk" Campaign to Orient', *MPW*, 21 Dec. 1918, p. 1,394.

30. S. B. Banerjea, 'Indian Notes', *MPW*, 4 Nov. 1916, p. 680 (the first appearance of this regular column).

31. Francisco Montero, 'Trade With South America', *MPW*, 27 Feb. 1915, pp. 1,269–70; 'Film News From Foreign Parts', *MPN*, 6 Nov. 1915, p. 61; Harold B. Meyerheim, 'Motion Pictures in Columbia', *CR*, 8 Nov. 1915, p. 557.

32. 'Here is "Cine-Mundial"', *MPW*, 18 Dec. 1915, p. 2,155; Jason S. McQuade, 'Chicago News Letter', *MPW*, 2 Oct. 1915, p. 83; W. Stephen Bush, 'The South American Market', 8 Jan. 1916, p. 217; 'Latin-American Trade', *MPW*, 18 Mar. 1916, p. 1,812.

33. 'South Americans Visit Vitagraph', *MPW*, 18 Dec. 1915, p. 2,192; 'Pan-American Conference', *MPW*, 25 Mar. 1916, p. 1,983.

34. W. Stephen Bush, 'A Note of Warning to Producers', *MPW*, 13 May 1916, pp. 1,135–6; Bush, 'Light Breaking in South America', *MPW*, 19 June 1916, p. 1,871.

35. 'Facts and Comments', *MPW*, 24 June 1916, p. 2,207; J. H. C., 'American Films in Brazil', *MPW*, 28 Oct. 1916, p. 531.

36. Hanford C. Judson, 'Big Possibilities For Pictures in the Orient', *MPW*, 1 Sept. 1916, p. 1,337; S. B. Banerjea, 'Indian Notes', *MPW*, 17 Nov. 1917, p. 997; '"Civilization" in South America', *MPW*, 21 Oct. 1916, p. 412; 'Read Talks of Foreign Rights', *MPW*, 25 Nov. 1916, p. 1,147; 'Porter Returns From South America', *MPW*, 25 Mar. 1916, p. 1,991.

37. W. Stephen Bush, 'Hungry for American Pictures', *MPW*, 11 Nov. 1916, p. 829; 'Facts and Comment', *MPW*, 28 Oct. 1916, p. 523.

38. 'Facts and Comment', *MPW*, 2 Dec. 1916, p. 1,299; W. Stephen Bush, 'Invading South America', *MPW*, 2 Dec. 1916, p. 1,331; J. H. C., 'American Film Invasion of South America', *MPW*, 30 Dec. 1916, p. 1,936.

39. W. Henry Robertson, 'Argentina', *CR*, 7 Apr. 1917, p. 83; E. T. McGovern, 'Export Items', *MPW*, 14 July 1917, p. 223.
40. L. J. Keene, 'Chile', *CR*, 7 Apr. 1917, p. 86; Frederic W. Goding, 'Ecuador', *CR*, 7 Apr. 1917, p. 87; F. G. Ortega, 'Film Export Notes', *MPW*, 21 Apr. 1917, p. 437; also 12 May 1917, p. 955; J. H. C., 'Dominating the Brazilian Market', *MPW*, 19 May 1917, p. 1,109; F. G. Ortega, 'Film Export Notes', *MPW*, 26 May 1917, pp. 1,270–1; F. G. Ortega, 'War and Exports', *MPW*, 29 Sept. 1917, p. 1,989.
41. F. G. Ortega, 'Wallach Arrives in New York', *MPW*, 4 May 1918, p. 703; F. G. Ortega, 'Our Future Trade With Latin America', *MPW*, 29 June 1918, p. 1,851; O. R. Geyer, 'Winning Foreign Film Markets', *Scientific American*, 20 Aug. 1921, p. 140.
42. George S. Messersmith, 'Motion Pictures in Dutch West Indies', *CR*, 25 Aug. 1916, p. 738; Samuel C. Reat, 'Photoplays Popular in Guatemala', *CR*, 25 Oct. 1916, p. 334; Francis J. Dyer, 'Motion-Picture Business in North Honduras', *CR*, 25 Oct. 1916, p. 329; Julius D. Dreher, 'Motion-Picture Shows Popular in Colon District', *CR*, 16 Nov. 1916, p. 630.
43. 'A Night at the Teatro Delicias', *MPW*, 13 Jan. 1917, p. 237; 'Export Items', *MPW*, 27 Oct. 1917, p. 530; George S. Messersmith, 'Dutch West Indies', *CR*, 21 Feb. 1917, p. 717; Alban G. Snyder, 'Panama', *CR*, 7 Apr. 1917, p. 86; F. G. Ortega, 'Random Shots About Export', *MPW*, 10 Mar. 1917, p. 1,545; F. G. Ortega, 'Film Export Notes', *MPW*, 16 June 1917, p. 1,768; 'Methods in Mexico', *MPW*, 22 Dec. 1917, p. 1,796; 'To Establish Fox Branch in Mexico', *MPW*, 29 Mar. 1919, p. 1,797.
44. 'Buyer From Australia Here', *MPW*, 19 Aug. 1916, p. 1,220; William C. Magelssen, 'Australia', *CR*, 14 Feb. 1918, p. 603; Walter H. Sully, 'Australian Theater Notes', *Mot*, 10 Mar. 1917, p. 504; 'Australian Showman Visits Seattle', *MPW*, 24 Mar. 1917, p. 1,924; 'Australasian Joins First National', *MPW*, 17 Nov. 1917, p. 1,921; Ad, *Wid's Year Book 1918*, n.p.; 'Like American Films', *Camera!*, 27 Oct. 1918, p. 1; F. G. Ortega, 'Trade Conditions in Far East Good', *MPW*, 24 Aug. 1918, p. 1,124.
45. From figures in Charles G. Winslow, 'Motion-Picture Business in New Zealand', *MPW*, 16 Jan. 1920, p. 308.
46. 'Essanay to Rent Direct', *Bio*, 19 Aug. 1915, pp. 569–70; 'The Essanay Company's New Policy', *Bio*, 19 Aug. 1915, p. 774.
47. 'Civus Britannicus', 'The Position of the British Producer', *Bio*, 9 Sept. 1915, p. 1,174.
48. 'Roy E. Aitken Returns From Europe With Glowing Report of the Outlook for Triangle Pictures Abroad', *The Triangle*, 5 Aug. 1916, p. 1; 'War and Exports', op. cit., p. 1,989; Horace Lee Washington, *et al.*, 'Motion Pictures in the United Kingdom', *CR*, 13 Apr. 1917, p. 173; quoted in 'American Films Popular Abroad', *Mot*, 1 Dec. 1917, p. 1,124.
49. J. A. Fleitzer, 'German Trade Notes', *MPW*, 13 May 1916, p. 1,143; Francis R. Stewart, 'Film Exhibitions in Germany', *CR*, 10 Feb. 1917, p. 570; 'Pictures in Germany', *Mot*, 17 Mar. 1917, p. 586; 'German Film Trust Carries Universal Title', *MPW*, 13 July 1918, p. 191.
50. 'The Film Trade in Holland', *Bio*, 16 Mar. 1916, p. 1,151; Walter H. Schulz, 'Switzerland', *CR*, 12 Dec. 1916, p. 970.
51. E. Haldman Dennison, 'Norway', *CR*, 15 Feb. 1917, p. 632; Axel Permin, 'Motion-Picture Theaters in Denmark', *CR*, 9 Nov. 1916, p. 530;

'Scandinavian Firm in New York', *MPW*, 9 June 1917, p. 1,631; Peter Cowie, *Swedish Cinema* (New York: A. S. Barnes & Co., 1966), p. 13; 'Le Développement de l'industrie cinématographique en Suède', *Ciné-Journal*, 21 Jan. 1920, n.p.; 'Cromelin Tells What Inter-Ocean is Doing', *MPW*, 29 Dec. 1917, p. 1,921.

52. F. T. F. Dumont, 'Motion Picture Situation in Greece and Italy', *CR*, 5 June 1915, p. 1,060; G. Kaczka, 'Film News From European Capitals', *MPN*, 21 Aug. 1915, p. 47; G. Kaczka, 'Film News From Foreign Parts', *MPN*, 25 Sept. 1915, p. 69; J. E. Jones, 'The Motion-Picture Business in Italy', *CR*, 9 Aug. 1915, p. 683; G. Kaczka, 'Film News From Foreign Parts', *MPN*, 9 Oct. 1915, p. 59.

53. Gentile Miotti, 'Italian Discontent With the British Film Tax', *Bio*, 21 Oct. 1915, p. 305; Leonard Donaldson, 'Our Allies and the Cinema: II, Italy', *Bio*, 28 Oct. 1915, p. 412; 'A Chat With the Marquis Serra', *Bio*, 12 Oct. 1916, p. 152; 'Facts and Comment', *MPW*, 28 Oct. 1916, p. 523.

54. Roger C. Tredwell, 'Italy', *CR*, 15 Feb. 1917, p. 631; Gualtiers I. Fabbri 'Cinematograph News From Italy', *Bio*, 12 July 1917, p. xviii; Francesco Manelli, 'Italian Letter', *MPW*, 1 Sept. 1917, p. 1,383; also 20 Oct. 1917, p. 373.

55. 'Looking Into the Moving Picture Future', *MPW*, 21 Dec. 1918, p. 1,399.

56. Calculated from H. C. MacLeon, 'Motion-Picture Industry in Italy', *CR*, 23 July 1920, p. 457.

57. Hermann Kinder and Werner Hilgemann, *The Anchor Atlas of World History*, vol. 2, trans. Ernest A. Menze (Garden City, New York: Anchor Books, 1978), p. 125; Chambers, op. cit., pp. 12, 37–9.

58. David B. Levis, 'Increased Use of American Films in France', *CR*, 14 Mar. 1916, p. 1,016; John Ball Osborne, 'France', *CR*, 12 Dec. 1916, p. 964; Paul H. Cram, 'Motion-Picture Trade in Southern France', *CR*, 30 Oct. 1916, p. 393; table computed from 'War and Export', op. cit., p. 1,988, with errors in addition corrected; Sadoul, op. cit., vol. 2, p. 48.

59. For a detailed analysis of these factors, see David Bordwell, Janet Staiger and Kristin Thompson, *The Classical Hollywood Cinema: Film Style and Mode of Production to 1960* (London: Routledge & Kegan Paul, 1985).

60. Henri Diamant-Berger, 'L'Inertie', *Le Film*, 20 May 1916, p. 5; Camille Bardou, 'De la Routine', *Le Film*, 1 July 1916, p. 7.

61. Quoted in 'Are American Producers Provincial?', *MPW*, 20 Jan. 1917, p. 343.

62. Bob Doman, 'Paris as Seen by a New Yorker', *MPW*, 17 Feb. 1917, p. 1,015; F. G. Ortega, 'Random Shots About Export', *MPW*, 10 Mar. 1917, p. 1,545; E. J., 'Interdiction d'importer', *Le Film*, 9 Apr. 1917, p. 7; 'Gaumont to Distribute Paramount Subjects', *MPW*, 9 Sept. 1918, p. 809; Henri Diamant-Berger, 'Exportation', *Le Film*, 29 July 1918, p. 5.

63. Harris N. Cookingham and John R. Putnam, 'Spain', *CR*, 12 Dec. 1916, pp. 967–8; Andre P. de la Mota, 'Pictures in Spain', *Bio*, 4 Jan. 1917, p. 30; 'From Spain', *MPW*, 16 Feb. 1918, p. 976; Frank J. Marion, 'Kalem Chief Writes of Spain as a Market', *MPW*, 23 Feb. 1918, p. 1,070; table computed from 'War and Exports', op. cit., p. 1,988, and F. G. Ortega, 'Foreign News and Comment', *MPW*, 24 Aug. 1918, p. 1,126.

64. W. Whattan Ward, 'Some Opinions of the Film Industry in Russia', *Bio*, 25 Nov. 1915, p. 870; '"The Fall of a Nation" in Russia', *MPW*, 30 Sept. 1916,

p. 2,120; T. Brooks Alford and John K. Caldwell, 'Russia', *CR*, 15 Feb. 1917, p. 635; 'Screen Industry of Russia', *MPW*, 30 June 1918, p. 2,080.

65. 'How War Affects Pictures', *MPW*, 2 Feb. 1918, p. 648.

66. 'Embargo on Films', *MPW*, 15 Sept. 1917, p. 1,671; 'Foreign Trade News', *MPW*, 9 Mar. 1918, p. 136a; 'Bar Export of Movie Films', *NYT*, 16 July 1918, p. 14; F. G. Ortega, 'Trade Conditions in Far East Good', *MPW*, 24 Aug. 1918, p. 1,124; 'Foreign News and Comment', op. cit., p. 1,126; 'Facts and Comments', *MPW*, 7 Sept. 1918, p. 1,408; also 30 Nov. 1918, p. 946; [Thomas] Imrie, 'Production Booming in Australia', *MPW*, 25 Jan. 1919, p. 532; 'American Movies May Be Imported Freely', *Japan Advertiser*, 28 Dec. 1918, p. 1; 'Export Regulations Handicap Film Trade', *MPW*, 25 Jan. 1919, p. 531.

67. 'Helping the Moving Pictures to Win the War', *Bio*, 18 July 1918, p. 8.

68. James R. Mock and Cedric Larson, *Words That Won the War: The Story of the Committee on Public Information 1917–1919* (Princeton: Princeton University Press, 1939), p. 134; 'Movies Mobilized to Aid in War Work', *NYT*, 29 July 1917, Sec. 1, p. 8.

69. 'Distribute American Films in Europe', *Mot*, 20 Oct. 1917, p. 812; 'American Cinema Aides Are Named', *Mot*, 10 Nov. 1917, p. 980; 'American Cinema Commission Preparing', *MPW*, 10 Nov. 1917, p. 842; 'Helping the Moving Pictures to Win the War', op. cit., p. 9.

70. 'Irwin Retires From Cinema Commission', *MPW*, 24 Nov. 1917, p. 1,152; George Creel, *How We Advertised America* (New York: Harper and Bros., 1920), pp. 274–6.

71. Mock and Larson, op. cit., p. 73; United States Committee on Public Information, *The Creel Report: Complete Report of the Chairman of the Committee on Public Information 1917: 1918: 1919* (1920; reprinted New York: Da Capo Press, 1972), pp. 195–6; 'Chance for Film Men in Spain', *Mot*, 19 Jan. 1918, p. 128; 'Opportunities in Spain, Says Marion', *MPW*, 19 Jan. 1918, p. 355; Frank J. Marion, 'Kalem Chief Writes of Spain as a Market', *MPW*, 23 Feb. 1918, p. 1,070.

72. 'America's Moving Picture Propaganda', *Bio*, 15 Aug. 1918, p. 19; 'Helping the Moving Pictures to Win the War', op. cit., p. 9; 'Congressmen Inquire About Picturemaking', *MPW*, 13 July 1918, p. 188; 'Baker Explains Movie Contract', *NYT*, 18 July 1918, p. 5; Mock and Larson, op. cit., p. 138.

73. Creel, op. cit., p. 273.

74. 'Hun Film Driven From Screen', *Bio*, 12 Dec. 1918, p. 9; Creel, op. cit., pp. 276–7; United States Committee on Public Information, op. cit., pp. 179, 147.

75. Creel, op. cit., pp. 277–81; United States Committee on Public Information, op. cit., pp. 244–6; L. B. N. Gnaedinger, 'Siberia Welcomes Moving Pictures', *MPW*, 30 Aug. 1919, p. 1,270; 'Herbert Griffin Home Again After Taking Films Into Siberian Wilds', *MPW*, 4 Oct. 1919, pp. 83–4.

76. United States Committee on Public Information, op. cit., pp. 51–2, 167; 'As Hart Sees It', *NYT*, 5 Jan. 1919, Sec. 4, p. 4; 'Helping the Moving Pictures to Win the War', op. cit., p. 9; 'America's Answer to the Hun', *Bio*, 25 July 1918, p. 7; 'America's Answer to the Hun', *Bio*, 1 Aug. 1918, p. 10; 'America's Effort', op. cit., p. 9.

77. 'How America Has Used the Moving Picture', *Bio*, 5 Dec. 1918, p. 8; 'Splendid Financial Showing for the Division of Films', *MPW*, 8 Mar. 1919,

p. 1,311; United States Committee on Public Information, op. cit., p. 50; 'Now
That the War is Over', *NYT*, 5 Jan. 1919, Sec. 4, p. 4; 'Facts and Comments',
MPW, 22 Feb. 1919, p. 1,028; 'Hart to Dissolve Division of Films', *MPW*,
22 Feb. 1919, p. 1,056.

Kevin Brownlow's *The War, the West, and the Wilderness* (New York: Alfred A.
Knopf, 1979), presents a very different interpretation of the Creel Committee
activities (see pp. 112–19). He argues that the Committee had little connection
with the industry and that the latter refused to co-operate with Creel. His
discussion seems to be based upon an assumption that the Division of Films
distributed mainly documentary materials; he mentions only Jules Brulatour as
having worked for Creel, seeming again to assume that Brulatour's 'National
Cinema Commission' (that is, the American Cinema Commission) was a
government organisation – when it was actually the NAMPI-sponsored group.
Brownlow ignores the many instances where film companies provided films for
Creel's programmes or distributed them commercially; instead he lays great
emphasis on a few anecdotes that evidence strife between the Committee and
members of the industry.

4 Maintaining the Lead, 1919–28

1. Herbert Howe, 'What Europe Thinks of American Stars', *Photoplay*, Feb.
1923, p. 41.
2. 'Most Important Event of the Year', *Wid's Year Book 1919* (1920), n.p.
3. Scheiber, *et al.*, op. cit., p. 324.
4. Dereck H. Aldcroft, *From Versailles to Wall Street 1919–1929* (Berkeley:
University of California Press, 1981), pp. 125–7, 148.
5. 'Production a-Plenty in Europe', *MPW*, 4 Oct. 1919, p. 155; W. Stephen
Bush, 'Our American Letter', *Bio*, 27 Nov. 1919, p. 74; ' "Panoraming"
Continent's Film Marts', *MPW*, 13 Dec. 1919, p. 793; 'America Alarmed!',
Bio, 1 Jan. 1920, p. 29.
6. 'Opinions on Foreign Outlook', *Wid's Year Book 1920* (1921), p. 257; C. S.
Sewell, 'Exchange Rate and Duping Driving Export Business to Other
Markets', *MPW*, 10 Jan. 1920, p. 231.
7. 'American Producers Directly Affected by Exporting Situation, Says
Howells', *MPW*, 28 Feb. 1920, p. 1,403; A. George Smith, 'English, French,
and Italian Films Will Reduce American Exportation', *MPW*, 28 Feb. 1920,
p. 1,423; 'Settlement of Peace Treaty Vitally Affects the Industry', *MPW*, 20
Dec. 1919, p. 951.
8. Carl Laemmle, 'The Higher Cost of Films', *Bio*, 1 Jan. 1920, p. 11; F. E.
Adams, 'The Higher Cost of Films', *Bio*, 8 Jan. 1920, p. 18; P. A. Powers,
'Huge Salaries, Foreign Exchange, and Competition Imperil Industry', *MPW*,
21 Feb. 1920, p. 1,201.
9. W. Stephen Bush, 'Austria Turns From German Films to Productions
Made in America', *MPW*, 3 Nov. 1923, p. 45; Sidney R. Kent, 'Distributing
the Product', in *The Story of the Films*, ed. Joseph P. Kennedy (Chicago: A. W.
Shaw Company, 1927), p. 231.
10. In my study of European film movements of the 20s, now in progress, I
shall deal at greater length with the 'German invasion' scare and the position
of the foreign film in the American market.
11. Walther Plugge, 'The German Quota Law', *International Review of*

Educational Cinematography, Nov. 1930, p. 1,278; Helmut Regel and Heinz Steinberg, *Der deutsche Stummfilm* (Köln: Arbeitsgemeinschaft für Filmfragen an der Universität zu Köln, 1963–4), p. B26; 'Film Exporters May Now Trade With German States', *MPW*, 26 July 1919, p. 483; 'Despite Embargo, Germany Will Become Excellent Market for American Films', *MPW*, 8 May 1920, p. 811; 'Eleanor O'Keefe Returns After Remarkable Trip Through Norway, Germany, Austria, and Poland', *MPW*, 27 Sept. 1919, p. 1,587; 'Exchange Rates and Duping Driving Export Business to Other Markets', *MPW*, 19 Jan. 1920, p. 231; 'German Cinematograph Companies Are Doing Their Best to Bar American Films', *MPW*, 20 Sept. 1919, p. 1,824.

12. Curt Andersen, *Die deutsche Filmindustrie: Aufbau, Gliederung, Aufgaben und volkswirtschaftlische Bedeutung* (München: Curt I. C. Andersen, 1930), p. 68; *JdF*, vol. 1, p. 32.

13. Figures from *JdF*, vol. 2, p. 284; *FYB*, 1924, pp. 61, 65; *JdF*, vol. 2, pp. 310–11.

14. *TIB*, no. 617, p. 21; *TIB*, no. 694, p. 22; *TIB*, no. 752, p. 32.

15. Plugge, op. cit., p. 1,278; Regel and Steinberg, op. cit., p. B26.

16. *JdF*, vol. 2, pp. 310–11; 'Laemmle Returning to us After Epochal Trip Abroad', *MPW*, 10 Oct. 1925, p. 458; 'Universal Confirms $4,000,000 Deal With uf a; Laemmle Off For Berlin', *MPW*, 5 Dec. 1925, pp. 415–16.

17. 'American Movies Get German Rights', *NYT*, 22 Nov. 1925, Sec. 1, p. 22; Heinrich Fraenkel, 'Universal Financing uf a?', *Bio*, 26 Nov. 1925, p. 23; Heinrich Fraenkel, 'Latest From Germany', *Bio*, 3 Dec. 1925, p. 31; 'Universal Confirms $4,000,000 Deal With uf a', op. cit., pp. 415–16; 'Universal on the Continent', *Bio*, 17 Dec. 1925, p. 26.

18. 'Universal Confirms $4,000,000 Deal With uf a', op. cit. p. 415; ' "U" Controls 85 Per Cent of us Distribution in Germany', *MPW*, 12 Dec. 1925, p. 528; W. Stephen Bush, 'Europe Views Universal-uf a Deal as Master Stroke by Carl Laemmle', *MPW*, 26 Dec. 1925, p. 749.

19. 'Red', 'News Flashes From the usa', *Bio*, 31 Dec. 1925, p. 27; 'American Film Men Make German Deal', *NYT*, 31 Dec. 1925, p. 10; Sumner Smith, 'Universal, Paramount and mg m Divide the German Field With uf a', *MPW*, 16 Jan. 1926, p. 221; Heinrich Fraenkel, 'Latest From Germany', *Bio*, 7 Jan. 1926, p. 47.

20. Heinrich Fraenkel, 'Latest From Germany', *Bio*, 7 Jan. 1926, p. 47; ibid., 28 Jan. 1926, p. 49.

21. 'Universal, Paramount and mg m Divide the German Field With uf a', op. cit., p. 221.

22. 'America Has Grip on German Movies', *NYT*, 11 Nov. 1925, p. 25; 'Germany Restricts Use of Our Films', *NYT*, 27 Dec. 1925, Sec. 8, p. 3; 'Declares uf a Faces New Financial Crisis', *NYT*, 11 Dec. 1926, p. 6; L'Estrange Fawcett, *Films, Facts and Forecasts* (London: G. Bles, 1927), p. 194; 'uf a Company Goes to Hugenberg', *NYT*, 22 Apr. 1927, p. 18; 'Berlin Cable', *MPW*, 2 Apr. 1927, p. 461.

23. Heinrich Fraenkel, 'Universal Renting in Germany', *Bio*, 9 Dec. 1926, p. 42; Heinrich Fraenkel, 'German–Russian Film Combine', *Bio*, 20 Oct. 1927, p. 26; *JdF*, vol. 5, pp. 170, 41, 155; 'F. N.'s German Organisation Launched', *Bio*, 11 Aug. 1927, p. 27.

24. Raymond Moley, *The Hays Office* (Indianapolis: The Bobbs-Merrill Company, 1945), p. 171; 'Work of the Hays Organization', *FYB*, 1926, p. 479.

25. Moley, op. cit., p. 175.
26. 'Film Industry Opposes Germany's Import Law', *MPW*, 29 Nov. 1924, p. 402.
27. 'L'Envers du cinéma', *Ciné-Club*, 20 Feb. 1920, pp. 14–16. Ellipsis in original.
28. Lionel Landry, *et al.*, 'Le Cabinet du Dr. Caligari', *Cinéa*, 11 Nov. 1921, p. 8.
29. 'Chez Erich Pommer', *Cinémagazine*, 4 July 1924, p. 11.
30. A few examples: Jean Tedesco, 'Pour un cinématographe international', *Cinéa-Ciné pour tous*, 1 Jan. 1925, pp. 4–5; Paul de la Borie, 'Le Film européen', *Cinémagazine*, 9 Jan. 1925, pp. 63–4; 'Les Idées de Fritz Lang', *Ciné Revue*, 6 May 1927, p. 2.
31. 'Les Projets de M. W. Wengeroff', *Cinémagazine*, 10 Oct. 1924, p. 54; 'French Film Firm Joins With Germany', *NYT*, 14 Dec. 1924, Sec. 1, p. 3; *JdF*, vol. 2, pp. 27, 29; 'Gaumont-Communiqué', *Ciné Revue*, 26 June 1925, p. 10.
32. William Marston Seabury, *Motion Picture Problems: The Cinema and the League of Nations* (New York: Avondale Press, 1929), pp. 148–9; Jean Tedesco, 'Suggestions à la Société des Nations', *Cinéa-Ciné pour tous*, 1 May 1925, p. 6; W. Stephen Bush, 'What Happened to the U.C.I.?', *MPW*, 30 May 1925, p. 515; 'Le Congrès international du cinéma', *Comœdia*, 10 Apr. 1925, p. 1; Bush, 'Film Congress Stands Postponed; America "Too Busy"', *MPW*, 1 Aug. 1925, p. 501.
33. *Compte Rendu Officiel du Congrès International du Cinématograph* (Paris: Chambre Syndicale Française de la Cinématographie, 1926), Introduction, n.p.; Seabury, op. cit., p. 149.
34. Quoted from *NYT*, 1 July 1926, in Seabury, op. cit., pp. 194–5.
35. *Compte Rendu*, op. cit., pp. 23–43; Seabury, op. cit., p. 358 (Seabury prints the resolutions in full, pp. 357–82).
36. Andor Krazsna Krausz, 'The European Kino-Congress', *Close Up*, Oct. 1928, p. 16.
37. 'Les Premières réalisations de l'Alliance Cinématographique Européenne', *Cinéa-Ciné pour tous*, 1 Jan. 1927, pp. 26–8; 'Big Anglo-German Film Pact', *Bio*, 15 Dec. 1927, p. 21; *TIB*, no. 542, p. 5; 'Deutsch-russische Film-Allianz', *LBB*, 10 Oct. 1926, p. 1; Heinrich Fraenkel, 'German-Russian Film Combine', *Bio*, 20 Oct. 1927, p. 26; 'Creditors Seize Four Reels of Eisenstein's Latest Film', *NYT*, 27 Sept. 1929, p. 27; *JdF*, vol. 4, pp. 58–9; Bryher, *Film Problems of Soviet Russia* (Switzerland: Territet, 1929), pp. 56, 76, 105; 'Französisch-Deutsche Film-Gemeinschaft Terra-Cinéromans', *LBB*, 23 Mar. 1928, p. 1; 'Pathé-Paris-British-International', *LBB*, 12 Apr. 1928, p. 1; 'UFA-Luce', *LBB*, 12 June 1928, p. 1; Mowatt M. Mitchell, 'Italian Industrial Conditions Still Lagging', *CR*, 9 July 1928, p. 70; 'Form Cartel to Fight America', *NYT*, 22 June 1928, p. 5.
38. 'US Considering Special Bureau to Watch Foreign Film Situation', *MPW*, 24 Jan. 1925, p. 323; 'Red', 'USA News Flashes', *Bio*, 18 Feb. 1926, p. 37; 'Gov't Aiding Foreign Sales', *FYB*, 1927, p. 925; 'Government Aid', *FDYB*, 1929, p. 1,002.
39. N. D. Golden, 'Department of Commerce Promotes Exports of Motion Picture Products', *FDYB*, 1934, p. 993; 'Government Aid', *FDYB*, 1929, p. 1,002; 'How the Government Aids the Film Industry', *FDYB*, 1931,

p. 1,005; N. D. Golden, 'American Motion Pictures Abroad', *TSMPE*, 9–14 Apr. 1928, p. 56.

40. 'Offer By Americans to Help British Films', *NYT*, 2 June 1926, p. 23; Sumner Smith, 'British Companies Get Finance Offer From Hays Office', *MPW*, 12 June 1926, p. 5; Sumner Smith, 'London Cable', *MPW*, 26 June 1926, p. 1; 'British Conference Ends; No Solution Offered', *MPW*, 14 Aug. 1926, p. 3; *TIB*, no. 542, pp. 1, 19–28.

41. 'Hays Condemns Discrimination Against American Film Industry', *MPW*, 6 Aug. 1926, p. 373; 'Der neue Parufamet-Vertrag', *LBB*, 11 Aug. 1926, p. 1; 'Ends Negotiations on Reich Film Policy', *NYT*, 15 Dec. 1926, p. 16; F. W. Allport, 'Import and Export Restrictions: Germany', *CR*, 5 Dec. 1927, p. 632.

42. 'Hays Agent confers on French Film Act', *NYT*, 21 Feb. 1928, p. 4; 'Hope for Respite on French Film Law', *NYT*, 23 Feb. 1928, p. 34; Moley, op. cit., p. 174; *TIB*, no. 617, p. 9.

43. Moley, op. cit., p. 174; 'Americans Reject French Film Plan', *NYT*, 6 Apr. 1928, p. 4; 'Hays Sees Herrick on Film Situation', *NYT*, 13 Apr. 1928, p. 9; 'Hays and Herriot Confer on Films', *NYT*, 14 Apr. 1928, p. 5; 'American Films End in France Tuesday', *NYT*, 29 Apr. 1928, p. 15; 'French Reconsider Film Restrictions', *NYT*, 2 May 1928, p. 4; 'Americans Accept French Film Plan', *NYT*, 4 May 1928, p. 4; *TIB*, no. 617, p. 8.

44. *TIB*, no. 542, p. 31; 'Hays Protests Film Ban', *NYT*, 24 Feb. 1929, Sec. 1, p. 2; *TIB*, no. 752, p. 63.

45. George R. Canty, 'History of the French Contingent Regulation', *CR*, 17 Aug. 1931, pp. 410–11; 'France Will Hear Our Film Complaint', *NYT*, 13 Apr. 1929, p. 7; 'Brief Survey of Activities of Motion Picture Producers and Distributors of America During 1929', *FDYB*, 1930, p. 571; *TIB*, no. 694, pp. 6, 13; 'France Ends Curb on American Films', *NYT*, 25 June 1931, p. 8.

46. 'Business in Wartime: No. 16: Internationalizing the American Idea', *Collier's Weekly*, 19 Oct. 1918, p. 26; Hill, 'Marion Says Trade Follows Films', *MPW*, 5 Apr. 1919, p. 54. 'Trade follows the film' became a sort of slogan after the war; for example, see Hays' use of it in a 1927 lecture given at Harvard, in 'Supervision From Within', in Kennedy, op. cit., p. 38.

47. Aldcroft, op. cit., p. 303.

48. C. J. North, 'Our Silent Ambassadors', *Independent*, 12 June 1926, p. 699.

49. Carl E. Milliken, 'Internal Developments in the Motion Picture Industry', *TSMPE*, 3–6 May 1926, p. 139; 'Will H. Hays Talks to Foreign Trade Council; "The Film as an International Salesman", Biltmore Address', *Hollywood Filmograph*, 24 May 1930, p. 20.

50. Tom Reed, 'Mr. Hays Has His Hands Full', *The Film Spectator*, 27 Nov. 1926, p. 13.

51. 'Hays Office Denies "Lid" is Placed on Foreign Film News', *MPW*, 11 June 1927, p. 401.

52. *TIB*, nos. 617, 694, 752, 797, 801, 815; all tables in the section, unless otherwise noted, are from these *Bulletins*.

53. Chester Lloyd Jones, 'French Motion Pictures Yielding to Foreign Competition', *CR*, 5 Feb. 1923, p. 353; 'The Statistical Ticker', *FYB*, 1927, p. 9; Edward Auger, 'Foreign Representation', *MPW*, 26 Mar. 1927, p. 436.

54. *TIB*, no. 617, p. 28; *TIB*, no. 694, p. 15; *TIB*, no. 752, p. 27.

55. 'The Statistical Ticker', op. cit., p. 9; 'Englishman Frankly Admits Intention of Invading American Picture Market', *MPW*, 1 May 1920, p. 659.

56. 'Foreign Representation', op. cit., p. 356; *TIB*, no. 617, p. 19.

57. Heinrich Fraenkel, 'Latest From Germany', *Bio*, 1 July 1926, p. 28.

58. *TIB*, no. 499, p. 8; *TIB*, no. 542, p. 5; 'Foreign Representation', op. cit., p. 356.

59. *TIB*, nos. 443, 617, 694; Einar Lauritzen and Gunnar Lundquist, *Film-Index 1929* (Stockholm: Film-Index, 1973); *TIB*, no. 752; John L. Bouchal, 'Motion-Picture Situation in Finland During 1930', *CR*, 23 Feb. 1931, p. 526.

60. Francis R. Stewart, 'Motion Pictures in Switzerland', *CR*, 14 Feb. 1920, p. 925; Kenneth M. Hill, 'Motion Pictures in Switzerland', *CR*, 6 Feb. 1928, p. 368; *TIB*, no. 542, p. 11; *TIB*, no. 617, pp. 2, 37; *TIB*, no. 752, p. 65; Charles W. Drew Jr., 'Motion Pictures in Belgium', *CR*, 3 Feb. 1920, p. 680; *TIB*, no. 617, p. 2; *TIB*, no. 694, pp. 27, 29; *TIB*, no. 752, p. 39; 'The Netherlands as a Motion Picture Market', *MPA*, 22 July 1929, p. 3.

61. Carol H. Foster, 'Austrian Motion-Picture Industry', *CR*, 20 May 1922, p. 572; *TIB*, no. 499, p. 26; John A. Embry, 'Motion Pictures in Austria', *CR*, 23 Jan. 1928, p. 227; *TIB*, no. 617, p. 251; *TIB*, no. 694, p. 55; *TIB*, no. 752, p. 60.

62. A. A. Osborne, 'Italy's Imports and Exports of Motion-Picture Films', *CR*, 16 June 1924, p. 692; Pierre Leprohon, *The Italian Cinema*, trans. Roger Greaves and Oliver Stallybrass (New York: Praeger, 1972), p. 51; Ernest H. Salvi, 'If Rightly Handled American Pictures Would Pay in Italy', *MPW*, 27 Jan. 1923, p. 323; 'Italian Producers Suspend Work', *Bio*, 21 Feb. 1924, p. 44d; Charles Simone, 'Distributing American Films in Italy', *MPW*, 28 Feb. 1925, p. 869; *TIB*, no. 499, pp. 40–41; Walter H. Scholes, 'Italian Motion Picture Industry', *MPA*, 29 Jan. 1930, p. 4; *TIB*, no. 617, p. 2; *TIB*, no. 694, p. 26; George R. Canty, 'Italian Film Trade', *CR*, 4 May 1931, p. 287; *TIB*, no. 752, p. 36.

63. Untitled, *MPW*, 26 July 1919, p. 559; O. S. Payne, 'Imports of Films into Spain in 1922', *CR*, 23 Apr. 1923, p. 223; *TIB*, no. 499, p. 47; 'Von Spanischen Markt', *LBB*, 26 Sept. 1927, p. 3; Charles A. Livengood, 'Motion Picture Situation in Spain', *CR*, 2 Apr. 1928, p. 49; *TIB*, no. 553, p. 39; *TIB*, no. 694, pp. 59, 61; *TIB*, no. 752, pp. 53–4; Prescott Childs, 'Motion Pictures in Portugal', *CR*, 31 Dec. 1928, p. 892.

64. 'Foreign News and Notes', *Bio*, 8 Dec. 1921, p. 25; table calculated from Vance Kepley Jr. and Betty Kepley, 'Foreign Films on Soviet Screens, 1922–1931', *Quarterly Review of Film Studies*, fall 1979, p. 431.

65. 'Possible Increased Markets for American Goods', *CR*, 3 Mar. 1919, p. 990; Graham H. Kemper, 'Motion Pictures in Bulgaria', *CR*, 14 Jan. 1920, p. 248; C. S. Sewell, 'American Films Practically Unknown in Baltic States, Says A. J. Xydias', *MPW*, 5 June 1920, p. 1,307.

66. Vladimir A. Geringer, 'Demand for American Films in Czechoslovakia', *CR*, 21 Aug. 1919, p. 964; Vladimir A. Geringer, 'Motion Pictures in Czechoslovakia and Austria', *CR*, 19 Aug. 1920, p. 852; Louis E. Van Norman, 'The Polish Moving-Picture Trade', *CR*, 21 Jan. 1921, p. 389; Don S. Haven, 'Opportunity for American Film Industry in Jugoslavia', *CR*, 3 Oct. 1921, p. 322.

67. W. S[tephen] B[ush], 'Austria Likes us Pictures But Money Bags Are Empty', *MPW*, 19 Aug. 1922, p. 567; H. C. Megill, 'American Motion Pictures in Zagreb', *CR*, 5 Feb. 1923, p. 354; Harold B. Quarton, 'The Estonian Motion-Picture Market', *CR*, 23 July 1923, p. 215; W. L. Lowrie,

'American Pictures Most Popular in Greece', *CR*, 28 Jan. 1924, p. 215; Digby A. Willson, 'The Hungarian Motion-Picture Market', *CR*, 29 Oct. 1923, p. 293; Emil Kokich, 'Motion Picture Situation in the Baltic States', *CR*, 17 Mar. 1924, p. 708.

68. Figures for total number of films, 1928, from George R. Canty, 'Film Items From Foreign Countries', *CR*, 29 Apr. 1929, p. 298.

69. Figures for 1927–9 from John W. Bailey Jr., 'Motion Pictures in Czechoslovakia', *MPA*, 13 Jan. 1930, n.p.

70. Figures for 1929 from Samuel Green, 'Motion Pictures in Bulgaria During 1929', *MPA*, 31 July 1930, p. 3.

71. Figures for 1926–8 from Leslie A. Davis, 'Market for American Motion Pictures in Yugoslavia', *MPA*, 29 Aug. 1929, p. 4.

72. George R. Canty, 'American Films Most Popular in Rumania', *CR*, 31 Mar. 1930, p. 852; Ely E. Palmer, 'Motion Picture Industry in Rumania', *MPA*, 22 Aug. 1929, p. 3; table's figures for 1925–9 from J. Rivers Child, 'Rumanian Market for Sound Films and Apparatus', *MPA*, 1 Feb. 1930, p. 4; for 1930 from Kenneth M. Hill, 'Rumanian Consumption of Motion-Picture Films in 1930', *CR*, 13 Apr. 1931, p. 107.

73. C. J. North, 'Developments of American Film Trade in the Last Decade', *CR*, 28 May 1928, p. 541; 'Far Eastern Trade Notes', *CR*, 7 Nov. 1919, p. 760; Alfred A. Winslow, 'Notes From New Zealand', *CR*, 12 Jan. 1921, p. 222; 'Far Eastern Trade and Economic Notes', *CR*, 12 Mar. 1921, p. 1,412; table based on Henry H. Balch, 'Australian Imports of Motion Pictures', *CR*, 31 July 1922, p. 299.

74. E. C. Squire, 'Far East: Drought and Restricted Finances in Australia', *CR*, 30 Jan. 1928, p. 269; 'Hit American Films New Zealand Sees', *NYT*, 13 Oct. 1926, p. 23; table from figures in H. P. Van Blarcom, 'Australian Imports and Censorship of Films', *CR*, 18 Apr. 1932, p. 165.

75. 'Glucksmann Gets Control of Metro's 1920 Entire Output For South America', *MPW*, 8 May 1920, p.849; Bernard H. Noll, 'Motion Pictures in Brazil', *CR*, 23 Apr. 1921, p. 490.

76. Rollo S. Smith, 'Motion Pictures in Chile', *CR*, 24 Apr. 1922, p. 236; A. Gaulin, 'Motion-Picture Market', *CR*, 25 Dec. 1922, p. 795; D. C. McDonough, 'Bolivia Likes American Films', *CR*, 5 Feb. 1923, p. 354; E. M. Lawton, 'The Sao Paulo Market For Motion Pictures', *CR*, 28 May 1923, p. 559; Amado Charles Jr., 'The Market for Motion Pictures in Venezuela', *CR*, 1 Oct. 1923, p. 23; table from George E. Seltzer, 'Films Censored in Brazil in 1929', *CR*, 7 Apr. 1930, p. 26; George S. Messersmith, 'The Motion-Picture Industry in Argentina', *CR*, 15 July 1929, p. 176.

77. A. C. Frost, 'Miscellaneous Items', *CR*, 20 Nov. 1922, p. 491; 'The Cuban Motion-Picture Market', *CR*, 25 June 1923, p. 817; L. W. James, 'American Motion Pictures Dominate Porto Rico Market', *CR*, 28 Jan. 1924, p. 215.

78. 'Mexico's Ban on Mexican Movie Villains Forbids All Pictures it Considers Propaganda', *NYT*, 11 Feb. 1922, p. 15; 'Seems Villainous', *MPW*, 16 Sept. 1922, p. 187; O. Gaylord Marsh, 'Motion Pictures in Yucatan', *CR*, 23 July 1923, p. 216; Warren Ulrich, 'The Mexican Market for Specialties', *CR*, 9 Nov. 1925, p. 327; 'Mexican Embassy Makes Clear Its Picture-Platform', *MPW*, 23 July 1927, p. 248.

79. Martin G. Scott, 'Motion-Picture Industry of Japan', *CR*, 26 Dec. 1929, p. 1,036; 'Censors American Films', *NYT*, 13 Nov. 1922, p. 9; E. R. Dickover,

'Distributing Motion Pictures in Japan', *CR*, 23 July 1923, p. 215; Robert Florey, 'L'Industrie cinématographique au Japon', *Cinémagazine*, 1 Dec. 1922, p. 300.

80. 'American Motion Pictures Help Japanese in Reconstruction Work', *NYT*, 20 Apr. 1924, Sec. 8, p. 4; 'Embassy Protests to Japan on Films', *NYT*, 15 June 1924, Sec. 1, p. 3; 'Japanese Boycott Fails', *NYT*, 17 June 1924, p. 5; 'Japan's Film Boycott Given Up as Failure', *NYT*, 13 July 1924, Sec. 2, p. 1.

81. Sumner Smith, 'US Losing Japanese Market; Exchanges Don't Make Expenses', *MPW*, 26 Feb. 1927, pp. 617–18; E. R. Dickover, 'Exhibition of Motion Pictures in Japan', *CR*, 5 Nov. 1928, p. 375; table from figures in the International Cinema Association of Japan, *Cinema Year Book of Japan 1936–1937* (Tokyo: Sanseido, 1937), p. 114.

82. *TIB*, no. 634, pp. 5, 9; table calculated from *Foreign Commerce and Navigation of the United States* (Washington: Government Printing Office), volumes for 1926 to 1934, and *Cinema Year Book of Japan 1936–1937*, op. cit., p. 114; Halleck A. Butts, 'High Lights of the Japanese Motion-Picture Industry', *CR*, 29 Aug. 1932, p. 359.

83. 'Trade Conditions Across the Pacific', *MPW*, 4 Oct. 1919, p. 156; 'Far Eastern Trade Notes', *CR*, 10 June 1920, p. 1,450; Jay Leyda has traced the film production of China during this period in *Dianying: Electric Shadows* (Cambridge, Mass.: The MIT Press, 1972), pp. 15–59; 'Far Eastern Trade and Economic Notes', *CR*, 12 Sept. 1921, p. 113; Lynn W. Meekins, 'Motion Pictures in China', *CR*, 26 Mar. 1922, p. 40; Stuart J. Fuller, 'Tientsin and Peking Markets for Motion Pictures', *CR*, 26 Mar. 1923, pp. 806–7; Leroy Webber, 'The Hongkong Motion-Picture Trade', *CR*, 29 Oct. 1923, p. 294; Richard C. Patterson Jr., 'The Cinema in China', *NYT*, 23 Jan. 1927, Sec. 7, p. 7.

84. Carl C. Hansen, 'Motion Pictures in Siam', *CR*, 28 Apr. 1924, p. 222; Parker W. Buhrman, 'American Motion Pictures in Java', *CR*, 28 Aug. 1922, p. 602; G. C. Howard, 'Growth of Motion-Picture Interest in the Philippines', *CR*, 20 May 1929, p. 476.

85. 'Trade Conditions Across the Pacific', *MPW*, 4 Oct. 1919, p. 156; 'Far Eastern Trade Notes', *CR*, 18 Oct. 1919, p. 380; S. S. Banerjea, 'The Cinema Trade in India', *Bio*, 13 July 1922, p. 29.

86. Erik Barnouw and S. Krishnaswamy, *Indian Film* (New York: Columbia University Press, 1963), pp. 38–55; George R. Canty, 'Film Production in India', *CR*, 23 Dec. 1929, p. 746; 'To Save the Hindu From Our Movies', *Literary Digest*, 31 Mar. 1928, p. 25.

87. Oscar S. Heizer, 'Cinema Theaters in Mesopotamia', *CR*, 12 Jan. 1920, p. 222; Thomas R. Owens, 'Motion Pictures in Iraq', *CR*, 10 Dec. 1923, p. 672; G. Bie Ravndal, 'Moving Pictures in Constantinople', *CR*, 4 Apr. 1920, p. 82; P. Knabenshue and I. Loder, 'American Motion Pictures in Asia Minor', *CR*, 26 Mar. 1923, p. 807.

88. James Loder Park, 'The Motion-Picture Industry in Arabia', *CR*, 24 Oct. 1927, pp. 231–2; Orsen N. Neilsen, 'The Motion-Picture Industry in Persia', *CR*, 28 Nov. 1927, p. 539; Henry S. Villard, 'Film Importers Face Difficulties in Persia', *CR*, 6 Apr. 1931, p. 38; Henry A. Villard, 'The Market for Motion Picture Films in Persia', *MPA*, 24 Feb. 1930, pp. 3–7; *TIB*, no. 694, p. 67.

89. 'Cinema Business in South Africa', *Bio*, 17 Feb. 1929, p. 24; P. J. Stevenson, 'South African Economic Notes', *CR*, 23 June 1921, p. 1,708; Harry

H. Morse, 'Motion Pictures in South Africa', *CR*, 11 Sept. 1922, p. 733; Fawcett, op. cit., pp. 58–9.
90. Frederic de Billiers, 'Motion-Picture Films in Cairo', *CR*, 3 Aug. 1920, p. 634; George R. Canty, 'Egyptian Film Market Expanding', *CR*, 2 Dec. 1929, p. 564; Charles E. Dickerson, Jr., 'Motion Pictures in Egypt', *CR*, 9 Sept. 1929, p. 689; Cecil M. M. Cross, 'Motion-Picture Situation in Portuguese East Africa', *CR*, 29 Oct. 1923, p. 292; Percy G. Kemp, 'Motion Pictures in the Canary Islands', *CR*, 30 July 1928, p. 297.

5 Surviving Talkies and the Depression, 1929–34

1. Clifford Howard, 'Hollywood Review', *Close Up*, June 1931, p. 112.
2. Gomery, 'The Coming of Sound', op. cit.
3. Gomery, 'The Coming of Sound', p. 379; Ernest W. Fredman, 'England and Sound', *FDYB*, 1929, p. 362; George R. Canty, 'European Interest in the Sound Film', *CR*, 23 July 1928, p. 231.
4. J. Douglas Gomery, 'Economic Struggle and Hollywood Imperialism: Europe Converts to Sound', *Yale French Studies*, 1980, p. 82.
5. *TIB*, no. 617, pp. 22–3; George R. Canty, 'Sound Film Developments in England, Germany, and Austria', *CR*, 3 Dec. 1928, p. 637; George R. Canty, 'British Company Joins with German Sound-Film Company', *CR*, 1 Oct. 1928, p. 54.
6. Dr Bruno Kiesewetter, 'The European Sound-Picture Industry', *Electronics*, Sept. 1930, p. 282; Kiesewetter's article includes a supplement, an excellent chart of the relations among the sound-film companies of the world; my own schematic diagrams of the European groups are adapted from the upper-right portions of this chart and from Kiesewetter's discussion. The whole chart is reproduced in Howard Thompson Lewis, *The Motion Picture Industry* (New York: D. Van Nostrand, 1933; reprinted Jerome S. Ozer, 1971), bet. pp. 78–9. Douglas Miller, 'Competing Talking Film Companies Organized in Germany', *CR*, 1 Oct. 1928, p. 54; Gomery, 'The Coming of Sound', p. 381; *JdF*, no. 4, p. 187; Nathan D. Golden, 'Sound Motion Pictures in Europe', *JSMPE*, Jan. 1930, p. 13; 'UFA to Make Sound Film', *NYT*, 9 Apr. 1929, p. 8.
7. Kiesewetter, op. cit., pp. 282–3.
8. Ibid., pp. 283–4; 'Europeans in $300,000,000 Sound Film Merger; Move is Seen as Union Against our Talkies', *NYT*, 2 July 1929, p. 9.
9. André Chevanne, *L'Industrie du cinéma, Le cinéma sonore* (Bordeaux: Librarie Delmas, 1933, p. 49; Sadoul, op. cit., vol. 6, pp. 372–3; Kiesewetter, op. cit. p. 284.
10. *JdF*, vol. 4, pp. 36–7; 'Jolson Talkie Wins Berlin Audiences', *NYT*, 4 June 1929, p. 29; 'Germans Win Talkie Suit', *NYT*, 21 July 1929, Sec. 1, p. 5; Gomery, 'The Coming of Sound', p. 382.
11. 'Seek World Compact on Talkie Devices', *NYT*, 24 July 1929, p. 14; Gomery, 'The Coming of Sound', pp. 382–3; 'Sues to Break Ban on American Talkies', *NYT*, 17 Nov. 1929, Sec. 1, p. 30.
12. Figures from *Monthly Summary of the Foreign Commerce of the United States* (US Department of Commerce), 1929–30.
13. Floyd Gibson, 'Audible Film Production in Germany', *NYT*, 9 Mar. 1930, Sec. 9, p. 6; Douglas Miller, 'Difficulties of the Spitzen Organization', *CR*, 18 Nov. 1929, p. 430.

14. Gomery, 'The Coming of Sound', p. 383; 'Warner Bros. Conclude Negotiations With the German Group', *Hollywood Filmograph*, 19 Apr. 1930, p. 26.

15. Gomery, 'The Coming of Sound', p. 384; 'World Patent Truce on Talkies Likely', *NYT*, 17 May 1930, p. 20; 'Hays to Seek Peace in Sound Film War', *NYT*, 18 June 1930, p. 4; Gomery, 'The Coming of Sound', p. 386; 'American Film Men and Germans Meet', *NYT*, 20 June 1930, p. 12; 'Clear Way to Pact on Sound Movies', *NYT*, 13 July 1930, Sec. 1, p. 8; 'Talkie Pact Signed With Reich Firms', *NYT*, 23 July 1930, p. 11; *TIB*, no. 752, p. 10; Kiesewetter, op. cit., p. 284.

16. *TIB*, no. 752, pp. 33, 35, 75; Gomery, 'The Coming of Sound', p. 421; 'Fox Movietone News Is Shown in Germany', *NYT*, 14 Sept. 1930, Sec. 3, p. 4.

17. Gomery, 'The Coming of Sound', p. 422; 'Aid French Studios on Film Recording', *NYT*, 9 Feb. 1932, p. 31; Gomery, 'Economic Struggle and Hollywood Imperialism', p. 87.

18. Gomery, 'The Coming of Sound', p. 422; Gomery, 'Economic Struggle and Hollywood Imperialism', pp. 87–8.

19. Clifford Howard, 'Hollywood Notes', *Close Up*, May 1929, pp. 93–4; 'Finds Talkies Spread Use of English Abroad', *NYT*, 15 Oct. 1929, p. 10; 'Talkies Set Vogue in Brazil for English', *NYT*, 18 Aug. 1929, Sec. 2, p. 21.

20. '"Talkies" in France', *NYT*, 4 Mar. 1929, p. 24; 'Views of Executives on the Foreign Situation for 1930', *FDYB*, 1930, p. 999; George R. Canty, 'Resumé of Central European Markets', *MPA*, 26 June 1930, p. 4.

21. T. O. Klath, 'The Swedish Film Market in 1929', *MPA*, 6 May 1930, p. 1; *TIB*, no. 694, pp. 5, 29; Jesse F. Van Wickel, 'Sound Films Popular in the Netherlands', *CR*, 9 Dec. 1929, p. 627; C. J. North, 'Our Foreign Trade', *FDYB*, 1930, p. 1,005.

22. Gomery, 'The Coming of Sound', p. 376; Chapin Hall, 'Stars Are Dimmed', *NYT*, 22 Mar. 1931, Sec. 8, p. 5; 'Talkies For Europe Baffle Audiences', *NYT*, 28 Dec. 1930, p. 4.

23. 'Foreign Language Films', *NYT*, 17 Nov. 1929, Sec. 9, p. 5; 'Fox to Film Italian-French Films Here', *Hollywood Filmograph*, 2 Aug. 1930, p. 7; '14 Foreigns By Warners to Date', *The Film Mercury*, 30 Jan. 1931, p. 4; Gomery, 'The Coming of Sound', p. 377; 'Paramount to Film Talkies in Europe', *NYT*, 27 Apr. 1930, Sec. 1, p. 10; 'Comment and Review', *Close Up*, Aug. 1930, p. 155.

24. 'Plenty of Work for Foreign Stars at MGM', *Hollywood Filmograph*, 16 Aug. 1930, p. 13; Clifford Howard, 'Hollywood Notes', *Close Up*, Dec. 1930, pp. 451–5; 'Much Foreign Activity on First National Lot', *The Film Mercury*, 7 Nov. 1930, p. 4.

25. C. J. North, 'Sound Dominates the World Market', *FDYB*, 1931, p. 1,001; Milton T. Houghton, 'Talking Pictures Shown in Chile', *CR*, 28 Apr. 1930, p. 240; Jesse F. Van Wickel, 'Sound Films Gain Popularity in the Netherlands', *CR*, 20 Oct. 1930, p. 174; C. Hooper Trask, 'Our Talkies in Germany', *NYT*, 15 June 1930, Sec. 8, p. 3; George Lewin, 'Dubbing and Its Relation to Sound Picture Production', *JSMPE*, Jan. 1930, p. 44.

26. 'RKO Putting Soft Pedal on Foreign Films', *The Film Mercury*, 3 Aug. 1930, p. 17; 'Studios Working on New Plan to Beat Foreign Situation', *The Film Mercury*, 8 Aug. 1930, p. 17; Walter Daniels, 'Europe Howling Down Talkies',

The Film Mercury, 28 Nov. 1930, p. 2; Valentin Mandelstamm, 'Le "Dubbing"', *Cinéa*, new series, Apr. 1932, p. 25; John Campbell, 'Paris Notes', *NYT*, 6 Dec. 1931, Sec. 8, p. 6.

27. 'Drop Foreign Players at MGM', *The Film Mercury*, 17 Apr. 1931, p. 4; 'Foreign Language Pictures', *NYT*, 31 May 1931, Sec. 8, p. 4.

28. Sylvester S. Roll, 'American Film Company Offices in Colombia', *CR*, 21 Sept. 1931, p. 736; Charles H. Ducote, 'The Motion-Picture Situation in Argentina', *CR*, 1 June 1931, p. 548; 'Progress in the Motion Picture Industry', *JSMPE*, Aug. 1932, pp. 117–18; C. Hooper Trask, 'On Berlin's Screens', *NYT*, 5 Feb. 1933, p. 4.

29. *FDYB*, 1933, pp. 986, 992–3; *FDYB*, 1934, p. 1,023; *TIB*, no. 694, p. 7; George R. Canty, 'Resumé of Central European Film Markets', *MPA*, 26 June 1930, pp. 5, 7.

30. C. J. North, 'Our Foreign Trade', *FDYB*, 1930, p. 1,005.

31. C. J. North and N. D. Golden, 'The European Film Market', *CR*, 12 Oct. 1931, p. 92.

32. Robert Murphy, 'A Rival to Hollywood?', *Screen*, July–Oct. 1983, pp. 96–106.

33. Grace A. Witherow, 'Foreign Trade of the United States in 1931', *TIB*, no. 808, 1932, p. 1.

34. General chart from 'Trade Trends', *CR*, 13 May 1933, p. 296, and 13 Apr. 1935, p. 244; film chart from *Monthly Summary of the Foreign Commerce of the United States*.

35. 'Silent versions Staging Comeback', *The Film Mercury*, 27 Feb. 1931, p. 4.

Appendix I
Chronologies

Sources: the information in these chronologies comes from a variety of articles too extensive to footnote individually. Chronologies 1 and 2 are basically surveys of the *MPW* and *Bio.* These publications did not usually give precise dates for agency or branch openings; hence dates are often those of the first mentions of the new offices by these journals.

1902: Nov. – Gaston Méliès opens **Star Film Agency** in New York City. (Star had distributed through AM & B until Feb. 1902.)

1904: 18 July – J. A. Berst comes to the USA, establishes **Pathé**'s branch.

1907: *c.* Mar. – Miles Bros. (New York) establishes London and Paris buying offices.
Signs with eighteen companies, including **R. W. Paul, Gaumont, Walturdaw, Internationale Kinematographer und Licht Effekt** and **Nordisk**.
Mar. – Kleine Optical appointed agent for **Charles Urban Trading Co. Ltd** (at about the time of the **Urban** and **Eclipse** merger).
Apr. – Williams, Brown & Earle (Philadelphia) appointed agent for **Hepworth, Cricks & Sharp** and **R. W. Paul**.
June – **Pathé** incorporates in New Jersey, builds printing laboratory.
Aug. – **Cines** opens New York office, first release 14 Aug.
Oct. – Williams, Brown & Earle increase output to two reels a week.
Dec. – **Warwick Trading Co.** signs Kleine Optical as Canadian representative, plans own American office.

1908: Early in year – Film Service Association forms.
Feb. – Formation of Biograph Association of Licensees.
Williamson & Co. advertises films; has office in New York.
Kleine Optical lists: **Gaumont, Urban-Eclipse, Lux, Raleigh & Roberts, Théophile Pathé** (French), **Gaumont, Urban-Eclipse, Warwick** (British), **Aquila, Carlo Rossi, Ambrosio** (Italian). (All under Biograph licences.)
Mar. – **Great Northern** opens New York office. (A few films had been sold by agents previously. Licensed by Biograph.)

1909: May – **Pathé** plans American studio.
Nov. – **Lux** opens own American branch.
Raleigh & Robert (Paris), agent for **Ambrosio**, signs with Film Import and Trading Co.

1910: Jan. – **Lux** office begins American releases.
Feb. – **Eclair** opens in New York.
Spring – re-organisation of independent groups. Motion Picture Distributing and Sales Co. merges with Associated Independent Film Manufacturers to form new Motion Picture Distributing and Sales Co., handling **Ambrosio, Eclair, Film d'Art, Lux, Great Northern, Itala.** (Operates until Apr. 1912.)
Apr. – **Pathé** opens New Jersey studio.
May – first **Pathé** American-made release.
June – Herbert Blaché purchases the **Gaumont Company of New York.**

1911: Apr. – **Cines** opens temporary New York office, looking for regular agent. (Has been releasing occasionally in the USA.)
c. Oct. – *Dante's Inferno* (Italian feature) sold states rights through Monopol Film Co.
Nov. – **Gaumont** announces George Kleine dropped as agent.

1912: Jan. – Kleine replaces **Gaumont** with **Cines**. Also picks up **Eclipse**.
Apr. – the Motion Picture Distributing and Sales Co. breaks up; Universal forms, also New York Motion Picture Co. Film Supply Co. gets: **Gaumont, Great Northern, Eclair** and **Lux.**
Aug. – **Itala** dropped by New York Motion Picture Co. **Itala** appoints American agent, Harry Raver, and goes over to feature films. **Great Northern** releasing **Ambrosio** and other European brands.
Sept. – **Ambrosio American Co.** formed in New York, to release through Universal.

1913: Jan. – Vivaphone Film & Sales Co. formed in New York. Representative for **Hecla** and **Hepworth.**
c. Aug. – R. S. Edmondson sets up **Film Releases of America** (importer).
Aug. – Kleine appointed agent for **Celio**. Also obtains world rights for *The Last Days of Pompeii* (**Ambrosio** feature).
Sept. – **Copenhagen Film Co. Ltd** gets New York agent.
Nov. – **Gloria** gets New York agent.
Midgar Features of New York signs **H. A. Muller** agency (German company).

1914: Early in year – **Eclair Film Co.** and various other **Eclair** subsidiaries formed in the USA.
Jan. – Formation of **Anglo-American Film Corp** (feature importer).
Feb. – **Nova Films Co.** (Rome) opens Philadelphia office, to sell states rights.
Mar. – **Pasquali American Co.** opens in New York.
Fire at **Eclair's** New Jersey studio.
Deluxe Attractions Film Co. to release twelve features a year (importer).

May – Motion Picture Sales Agency currently handling **Film d'Art, Aquila, Clarendon** and **Regent.**

Gaumont selling states rights.

Cosmotfotofilm formed, has agency for **London Film Co.** and others (importer).

May to June – **Pathé** breaks with General Film Co., opens own exchanges.

July – **Pasquali American** reorganised after success of *Last Days of Pompeii*; plans to produce in the USA.

Pathé ceases own production except serials, goes over to independent distribution.

Aug. – At beginning of war, much of **Eclair** staff called back to French military. Negatives on hand for eight months; foresee production continuing in London and Italy.

Raver, **Itala**'s agent, says **Itala** product will continue to be supplied.

Sept. – **Pasquali** films reported difficult to obtain.

Oct. – Charles Pathé comes to the USA for extended stay.

Sept.-Oct. – **Pathé** releasing only *Pathé Daily News*, twice a week, through Eclectic.

Nov. – **Bishop, Pessers & Co.** sends representative to establish an American office.

Charles Pathé says he will concentrate on the American market and Eclectic. Eclectic now releasing **Pathé** fiction films as well as the *Daily News*.

Late 1914, early 1915 – Eclectic replaced by the **Pathé Exchange.**

1915: Jan. – **Gaumont** soliciting scenarios for American production, releasing no films.

Feb. – **Hepworth American Film Corp.** selling states rights.

Ben Blumenthal, importer, selling **Gloria** and **Milano** states rights.

Savoia Company of America recently formed.

Mar. – **Great Northern** selling states rights.

Apr. – **Itala** reportedly negotiating to sell through the **Pathé Exchange;** agent, Raver, handling only *Cabiria* and other specials.

June – **Itala** plans American production of a Maciste film.

c. Aug. – **Ambrosio** representatives sell some films to Universal, appoint an American agent.

1 Sept. – **Société Française des Films et Cinématographes Eclair** sues **Eclair Film Co.** and other subsidiaries to recover stock turned over to holding company by American company official.

Oct. – Universal to distribute a major **Hepworth** feature, *My Old Dutch*.

Nov. – **Great Northern** begins regular feature releases, with two four-reelers a month, as Polar Bear Features.

Dec. – **Hepworth** official comes to the USA to trade-show films and try to get back into American market.

C. Ambrosio to the USA, looking for new **Ambrosio** agent for the USA, to try to get back into the American market.

1916: Feb. – C. Ambrosio leaves having sold two **Ambrosio** features.

June – C. Jourjon, **Eclair** president, plans to come to the USA and re-organise the **Eclair Film Co.** when he obtains leave (and if the German offensive at Verdun fails!).

Nov. – Chester Beecroft sets up the **Overseas Distributing Co. of America.**
It sells **American Film Co.** and **Mutual** films abroad (importer/exporter).

1917: Feb. – Paul Cromelin and others start the **Inter-Ocean Film Co. Ltd,** mostly to buy European rights of American films (importer/exporter).
May – **Max Glucksmann** (South American distributor) establishes American buying office, with brother Jacobo as manager.
June – **John Olsen & Co.** opens New York office (transferring from London). Buys American films for **Fotorama, Swedish Biograph** and **Scandinavian Film Central** (three large Scandinavian distributors).
Jourjon has now investigated **Eclair** in the USA. Suit dropped. Production planned to resume.
July – **Export and Import Films Co.** formed in New York (importer/exporter).
Sept. – Foreign Buyers Association formed. Group of buyers to deal directly with American firms, buy world rights in packages. Also to lobby.

1918: Jan. – **Central American Film Co.** (Havana) opens New York buying office to obtain American films for Cuba, Santo Domingo, Puerto Rico, Jamaica, Venezuela, Colombia, Panama, Central America.
Early in year – **Robertson-Cole Co.,** a general export firm, begins handling films.
Wid's Year Book lists import/export agents: **M. H. Hoffman, J. Frank Brockliss, David P. Howells, Windmill Motion Pictures** and **Export and Import Film Co. Inc.**
Mar. – **Gaumont** drops Mutual as its distributor and goes states rights.
June – **Inter-Ocean** has so far exported only. Now in market for British films for American market.

1919: Early – *Wid's* ads for exporters: **J. Frank Brockliss, Inter-Ocean, David P. Howells, Export and Import, Gillespie Bros., Les Films Albert Dulac.** Also a *Wid's* ad for the **Swedish Biograph** office in New York.
Feb. – **Apollo Trading Corp.** (Chester Beecroft) started (exporter).
Apr. – **Robertson-Cole** signs reciprocal agreement with **Jury's Imperial Pictures. World-Wide Distributing Corp.** opens in New York (importer/exporter).
June – **Charles Delac Vandal & Co.** (French) appoints Adolphe Osso New York agent, for export and import.
July – **Atlantic Cinema Corp.** starts in New York (Ben Blumenthal president) (exporter).
Max Glucksmann begins buying American films for all Latin America, not just own circuit.
Aug. – **Compagnie Cinématographique Albert Dulac** to open New York office to be called **Les Films Albert Dulac of Paris.** Plans to release French films.

Guy Croswell Smith Ltd formed to export specials (for example signs *Broken Blossoms* world rights) (exporter).

Dec. – **David P. Howells,** exporter, opens Scandinavian branch to sell American films.

1920: Early – *Wid's* exporters' ads for: **Inter-Ocean, Export and Import, Sidney Garret Inc., Criterion Pictures, Falkner-Tyrol Productions.**

Feb. – Ben Blumenthal, of **Export and Import,** importing Swedish pictures.

May – **David P. Howells Inc.** absorbs **J. Frank Brockliss Inc.**

July – **Hepworth Picture Plays Inc.** opens in New York.

Sept. – Charles Pathé resigns as president of the **Pathé Exchange**.

6 Dec. – **Stoll Film Corp. of America** (British subsidiary) opens to distribute through the **Pathé Exchange**.

1921: Early – *Wid's* listings of importers/exporters: **William A. Vogel, Herz Film Corp., Overseas Film Trading Co., Luporini Bros., Ernest Shipman, Export and Import Film Co.**

c. Apr. – **Stoll Film Co.** goes out of business, signs over its distribution rights to the **Pathé Exchange**.

July – American stockholders acquire control of the **Pathé Exchange**, with Charles Pathé retaining minority holdings.

Aug. – **International Pictures of America** (William H. Brady) formed (importer/exporter).

1922: Early – *Film Year Book* import/export listings: **Motion Picture Enterprises, Export and Import, William A. Vogel, Herz Film Corp., David P. Howells, Inter-Globe Export Corp., Reginal & Warde, Far East Film Corp., Edward L. Klein Co.**

Feb. – **Luxor Pictures Corp.** formed.

1923: Early – *Film Year Book* import/export listings: **CBC Film Sales, Luporini Features Inc., Export and Import, Apollo Trading Corp., Inter-Ocean Film Corp., David P. Howells, William M. Vogel, Herz Film Corp., George E. Kann Corp.** (exporter only), **Inter-Globe Export Corp., Chipman Ltd, Ferdinand H. Adam** (foreign buyer), **Ernest Mattsson Inc.** (Swedish importer/exporter), **Edward L. Klein Co., Hi-Mark Sales Co., Max Glucksmann** (Latin American buyer), **The New York Buying Office.**

1924: Early – *Film Year Book* import/export listings: **Cranfield & Clarke, Ritz International Corp., Simmonds-Kann Enterprises, Export and Import Film, Inter-Ocean Film Corp., Richmond Pictures Inc., Henry R. Arias, Hi-Mark Sales Co., Frederick W. Kilner, David P. Howells, John H. Taylor Film Corp., Max Glucksmann** (Latin American buyer), **Edward L. Klein Co., Chipman Pictures Corp., Ernest Mattsson** (Swedish importer/exporter), **Ferdinand H. Adam, Inter-Globe Export Corp., Akra Pictures Corp., Apollo Trading Corp., Seven Seas Film Corp., Capital Productions Co., U. Ono** (Japanese buyer), **Donald Campbell.**

Sept. – **Hepworth's** American office closes, turns over sales to an import firm, **Cranfield & Clarke.**

1925: Early – *Film Year Book* import/export listings: **Export and Import, Edward L. Klein, Richmont Pictures Inc., Inter-Ocean Film Corp., Hi-Mark, Akras Pictures, Capital Production Exporting Co., Exhibitors Film Exchange, Simmonds-Kann Enterprises, Apollo Trading, Inter-Globe, J. H. Hoffberg Co., Ferdinand H. Adam** (foreign buyer), **Massce & Co., Ernest Mattsson** (Swedish importer/exporter), **Class Play Picture Corp., Magnus Film Corp., Donald Campbell, U. Ono** (Japanese buyer), **Cranfield & Clarke, Roy Chandler** (Latin American buyer), **M. Ramirez Torres, Jawitz Pictures, Chipman Pictures Corp.**
Jan. – Formation of UFA-USA announced.
June – Schubert cinema chain signs with UFA to show *Siegfried* in its houses. Two American companies negotiating reciprocal distribution with UFA.
Aug. – UFA announces it has decided against reciprocal agreement, will continue to negotiate American rights film by film. Says twenty of its thirty-six films for the year will be imported into the USA.

1926: Early – *Film Year Book* import/export listings: **Export and Import, Richmont, Edward L. Klein, Hi-Mark Film Sales, Ednella Export, Capital Production Exporting, Argentine American Film Corp., Ferdinand H. Adam** (foreign buyer), **Inter-Globe Export, Ferdinand V. Luporini, J. H. Hoffberg, Donald Campbell, Cranfield & Clarke, Apollo Trading Corp., Class Play Pictures, Ernest Mattsson** (Swedish import/export), **Seventh Avenue Film, Exhibitors Film Exchange, U. Ono** (Japanese buyer), **Edward Augier** (buyer), **Jawitz Pictures, G. De Arana, Massce Co.**
c. Dec. – **Amkino** opens, American branch of **Sovkino.**

1927: Early – *Film Daily Year Book* import/export listings: **Export and Import Film, Hi-Mark Productions, Capital Production Exporting, Argentine American Film, Ferdinand V. Luporini, Ferdinand H. Adam** (foreign buyer), **Inter-Globe, Massce & Co. ALA Film Trading Corp., Ernest Mattsson** (Swedish importer/exporter), **J. H. Hoffberg, Donald Campbell, Artlee Pictures, Guaranty Pictures, European Phoenix Features Corp., ABA Film.**
July – A New York agent opens an office for **Filmwerke Staaken** and **Phoebus-Film A-G** (German companies).
Nov. – UFA announces plans for its own Broadway cinema; ten films per season will be distributed by MGM and Paramount, but UFA will expand production and distribute an additional ten to twenty directly in the USA.

CHRONOLOGY 2: AMERICAN FIRMS' FOREIGN OFFICES AND REPRESENTATIVES, 1894–1927

1894: 30 Aug. – Maguire & Baucus, a New York export company, already have **Edison** foreign rights for South America, West Indies, Australia and Mexico, request European rights.

c. Oct.-Nov. – Continental Commerce Co., London (F. L. Maguire) opens **Edison** Kinetoscope business for Europe.

1895: 28 Jan. – Maguire & Baucus open a Kinetoscope parlour in Mexico City.

1896: Maguire & Baucus begin selling projecting Kinetoscopes abroad.

1897: *c.* Mar. – sole agency abroad taken from Maguire & Baucus; **Edison** films are sold abroad by jobbers as well.

1903: Dec. – National Phonograph Co. Ltd, **Edison** subsidiary in London, begins direct sales of Edison films in Europe.

1906: **Vitagraph** opens London branch office.
    Dec. – **Edison-Gesellschaft MBH** has recently opened a film showroom and special department in Berlin. Catalogues published in German, Russian, Italian, with French-language version planned.

1907: **Vitagraph** begins building Paris printing laboratory.

1908: *c.* Apr. – **Vitagraph** opens Paris lab.

1909: Mar. – **Lubin** has agent in Berlin; supplies Europe, including Britain.
    Apr. – **Lubin** has London office.
    May – **AM & B** first listed in *Bioscope*'s release schedule, Britain. **Vitagraph** ad lists agents in Barcelona, Budapest, Turin, Buenos Aires, Berlin, Hamburg and Copenhagen.
    By July – **AB**, **Lubin** and **Selig** handled by Markt & Co. (for Britain and Continent).
    Sept. – **Essanay**'s London office opens; first release 9 Oct.
    Dec. – Markt & Co. (British agent for **AB, Selig, Lubin**) opens Berlin office.

1910: Jan. – **Bison** agent is the London Cinematograph Co.
    Apr. – Markt & Co. now **AB**'s sole representative for Europe, Asia, Africa and Australasia.
    Imp's British agent to be J. Frank Brockliss (with rights for France, Belgium, and the French colonies).
    May – **Bison**'s French agent is Aubert.
    Imp opens main foreign office in Berlin.
    Vitagraph is reported to be printing films in eight languages at Paris lab; also going to two reels a week in London.
    June – **Kalem**'s British agent is Kineto Ltd.
    Imp begins European releases.
    July – **Selig** lists agents in London, Moscow, Berlin, and Vienna.
    Aug. – **Essanay** has Berlin agent.
    Sept. – Brockliss adds a second **Imp** release per week.
    Thanhouser to release through Gaumont (London).
    Markt & Co. (agent for **AB, Selig, Lubin**) opens Milan office.
    Centaur and **Nestor** represented in Britain by Walturdaw.

Champion's agent abroad is R. Prieur (an agent based in London and Paris).

Powers is represented in Britain by J. Frank Brockliss.

Nov. – **Kalem** releasing through Markt & Co. in Britain.

Announcement of opening of the **American Film Trading Co.** of London (Roy Aitken, manager). Soon changes name to the **Western Import & Film Co.**

1911: Jan. – First release of **Flying 'A',** through the **Western Import & Film Co.,** set for Feb.

Mar. – First release of **Reliance** films in Britain, through the Tyler Film Co.

Bison also now releasing through Tyler.

Apr. – **Solax**'s first release in Britain, through Gaumont (London).

Bison films going on European market through Lux (Paris).

R. Prieur has just signed **Nestor**'s European agency for Lux.

Markt & Co. (**AB, Lubin, Kalem**) opens Paris branch; now has Berlin, Barcelona, Vienna, Moscow, Paris, Alexandria, Brussels and Rome.

16 Apr. – **Selig** leaves Markt & Co. for direct selling in Britain.

Apr. – **Champion**'s British agent now the Universal Film Co. (unconnected with later American firm of that name).

May – **Selig** increases British releases to three reels a week.

June – **Kalem** lists branches at New York, London, Berlin.

July – **Moose Head** films first released in Britain, through Cosmopolitan.

10 Aug. – **Rex** opens London branch office, plans openings in Copenhagen and Vienna in next month.

Aug. – **Crystal** releasing in Britain through the E. S. Williams Bioscope Co.

Sept. – **Rex**'s first British release.

Majestic to begin British releasing through the **Western Import & Film Co.**

Carson releasing in Britain through Walturdaw.

Atlas releasing through R. S. Edmondson (London).

Oct. – **Essanay** opens Berlin branch.

Lubin claims agents in Chicago, London, Berlin, Vienna, Manila, Moscow, Barcelona, Rio de Janeiro, Milan, Sydney.

Thanhouser now sold in Britain through Pathé.

Nov. – **Comet** releasing through American Film Releases (London).

Gaston Méliès' **American Wild West** to be sold through J. Frank Brockliss (London).

16 Nov. – **American Company (London) Ltd** opens to sell all **Flying 'A'** films directly in Britain.

c. mid 1911 – MP Sales Agency, a London sales firm, opens a Paris office.

1912: Jan. – **Selig** lists branches in London, Berlin, St Petersburg.

Kalem lists branches in London, Berlin, Paris.

Essanay lists branches in London, Berlin, Barcelona.

Lubin lists branches in London and Berlin.

Feb. – **Champion** now selling through J. Frank Brockliss (London).

Selig adds an agent in Budapest.

Mar. – **Brooklyn** releasing through the **Western Import & Film Co.** (London).

Apr. – **AB, Lubin, Kalem** now releasing in Britain through the MP Sales Agency.

Bison releasing through Cosmopolitan (London).

Reliance releasing through the **Western Import & Film Co.** (London).

Republic releasing through American Film Releases (London).

Bison 101's French releasing through Paul Hodel (Paris).

Vitagraph gets Romanian agent.

May – **Solax** now releasing through the American and Continental Film Co. (London).

June – **Broncho** releasing through the **Western Import & Film Co.** (London).

American Standard's first British release, through Tyler.

Aug. – Announcement that Itala will continue as **Bison 101**'s European agent.

Sept. – Compagnie Cinématographique Brésilienne to represent **Vitagraph, Edison, Lubin, Essanay** in Brazil.

Oct. – **Thanhouser** switches over to the **Western Import & Film Co.** (London).

Invicta Film Co. (London) to release **Victor, Gem, Bison 101**.

Nov. – **Thanhouser** and **Brooklyn** in Berlin, switch from the Carpatia Co. to the Skandinavisk Film Co. as agent.

Dec. – the J. D. Williams Amusement Co. buys Australian rights for **AB, Essanay, Kalem, Méliès, Selig**.

1913: Feb. – **Warner's Features** releasing through Casanova Ardarius (Barcelona).

Comet now releasing through R. Prieur in Britain.

Mar. – **Selig** lists foreign branches as London, Berlin, St Petersburg, Paris, Budapest, Rio de Janeiro.

Louis Aubert (Paris) releasing **Solax, Rex, Méliès Wild West**.

Apr. – **Keystone**'s first British release, through Tyler.

Western Import & Film Co. picks up **Keystone, Kaybee, Broncho**.

Ruffell's Imperial (Britain) releasing **Ramo** and **Ryno**.

Warner Feature Film Co. opens branch in London.

May – **Michigan Pictures** releasing through Pathé abroad.

June – **Lubin** has recently opened a main European office in London (for publicity and business purposes only; it still releases through the MP Sales Agency).

Frontier's first British release, through R. Prieur.

July – **Selig** building own quarters in London.

Warner's first release in Britain.

Lubin begins direct selling through its London office.

Aug. – **Vitagraph** begins building a Paris production studio.

Ramo signs with the General Film Agency (London).

Sept. – **Lubin** gets a Paris agent, the Mondial Film Co.

Famous Players Film Co. Ltd opens in London.

Oct. – **Domino** and **Apollo** sign with the **Western Import & Film Co.** (London).

Current American offices and agencies in Paris: **Selig**, agent Charles Helfer; **Kaybee, Keystone, Bison 101, Reliance**, agent Paul Hodel;

Lubin, agent Mondial; **Thanhouser, Biograph, Kalem, Lubin,** agent, the MP Sales Agency; **Vitagraph, Edison,** and **Essanay,** own offices; **Rex** and **Solax,** agent Louis Aubert.

22 Oct. – **Universal**'s British branch, the **Trans-Atlantic Film Co.,** opens; to release **Imp, Powers, Rex, Bison 101, Nestor, Gem, Victor, Frontier, Crystal.**

Nov. – **Western Import & Film Co.** (London) releasing **Keystone, Broncho, Punch, Thanhouser, Kaybee, Majestic, Reliance** and others.

Universal opens branches in Berlin and Copenhagen.

Ammex Motion Picture Co. (California) and the **Blaché Co.** sign with R. Prieur (London and Paris).

Thanhouser Films Ltd opens in London.

Dec. – **Trans-Atlantic**'s first British releases.

Universal organising Paris branch.

Majestic and **Reliance** have split off from the **Western Import & Film Co.** to form **New Majestic** (London).

1914: Jan. – **Thanhouser** signs Eclipse as agent for France, Belgium and Holland.

Nevada brand signs with Cosmopolitan (London) as agent; first release, 1 March.

9 Jan. – **Trans-Atlantic Film Co. Ltd**'s first French releases (**Bison 101, Gem, Victor, Powers**).

Feb. – **Western Import & Film Co.,** London, opens a Paris branch.

Buffalo Bill's Wild West Pictures to release through the Motograph Co. (London).

6 Feb. – **Thanhouser** gets own Paris exchange.

Mar. – **Western Import & Film Co.** begins releasing in France (**Broncho, Kaybee, Majestic, Thanhouser, Keystone**).

Nestor, Luna, American films released in France for first time, through the UNMC.

May – American firms' offices or agents in France: **Selig,** through the Agence Générale Cinématographe; **Biograph, Kalem,** through the MP Sales Agency; **Edison, Vitagraph, Thanhouser,** own offices; **Selig, Standart,** through Charles Helfer; **American Blaché, Gloria Blaché,** through R. Prieur; **Imp, Nestor, Crystal, Gold Seal, Rex, Bison 101,** through **Trans-Atlantic; Kaybee, Keystone, Thanhouser, Broncho,** through the **Western Import & Film Co.**

June – **Balboa** gets agent in London, for all Europe.

Sam Goldfish sets up central distribution offices in London for all Europe, for **Lasky, Famous Players** and **Bosworth.**

July – Goldfish has signed agents for various countries for **Lasky, Famous Players, Bosworth:** Walker for Britain; Dusseldorfer Film-Manufactur for Germany, other for France, Russia.

Life Photo Film Corp. signs with the American and Continental Film Co. (London).

Aug. – After war begins, Paris studio of **Vitagraph** closed, printing being done in Britain.

Balboa agent in Britain is Bishop, Pesser, & Co.

MP Sales Agency's Paris branch closes.

Sept. – **Selig** transferring its stock from Paris to Eclipse's London plant (Eclipse is responsible for Selig's printing in Europe).

Vitagraph, Selig, Lubin lay in supplies of negatives in London.

Oct. – **Universal** representative goes to South America to see about shifting business there from Europe.

1915: Jan. – **Trans-Atlantic** currently has branches in Denmark, Norway, Sweden, Russia, France, Spain, Italy and the Balkans.

Feb. – **Kinetophote Corp.** gets British agent.

Famous Players Film Co. British branch releasing **Famous Players** and **Lasky.**

Mar. – Bishop, Pesser, & Co. signs as British agent for **Balboa, Nemo, White Star, Life Photo Film, Sawyer's Films, Picture Playhouse, Flamingo** and **Sterling Camera.**

Apr. – **American**'s Croydon printing plant nearing completion.

May – Anglo-American Film Co., London, becomes agent for **Alliance.**

Winick and Brock become agents for **World,** for world rights outside Canada and the USA; headquarters in London.

Selig has moved to new London offices. Branches in Paris, Copenhagen, Moscow, Barcelona and Buenos Aires.

July – **AB** and **Kalem** get German agent, Nordische.

Aug. – Ruffell's Exclusives trade-show first **Metro** films in London.

Oct. – **Essanay** to rent directly to theatres in Britain, forms **Essanay Film Service Ltd.**

David Horsley's representative opens office in London, to handle **Horsley, Mina,** and **Cub.**

Fox opens first foreign branch, in Montreal.

Nov. – **Raver-Thomas** feature company signs the International Cinematograph Corp., as British representative.

Dec. – **Trans-Atlantic** announces that since January it has opened an office in Amsterdam, closed one in the Balkans.

Fox opens branches in Argentina and Brazil.

1916: **Universal** opens branches in Japan and India.

Jan. – Australasian buys Australian rights for **Triangle** films. Canadian rights also sold.

Feb. – Australasian buys exclusive rights for **Equitable Films.**

c. Mar. – **Fox** opens chain of offices in England and Scotland.

Mar. – **Trans-Atlantic** sell **Universal Bluebirds** for Britain to Gaumont.

Apr. – Australasian opens a theatre in Sydney for **Triangle** films.

Metro signs Co-operative Film Exchange as British agent.

Fox Film Co. Ltd opens in London.

William Fox Photoplays (Australasia) Ltd formed. (**Fox** now has offices in Australia, England, Scotland, Canada, Brazil, Argentina.)

Famous Players and **Lasky** sign rights for South Africa; now report to have representation everywhere except Asia and belligerent countries.

May – **Western Import & Film Co.** releases first **Ince-Triangles** in Britain. Monatfilm signs as **Famous Players** and **Lasky** agent for France.

1 May – **Vitagraph** begins renting features (not shorts) directly in Britain.

June – Prieur signs as agent for **Ray Comedies** for Europe and Australia.

July – Monatfilm signs to release **Keystone-Triangles** in France.

   Famous Players-Lasky forms – plans to push into Asia and South America. Still handled by World's Films for Britain.

   Vitagraph gets German representative.

Aug. – **Fox** setting up Paris office.

   American begins renting directly in Britain, opening the **Flying 'A' Film Service** (dealing in **Flying 'A', Vogue, Signal, Mustang, Beauty**).

   Mutual Chaplins sold to J. D. Walker, Britain.

c. Sept. – **Universal** opens Singapore office.

Nov. – **Famous Players-Lasky** representative goes to Australia.

   Trans-Atlantic sells exclusive rights for **L-KO, Nestor, Victor** and **Imp** comedies, to Gaumont in Britain.

Dec. – **Mutual** sells rights for Denmark, Norway, Sweden and Russia.

   In past year, **Fox** has opened offices in London and seven branches in Britain, Buenos Aires, Sao Paulo and Rio de Janeiro.

1917: Jan. – **World Film Corp.** signs Gaumont British for Britain, for **Brady-Made** features.

   Western Import & Film Co. signs for **Selznick Pictures** (independent features).

Feb. – **Universal** has new branch in Java.

   Famous Players-Lasky signs exclusive agent for Argentina, Paraguay and Uruguay (Sociedad General Cinematografica of Buenos Aires).

Mar. – **Triangle** appoints Spanish agent.

   Famous Players-Lasky acquires controlling interest in Australia Feature Films Ltd (a distribution company).

   Goldwyn launches worldwide publicity campaign preparatory to setting up an export network.

   South American Film Service Corp. (New York) opens a branch in Buenos Aires, representing **Metro, World, Universal, Bluebird, Mutt & Jeff** and others.

Apr. – **Fox** has recently set up offices in Norway, Sweden, Spain and Portugal, Uruguay and Paraguay.

   Mutual gets agent in Australia.

May – Sociedad General Cinematografica (Buenos Aires) handling **Triangle** and **Vitagraph,** has been handling **Famous Players-Lasky** for two months.

June – **Famous Players-Lasky** films (including **Artcraft** and various independents) are sold to John Olsen and Co. (New York) for Scandinavia.

   Mutual has recently signed with export firm, the Oceanic Film Corp.

Aug. – **American** signs with a foreign distribution syndicate, for Russia, Norway, Sweden and Denmark; has recently signed for Spain and Portugal, China and Japan.

Sept. – **Triangle** has recently opened an office in Italy; it has signed rights for Uruguay, Chile, Paraguay and Argentina to Sociedad General Cinematografica.

Oct. – **Fox** expands foreign-department facilities. Has recently sold for: British possessions, Spain and Portugal, Peru, Bolivia, Chile, Central America.

Goldwyn's foreign-export department organized.

Nov. – **Paramount** distributing in France through Gaumont.

Triangle distributing in France through Eclipse.

15 Nov. – **Paramount House** opens distribution headquarters in Australia.

Dec. – Export & Import Film Corp. buys **Metro**'s entire foreign rights. Sells rights for Spain, France, Italy, Switzerland, Holland, the Balkans to the Mundesfilm Corp. of Paris.

1918: Jan. – Inter-Ocean Film Co. gets British rights to **Paralta.**

Paramount-Artcraft has sold agencies for West Indies and Central America to a Havana company.

Feb. – **Famous Players-Lasky** has recently signed with Gaumont for distribution in France, Switzerland, Belgium and Egypt, for **Paramount** films (had done only **Pallas** and **Morosco**).

Mar. – **Goldwyn** has just signed rights: for Australia and Tasmania to J. C. Williamson; for New Zealand to New Zealand Picture Supplies; for Sweden, Norway, and Denmark, to John Olsen and Co.; for Chile, Bolivia, Peru and Ecuador, to the Co-operative Film Corp.; for South Africa, to the South African Film Trust; for India and Burma, to K D & Brothers; for Argentina and Uruguay, to Saenz & Gonzalez; for Puerto Rico and San Domingo, to the Agencia General Cinematografica; currently negotiating Spain, Italy and France.

Triangle releasing in France through Eclipse; signs with Max Glucksmann, for South America.

Apr. – **Goldwyn** signs British rights to the newly formed Stoll Film Co.

June – **Universal** now has twenty foreign exchanges, including Manila, Japan, Java and India.

Oct. – **Paramount**'s representative returns from establishing the **South Pacific Paramount Co.** in Santiago, Chile – for Chile, Peru and Bolivian distribution.

Late 1918 – **Fox Film Société Anonyme** opens in Paris and Brussels.

1919: Feb. – **Fox** signs with Granados Diaz for distribution in Venezuela. (Now circulates in all South American countries except Colombia.)

Mar. – **Fox** representatives go to Mexico to set up office.

Apr. – **American**'s representative back from Europe – has agent in Britain, has sold Scandinavian rights to John Olsen and Co. and rights for most of Europe to Cinématograph Harry (Paris).

Aubert releasing some **Fox** films in France.

May – **Universal** opens Mexico City branch.

Fox representative returns after establishing twelve exchanges in France and Italy. (Now lacks only Germany and Austria to cover world.)

Vitagraph gets agent for Mexico, Guatemala and San Salvador.

June – Walturdaw to distribute **First National** features in Britain for 1920.

July – **Fox** now has twenty-three American branches, six Canadian, twenty-three European, also branches in Argentina/Uruguay, Brazil, Australia, New Zealand.

Aug. – **Selig Polyscope** closes London office.

Vitagraph buys Ruffell's exchanges in Britain.

c. July to Sept. – **Metro** signs with Jury's Imperial Pictures, Ltd (London).

Sept. – after two and a half years, **Paramount** reported one of largest exchange systems in Australia.

Vitagraph has recently re-opened Paris office and lab.

Oct. – **Selznick Pictures Ltd** about to register in Britain, to buy and sell independent features.

Nov. – **Goldwyn** backs out of distribution contract with the Stoll Film Co. in Britain.

1920: Jan. – **Paramount-Artcraft** have been distributing in France, Belgium, Switzerland and Egypt through Gaumont; now adds Holland, Turkey and Greece.

Selznick signs one-year contract with South African Film Trust.

Paramount-Artcraft signs Danish-American Film as agent for Germany, Austria, Hungary, Poland, Ukraine, Czechoslovakia, Yugoslavia, Romania and Bulgaria (takes effect in March).

Feb. – **Vitagraph** selling direct only in Britain. Has agents for France and Belgium, Scandinavia, Australia, South Africa, Argentina, Chile and Peru, Spain, Cuba, Brazil, Puerto Rico, Mexico and the Philippines.

Fox declares it has direct dealing with every major city in Europe, the Orient, Australia and South America (with a total of 26 foreign offices).

Apr. – **Goldwyn Ltd** opens in Britain.

Universal opens an office in Sydney.

May – **Fox** opens a branch office in Algiers.

Walturdaw signs to distribute **Selznick** films.

July – **Metro** is being distributed in Britain by Jury's Imperial, in France by Mundus Film.

Famous Players-Lasky signs exclusive contract with UFA for Germany, Austria, Poland, Turkey, Bulgaria, Holland and Switzerland.

Aug. – **UA Corp. Ltd** opens in London as head branch of world distribution.

Oct. – **First National** contract sold by Walturdaw to the International Film Distributing Co., London.

Goldwyn Far Eastern representative back from forming Japanese branch, also signed agents for China, Manila, Singapore and Java, Australia and New Zealand, and India.

Construction of **Famous Players-Lasky British Producers Ltd** studio completed.

Nov. – **Famous Players-Lasky**'s Indian exchange ready to open; centre of network for India, Burma, Mesopotamia, Ceylon, Straits Settlements, Java and others.

Selznick's representative back from setting up European exchanges: head office in Paris, nine branches in Britain, France, Belgium.

Trade shows of first two features made in **Famous Players-Lasky**'s British studio.

1921: Jan. – **Goldwyn** representative returns from setting up exchanges in Holland, Stockholm (Scandinavia and Finland), Milan and Barcelona.

Mar. – **UA** will distribute directly: exchanges now in London, with four British branches, and in Paris.

UA representative to Berlin to set up head office for Continent.

UA representative to Havana to set up office.

Apr. – **Fox** representative organising office in Copenhagen, to open 1 May.

Universal now has four branches in Australia, three in New Zealand.

UA representative goes to France to set up Paris branch.

June – **UA** gets Australian agent.

Aug. – **Selznick** representative departs for Scandinavia to sell rights. Now distributing through agents in Britain, France, Switzerland, Belgium, Australia, Eastern Europe, Argentina, Germany, Cuba, Puerto Rico and the Far East.

Sept. to Oct. – **Société Anonyme Française des Films Paramount** to begin releasing in France.

Dec. – **UA** opens **United Artists (Australasia) Ltd,** a series of exchanges.

1922: **Universal** opens a direct-sales office in Italy (claimed to be first such American office there).

Jan. – **Fox** signs Middle East Films Ltd as agent in Orient, except Japan.

Paramount signs for distribution of films in six South American countries with Max Glucksmann. Already has other South American countries, as well as Central America and the Caribbean.

Paramount signs group of films to Mexican agent; already has branch office there as well.

Goldwyn signs for distribution in parts of Central and South America.

17 Mar. – **First National Pictures Ltd** begins trade shows in Britain.

Apr. – **UA** sends representatives to set up Japanese office. Now has offices in Rome and Stockholm as well. Negotiating South American rights.

May – **Universal** opens the **European Motion Picture Co. Ltd** in Britain (had distributed through **Trans-Atlantic,** then FBO Ltd).

June – **First National** has signed for Belgium, Holland and Switzerland; also through Luporini Brothers for Italy. Portions of production sold for South America, South Africa, Japan, Australia, China, India, Straits Settlements, etc.

Famous Players-Lasky signs Scandinavian agent (Carl York and W. W. LeMat).

Aug. – **Famous Players-Lasky**'s Tokyo branch opens.

Sept. – **Goldwyn** signs agents for Japan (Yanuma), Cuba (Liberty), Puerto Rico (Selection) and Australasia (Australasian).

Goldwyn and **Vitagraph** bought for Brazilian exchange by the New York Film Exchanges.

Oct. – **First National** has own exchanges in Britain, France, Sweden and Germany. Chipman Ltd gets **Metro** films for Caribbean.

Nov. – Film Booking Office Ltd gets **Warner**'s features for Britain, 1922–3.

Dec. – During 1922, **Paramount** opened exchanges in French provinces; new branches in Brussels, Switzerland, Algiers, Cairo and Constantinople. Agents signed for Scandinavia.

Branches for Famous-Lasky Film Service Ltd opened in Singapore and Java.

1923: Mar. – **Fox**'s recent branch-office openings: Cuba, Mexico, Holland, Czechoslovakia and Japan.

May – Pathé Exchange signs Robert Wilcox & Co., as Central America and Caribbean agent.

July – J. Frank Brockliss, as **Metro**'s representative, signs its output to the Foreign Film Co., Berlin.

First National goes to a policy of direct distribution abroad as of 1 July. Opening exchange in Switzerland; has them in Stockholm, Christiania and Denmark.

Universal opens office in Christiania, plans one in Stockholm.

Fox branches opening in Bombay, Amsterdam and Rome.

Aug. – **Fox** representative goes to Tokyo to open a branch office and system of exchanges.

Sept. – Great Japanese earthquake damages or demolishes offices of companies in Japan: **Fox, Famous Players-Lasky, Universal** and a branch of the Export and Import Film Co.

Nov. – **Fox** has opened a branch in Vienna.

Dec. – **Fox** has opened a branch in Stockholm.

1924: Jan. – **First National** sends representative to open head office for Japan at Kobe, with a series of exchanges.

June – Gaumont signs several-year contract for **Warner Bros.** films.

Pickford films sold to Terra for Germany, Eastern Europe, Russia, Egypt, etc.

July – **MGM** recently merged: branches in London, Paris, Berlin, Stockholm, Copenhagen and Barcelona.

Aug. – **Warner Bros.** claims to have 100% representation throughout the world.

Oct. – **Famous Players-Lasky** representative returns; **Famous Players-Lasky** now owns a first-run theatre in London; opens branches in Holland and Rome.

Dec. – **Famous Players-Lasky** distributing in Germany through National Films.

Warner Bros. signs Jacques Haik as agent for France, Belgium, Holland, Switzerland, Italy, Spain, Portugal and Near East, for 1924 films.

1925: Jan. – **Paramount** announces three new exchanges opening within sixty days: Athens, Sofia (Bulgaria) and Constantinople. (Now up to forty-five international exchanges and agents.)

Feb. – **MGM** rights for Germany sold to Phoebus.

As of this month, only **Universal, UA** and **Fox** dealing directly in Italy.

May – **Warner Bros.** buys Vitagraph, gets fifty exchanges: twenty-six American, four Canadian, ten British, ten on Continent.

Société Anonyme Gaumont-Metro-Goldwyn recently formed. **MGM** to distribute, controls all Gaumont theatres.

First National opens own distribution network in France.

June – **Paramount Films SA** formed, opens offices in Buenos Aires and Santiago, Chile. Serves most of South America except Brazil.

July – **First National** opens German branch, Transocean Films.

UFA buys rights to forty **MGM** films to 1925–6 season.

209

Aug. – **Paramount** does not renew contract with National Film for Germany.

UA buys substantial interest in International Film A-G, Berlin (Ifa Film Verleih).

Summer – **Universal** opens an exchange in Poland.

Sept. – **First National** continues direct rental push: Paris and seven branches in Europe; ten in Britain; agents in Switzerland, Germany, Italy, Spain and Austria.

Producers Distributing Corp. has opened British branch in London, with eight exchanges. Signed with National Film A-G, for Germany; F. de Sacadura, Paris, for France, Belgium, Switzerland, Spain, Portugal and Italy.

Oct. – **Universal** signs exclusive agency for Germany with Filmhaus Bruckmann.

Late Nov. – **Universal** agrees to loan UFA 15 million marks, with a mutual distribution agreement.

Dec. – **Producers Distributing Corp.** signs Far Eastern rights: China (China Theatres), Japan (U. Ono), Philippines (Lyric Film Exchange), India (Madan Theatres).

30 Dec. – **Parufamet** contract signed. **Universal** gets ten films per year distributed.

1926: Jan. – **Producers Distributing Corp.** opens branch in Prague, soon to open in Geneva, Brussels, Stockholm. Contract sold for Holland.

Feb. – **Famous Players-Lasky, First National** and **MGM** amalgamate their Central and Eastern European offices into a single distribution company: Fanamet. To begin operation in the fall.

Apr. – **Warner Bros.** signs contract with Bruckmann for Germany.

May – Ifa Film Verleih (**UA**) signs deal with Phoebus for access to its theatre chain (Germany).

First National plans opening own renting office in Germany.

June – **UA** has just opened office in Rio de Janeiro, one soon to open in Cristobal (Panama) for Central America and Caribbean. Also has new branch at Capetown, South Africa.

July – **First National** delays by one year the opening of its direct-distribution office in Berlin.

Sept. – **FBO** signs agency for Britain: Ideal Films Ltd.

Warner Bros. contract with Gaumont expires; it begins direct distribution through its recently acquired Vitagraph exchanges.

Oct. – **Tiffany** planning own exchange in Havana.

Dec. – **Universal** opens own distribution offices in Vienna and Berlin (the latter is Universal-Matador, with its name changed to Universal-Film-Verleih in May 1928).

1927: Apr. – **Columbia** signs entire output to Film Booking Offices Ltd for Britain.

First National again announces office opening in Germany.

May – **FBO**'s output sold to Tozai-Eiga in Japan.

Aug. – **First National**'s German branch, Defina (Deutsche First National) opens – also to distribute Deutsche Film Union (Defu) films, due to 1 : 1

quota. Second **Parufamet** contract reduces **MGM** and **Paramount**'s share of UFA theatres' screen time from 75% to 33.3%.

Sept. – **Loew's** buys controlling interest in Jury-Metro-Goldwyn.

Nov. – **Universal** drops ten-films-per-year contract with UFA.

1928: 1 Jan. – Fanamet dissolved (due to **First National**'s link-up with Defu).

CHRONOLOGY 3:   EUROPEAN QUOTAS, 1921–34

Sources: TIB series, FDYB, CR, JdF, MPW

1921: 1 Jan. – **Germany** institutes quota: 15% of negative footage produced in Germany in 1919 allowed in, 1921–4. (1,200 kg, estimated 180,000 metres).

1925: 1 Jan. – **Germany** switches to 1 : 1 quota for features imported.
  Italy – exhibition quota: one week in every two months, theatres must show an all-Italian programme.
  Hungary – every film exchange handling twenty or more films per year must produce one Hungarian film.

1926: **Hungary** – importers must sponsor one Hungarian film for every thirty imported.
  3 Sept. – **Austria** institutes a two-year quota of 20 : 1. Twenty import licences granted a producer for every domestic film made (licences can be sold).

1927: 1 Jan. – **Austria** lowers 20 : 1 quota to 10 : 1.
  1 Apr. – **Britain**'s Quota Act: renters must handle 7.5% British films, graduating to 20% by 1935–6 season. (Begins at 5% for exhibitors.)
  6 May – **Portugal**: Each programme must include at least one 300-metre (one reel) film made domestically.
  1 Oct. – **Italy**: Exhibition quota decrees 10% of screen time must be Italian films. (Not enforced due to lack of domestic films.)
  Oct. – **Austrian** quota adjusted to 18 : 1, retroactive to 1 Jan.
  Nov. – New **German** Kontingent system for 1 Apr. 1928 to 30 June 1929 specifies number of imports based on estimated needs of market; of 260 features, ninety held in reserve and 170 given to German companies on basis of 1926 and 1927 distribution. (Approximately a 1 : 2 system.)

1928: 1 Jan. – **Austrian** quota put back to 20 : 1.
  1 Jan. – **Hungary** gives option: either one Hungarian film must be produced for every twenty imported or a heavy surcharge must be paid on imports.
  12 Mar. – **France** institutes 7 : 1 quota with licences granted only on basis of French film exports. (Negotiations with American industry result.)
  1 May – **French** export rule abolished, replaced with straight 7 : 1 quota.
  24 Aug. – **Italy** agrees to class as Italian films those of foreign countries which import Italian films.

5 Dec. – **Austrian** quota becomes 23 : 1, retroactive to 1 Jan.

13 Dec. – **German** quota allotment for 1 July 1929 to 30 June 1930 set up: 210 import licences to be issued.

1929: 1 Jan. – **Austrian** quota returns to 20 : 1.

1 Feb. – **German** Kontingent system extended till June 1931. Of 210 import licences, 160 to German distributors in proportion to the number of German films they handled in 1928–9; other 50 to companies exporting German films. (Works out to a 1 : 2.5 quota.)

1 Apr. to 24 Sept. – American offices in **France** close in response to proposed 3 : 1 quota.

27 May – **French** adopt 4 : 1 quota, but boycott continues.

19 Sept. – **France**'s new quota renews old 7 : 1 basis for licensing imports. Extended to 30 Sept. 1930 or one more year if no agreement is reached by 1 May 1930.

1930: 1 May – no agreement is reached; the **French** quota of 7 : 1 extended to 30 Sept. 1931.

July – **German** quota reserves two-thirds of permits for silent films (90 sound permits, 129 silent actually issued).

1 Oct. – **Hungarian** 20 : 1 quota dropped, substitutes unlimited import licences at fixed fees.

1931: 1 July – **France** abolishes quota for countries with no restrictions on French imports for one-year period. Negotiations begin with Germany, only country with a quota affecting France.

July – **Austria** lowers number of import certificates needed per film from three to one and a half, fixes price of certificates.

1 July – **German** quota renewed on same basis for a year. For 1931–2 season, 105 sound, 70 silent licences. (Based on number of German films distributed in previous eighteen months.)

1932: 23 Apr. – **Czechoslovakia** institutes quota of 240 features per year (later reduced repeatedly, finally to 120). Certificates are required, which rise steadily in price. American firms respond with boycott.

1 July – **Germany** restricts dubbed imports to 50% and dubbing must be done in Germany.

29 July – **France** bans dubbed versions not dubbed in France. Restrictions declared on the number of theatres in which original-language versions can be shown.

1933: 24 July – Only 140 dubbed films can be released in **France** in the year ending 30 June 1934; dubbing must still be done in France. Theatre restrictions continue.

1934: 26 June – 94 dubbed films allowed into **France** for upcoming six months. Theatre restrictions continue.

Appendix II
Tables

Number of foreign vs. American short films in the American market, 1907–14

Source: Periodic samplings of *MPW*'s schedule of releases. Figures indicate the number of titles in release within a given week, with some titles repeating from one period to the next. The table does not include states rights releases.

MPW issue	Total	Domestic No.	%	Total foreign No.	%	Licensed foreign No.	%
27 Apr. 1907	150	61	40.7	89	59.3		
15 June	106	44	41.5	62	58.5		
10 Aug.	197	83	42.1	114	57.9		
23 Nov.	311	126	40.5	185	59.5		
28 Mar. 1908	126	70	55.6	56	44.4		
2 May	274	96	35.0	178	65.0		
11 July	239	84	35.1	155	64.9		
26 Sept.	176	86	48.9	90	51.1		
14 Nov.	146	43	29.5	103	70.5		
16 Jan. 1909	188	102	54.3	86	45.7	60	31.9
6 Mar.	192	107	55.7	85	44.3	66	34.4
10 Apr.	191	107	56.0	84	44.0	65	34.0
12 June	239	112	46.9	127	53.1	94	39.3
7 Aug.	242	143	59.1	99	40.9	84	34.7
16 Oct.	273	175	64.1	98	35.9	82	30.0
18 Dec.	326	180	55.2	146	44.8	107	32.8
19 Feb. 1910	226	144	63.7	82	36.3	45	19.9
16 Apr.	284	176	62.0	108	38.0	53	18.7
18 June	383	211	55.1	172	44.9	55	14.4
20 Aug.	391	239	61.1	152	38.9	67	17.1
15 Oct.	321	214	66.7	107	33.3	45	14.0
17 Dec.	353	231	65.4	122	34.6	71	20.1
18 Feb.1911	210	149	71.0	61	29.0	31	14.8
15 Apr.	302	208	68.9	94	31.1	46	15.2

MPW issue	Total	Domestic		Total foreign		Licensed foreign	
		No.	%	No.	%	No.	%
17 June	293	204	69.6	89	30.4	43	14.7
19 Aug.	393	257	65.4	136	34.6	85	21.7
14 Oct.	343	240	70.0	103	30.0	57	16.6
16 Dec.	384	279	72.7	105	27.3	63	16.4
12 Feb. 1912	81	56	69.1	25	30.9	13	16.0
(one week only)							
13 Apr. 1912	527	364	69.1	163	30.9	92	17.5
13 July	348	216	62.1	132	37.9	73	21.0
(From this point, figures include only films released within a single week.)							
18 Aug.	94	73	77.7	21	22.3	15	20.2
9 Sept.	93	67	72.0	26	28.0	16	17.2
14 Oct.	100	73	73.0	27	27.0	14	14.0
10 Nov.	99	60	70.7	29	29.3	15	15.2
16 Dec.	103	71	68.9	32	31.1	16	15.5
20 Jan. 1913	106	77	72.6	29	27.4	14	13.2
16 Feb.	112	83	74.1	29	25.9	14	12.5
9 Mar.	119	94	79.0	25	21.0	14	11.8
7 Apr.	116	88	75.9	28	24.1	18	15.5
12 May	108	82	75.9	26	24.1	16	14.8
9 June	106	85	80.2	21	19.8	12	11.1
14 July	108	88	81.5	20	18.5	12	11.1
11 Aug.	109	87	79.8	22	20.2	10	9.2
15 Sept.	106	83	78.3	23	21.7	12	11.3
13 Oct.	107	84	78.5	23	21.5	10	9.3
10 Nov.	102	82	80.4	20	19.6	12	11.8
8 Dec.	104	86	82.7	18	17.3	11	10.6
12 Jan. 1914	98	81	82.7	17	17.3	9	9.2
9 Feb.	110	84	76.4	26	23.6	11	10.0
9 Mar.	108	89	82.4	19	17.6	12	11.1
13 Apr.	95	81	85.3	14	14.7	12	12.6
11 May	87	77	88.5	10	11.5	8	9.2
8 June	84	70	83.3	14	16.7	12	14.3
13 July	96	81	84.4	15	15.6	12	12.5
17 Aug.	91	77	84.6	14	15.9	12	13.2
14 Sept.	88	81	92.0	7	8.0	5	5.7
5 Oct.	92	87	94.6	5	5.4	3	3.3

Number of American vs. other films – Britain, 1911–19

Source: The *Bioscope*

Period	Total no. of films	No. of American films	% American	No. of British films	% British
9–29 Jan. 1911	262	68	26.0	51	19.5
11 Sept.–1 Oct.	295	109	36.9	48	16.3
25 Dec.–14 Jan. 1912	304	132	43.4	50	16.5
30 June–21 July	377	172	45.6	57	15.1
29 Dec. 1912– 19 Jan. 1913	447	203	45.4	62	13.9
2–23 Mar.	457	226	49.5	55	12.0
28 June–20 July	458	221	48.3	37	8.1
7–27 Dec.	455	260	57.1	61	13.4
4–24 Jan. 1914	300	207	69.0	61	20.3
29 Mar.–18 Apr.	505	284	56.2	63	12.5
28 June–8 July	423	225	53.2	63	15.0
9–29 Aug.	377	195	51.7	68	18.0
30 Aug.–19 Sept.	424	221	52.1	65	15.3
20 Sept.–10 Oct.	349	193	55.3	73	20.9
11–31 Oct.	331	194	58.6	77	23.3
8–28 Nov.	337	198	58.8	77	22.9
3–23 Jan. 1915	369	204	55.3	91	24.7
7–27 Mar.	369	205	55.6	87	23.6
2–22 May	328	181	55.2	86	26.2
5–26 Sept.	289	177	61.3	74	25.6
June 1916	269	168	62.5	46	17.1
Oct.	201	147	73.1	32	15.9
Dec.	165	116	70.3	37	22.4
Feb. 1917	160	117	73.1	32	20.0
Apr.	118	87	73.7	26	22.0
Aug.	144	112	77.8	25	17.4
Sept.	110	87	79.1	17	15.5
Dec.	112	92	82.1	16	14.3
Apr. 1918	109	80	73.4	23	21.1
Oct.	94	52	55.3	36	38.3
Dec.	79	47	59.5	26	32.9
Mar. 1919	100	54	54.0	35	35.0
June	114	82	71.9	28	24.6
Sept.	98	62	63.3	28	28.6
Jan. 1920	128	60	46.9	59	46.1

TABLE A.III

Percentage of American exports to various world areas (footage and value) 1913–34

Source: Computed from: *Foreign Commerce and Navigation of the United States* (Washington: Government Printing Office, 1917–35).

Year	Europe Footage	Europe Value	North America Footage	North America Value	South America Footage	South America Value	Asia Footage	Asia Value	Oceania Footage	Oceania Value	Africa Footage	Africa Value
Fiscal years:												
1913	55.2	57.9	33.7	33.4	2.5	1.7	2.4	1.5	6.2	5.5	0.028	0.03
1914	39.0	41.6	44.6	45.7	1.4	1.2	1.7	1.5	13.0	10.1	0.029	0.03
1915	38.5	38.7	41.4	41.4	2.6	1.9	2.5	1.9	14.9	16.1	0.0027	0
1916	79.8	71.8	11.1	15.8	1.7	1.9	2.1	1.8	5.3	8.6	0.03	0.1
1917	57.6	53.1	19.0	20.7	7.4	7.4	6.2	5.7	9.6	12.6	0.3	0.5
1918	32.6	38.8	29.2	27.9	14.2	11.2	7.6	6.1	14.7	14.7	1.7	1.4
1918 (2nd half)	29.4	45.1	24.8	22.3	17.6	13.1	7.6	5.4	20.4	13.9	0.1	0.1
Calendar years:												
1919	44.6	49.0	20.2	20.9	11.2	9.6	10.7	8.6	12.2	10.8	1.1	1.0
1920	40.3	41.2	20.0	23.6	14.7	13.2	12.2	10.3	11.2	10.6	1.5	1.1
1921	29.8	31.5	22.6	24.4	17.0	16.0	12.0	11.3	17.0	15.6	1.5	1.1
1922												
Neg.	67.4	78.9	13.2	7.5	14.9	8.6	4.1	4.7	0.3	0.2	0.2	0.2
Pos.	20.8	21.9	24.8	24.2	20.9	21.3	13.9	13.7	17.6	16.9	2.1	1.9
1923												
Neg.	65.2	86.6	21.5	7.9	9.0	3.5	3.2	1.6	0.9	0.4	0.3	0.1
Pos.	21.2	22.3	26.4	26.1	20.2	19.9	13.3	12.2	16.2	17.0	2.6	2.5

Year	Europe Footage	Value	North America Footage	Value	South America Footage	Value	Asia Footage	Value	Oceania Footage	Value	Africa Footage	Value
1924												
Neg.	84.9	96.7	4.7	0.9	3.3	0.8	5.4	0.8	1.5	0.6	0.1	0.1
Pos.	31.5	30.7	23.0	23.8	16.5	16.6	13.2	12.9	13.3	13.1	2.5	2.9
1925												
Neg.	90.2	97.3	7.6	1.9	0.5	1.0	0.9	0.4	1.0	0.3	0.02	0.01
Pos.	34.5	32.8	21.5	23.4	18.3	18.9	10.8	9.8	13.1	12.8	1.9	2.3
1926												
Neg.	76.3	92.0	9.2	3.6	5.9	2.8	4.4	0.9	1.7	0.3	2.4	0.4
Pos.	27.1	27.9	22.2	22.2	22.8	23.6	10.7	10.0	15.1	14.1	2.0	2.2
1927												
Neg.	63.2	90.2	7.5	3.5	3.8	0.8	17.0	4.2	3.3	0.8	5.3	0.5
Pos.	28.6	27.8	18.7	19.5	24.9	25.5	10.8	10.4	14.8	14.4	2.1	2.4
1928												
Neg.	75.2	89.4	7.9	6.5	3.5	0.6	5.6	1.6	5.3	1.2	2.5	0.6
Pos.	30.0	30.2	17.1	17.8	25.3	25.8	11.1	10.5	14.3	13.1	2.1	2.6
1929												
Neg.	68.7	88.3	12.8	6.0	1.5	0.6	3.9	1.1	7.8	3.0	5.2	0.9
Pos.	38.1	36.2	16.6	19.6	19.8	20.6	10.6	9.3	12.3	11.7	2.5	2.6
1930												
Neg. sil.	63.9	85.9	12.0	4.1	2.7	1.0	9.5	4.0	10.7	4.6	1.2	0.5
Neg. sd.	85.8	94.4	5.0	2.1	1.3	0.3	0.9	0.2	7.3	3.0	0	0
Pos. sil.	29.6	29.7	20.2	18.7	28.1	31.8	14.5	12.2	4.3	4.3	3.3	3.4
Pos. sd.	49.2	52.8	17.2	18.8	11.9	9.4	7.9	6.2	11.3	10.6	2.1	2.2

Year	Europe Footage	Value	North America Footage	Value	South America Footage	Value	Asia Footage	Value	Oceania Footage	Value	Africa Footage	Value
1931												
Neg. sil.	62.5	86.1	10.8	4.7	11.3	3.8	7.4	3.0	7.4	2.1	0.5	0.2
Neg. sd.	68.9	83.0	13.2	6.8	0.5	0.2	1.8	0.8	15.4	9.1	0.1	0.1
Pos. sil.	19.2	23.8	23.1	20.9	35.0	35.7	12.7	10.6	3.2	2.2	6.8	6.9
Pos. sd.	38.1	39.6	23.2	22.5	18.5	17.4	10.4	9.8	5.3	5.6	4.5	5.2
1932												
Neg. sil.	17.3	32.4	69.6	60.9	1.4	1.3	2.7	2.2	8.6	2.8	0.4	0.4
Neg. sd.	55.8	77.0	30.6	14.8	0.04	0	1.3	0.5	12.3	7.6	0.03	0
Pos. sil.	17.4	28.4	30.8	26.4	21.9	17.8	22.0	20.4	2.0	2.3	5.8	4.8
Pos. sd.	32.7	32.4	27.0	25.8	18.6	18.4	13.5	13.4	5.4	5.9	2.8	4.1
1933												
Neg. sil.	6.2	10.9	75.8	82.2	3.7	1.1	4.2	2.6	9.9	3.1	0.2	0.2
Neg. sd.	43.1	65.8	43.9	27.3	5.8	2.2	0.4	0.2	6.6	4.4	0.01	0
Pos. sil.	10.5	26.5	27.8	32.0	28.6	14.6	29.2	20.6	1.4	2.6	2.4	3.7
Pos. sd.	33.6	34.3	24.1	21.7	20.8	20.7	12.8	11.9	4.8	5.2	3.9	6.2
1934												
Neg. sil.	4.3	5.4	80.9	89.3	3.2	1.1	1.5	1.0	9.7	3.1	0.4	0.2
Neg. sd.	40.3	55.4	46.0	33.5	1.9	1.7	4.2	4.0	7.6	5.5	0.01	0
Pos. sil.	16.4	31.7	47.6	52.0	21.4	5.3	10.6	6.6	2.4	1.9	1.6	2.4
Pos. sd.	35.9	36.0	22.3	20.2	22.6	25.3	11.6	11.1	4.2	4.1	3.4	3.2

TABLE A.IV

Percentage of American shares of foreign markets, 1930–4

Source: 'An International Survey of Motion Picture Markets', FDYB (1931–5). (Where the USA is not in first place, the leading country's share is shown in brackets, if available.)

Country	1930	1931	1932	1933	1934
Argentina	90	90	?	?	88
Australia	(no estimates given)				
Austria	50	40 (50 German)	35 (55 German)	30 (60 German)	30 (60 German)
Bahamas	?	?	?	80	90
Belgium	70 (50 French)	40 (50 French)	15 (50 French)	80 – Flemish / 40 – French	?
Bermudas	90	90	90	90	90+
Bolivia	?	80	90	95	98
Britain	75	(no estimates given thereafter)			
British Malaya	71	74	76 (first six months)	72	63
Bulgaria	15 (55 German)	?	35 (38 German)	36 (45 German)	49
Ceylon	85	85	85	65	60
Chile	90	90+	98	85	97
China	83	83	80	80	75
Colombia	90	90	95	95–98	96
Costa Rica	90	90	?	?	?
Cuba	95	98	98	98	?

Country	1930	1931	1932	1933	1934
Czechoslovakia	43	51	44	22 (41 German)	9 (41 German)
Denmark	58	49 (49 German)	49 (49 German)	57	63
Dominican Republic	90	90	90	90	95 (First nine months)
Ecuador	80	80	80	95	99
Egypt	70	70	70	75	80
Estonia	75	75	58	45	60
Finland	60	68	43	65	60
France	48	49.6	48.6	42	?
Germany	32	34	26	21	31
Greece	50 (47 German)	? (46 German)	? (59 German)	46 (65 German)	57 (53 German)
Guatemala	90	90	95	95	92
Haiti	95	95	20 (rest French and German)	65	90
Hawaii	98	?	?	?	?
Holland	75	41	?	42	44
Honduras	90	90	90	95	95
Hungary	60	51	44 sd / 41 sil	55	61
India	80	80	80	80	65
Italy	65	65	65	65	65
Jamaica	90	90	90	80	65
Japan	22 (75 Japanese)	22 (75 Japanese)	12 (85 Japanese)	13 (84 Japanese)	11 (86 Japanese)

Country	1930	1931	1932	1933	1934
Latvia	40	48	50	65	59
Lithuania	?	?	?	50	40 (50 German and Austrian)
Mexico	98	98	98	95	90
Netherlands East Indies	?	?	?	?	50+
New Zealand	88	89	79	76	70
Nicaragua ('nearly all' reported as American share for each year)					
Norway	?	?	?	?	56
Palestine	?	95	? (the USA reported in first place, 1932–4)		
Panama	100	100	100	100 –	?
Paraguay	95	95	95	95	90
Persia	?	(the USA in fourth place, with France in first, 1931–2)		(the USA third, Germany first)	?
Peru	90	90	90	95	95
Philippines	95	90	80+	80+	?
Poland	75	75	58	87	60
Portugal	80	80	66	62	? (to mid 1935)
Puerto Rico	95	95	96	? (first six months)	98
Romania	50	40 (45 German)	45	50	?
Russia (no estimates given)					
South Africa	80	85	85	80	?
Spain	85	70–80	70–80	70	53

Country	1930	1931	1932	1933	1934
Sweden	75	65	65	50	50
Switzerland	50	?	?	30 – French area (35 French) 35 – German area (60 German)	?
Syria	75	65	?	?	25 (75 French)
Turkey	80	15 (70 French)	40	47	59
Uruguay	95	85	65–75	65–75	90–95
Venezuela	85	90	90	90	90
Yugoslavia/Albania	65	65	65	80 (Albania)	60 (Albania)

Appendix III
Charts

Source: Figures from *Monthly Summary of the Foreign Commerce of the United States* (us Department of Commerce).

CHART 1

Total footage imported into America 1911–34

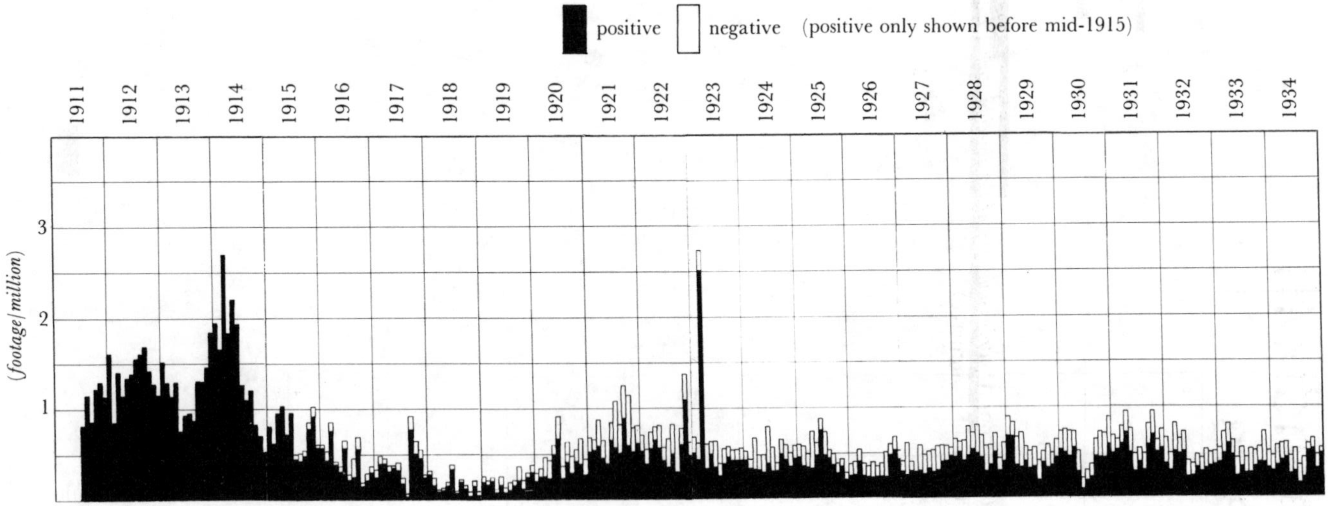

■ positive   □ negative   (positive only shown before mid-1915)

(*footage/million*)

CHART 2

Total footage exported from America 1911–61

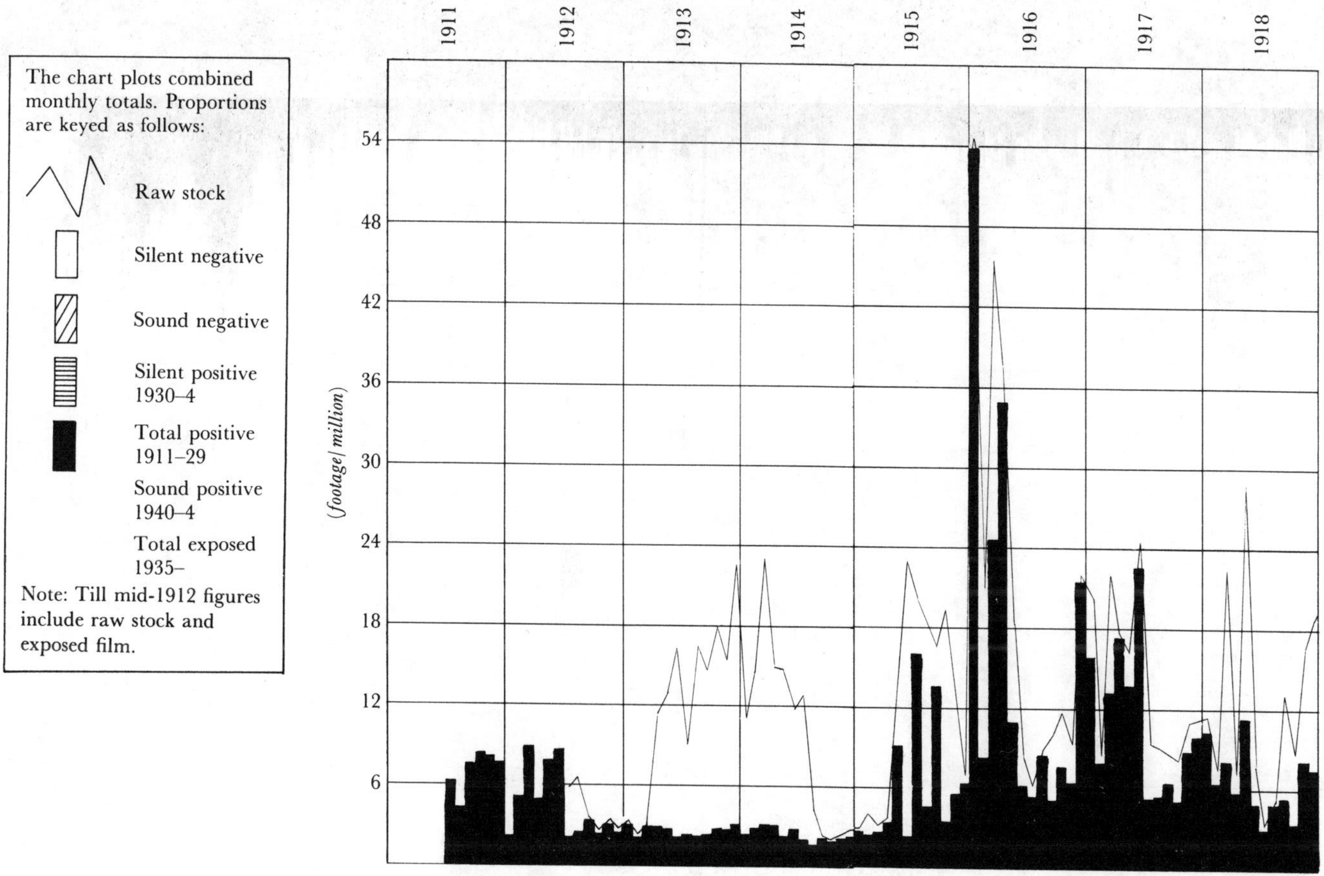

The chart plots combined monthly totals. Proportions are keyed as follows:
Raw stock
Silent negative
Sound negative
Silent positive 1930–4
Total positive 1911–29
Sound positive 1940–4
Total exposed 1935–
Note: Till mid-1912 figures include raw stock and exposed film.
1911
1912
1913
1914
1915
1916
1917
1918
54
48
42
36
30
24
18
12
6
(footage/ million)

Continued

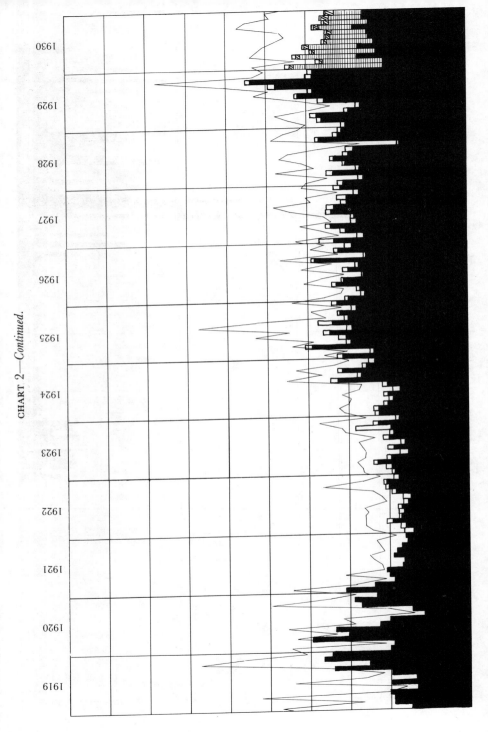

CHART 2—Continued.

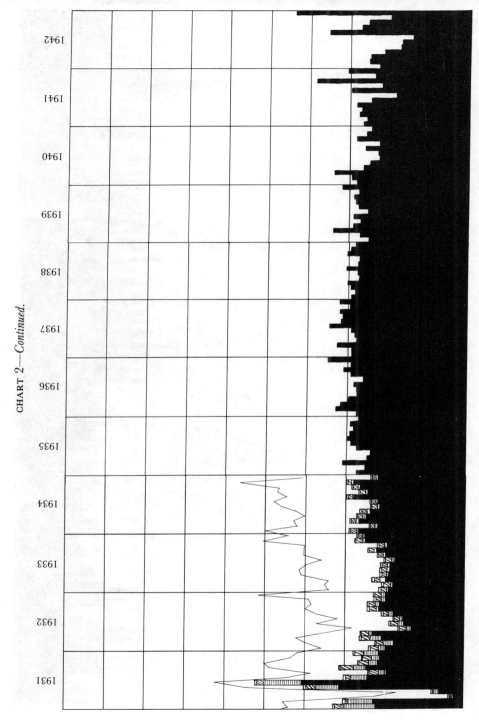

CHART 2—Continued.

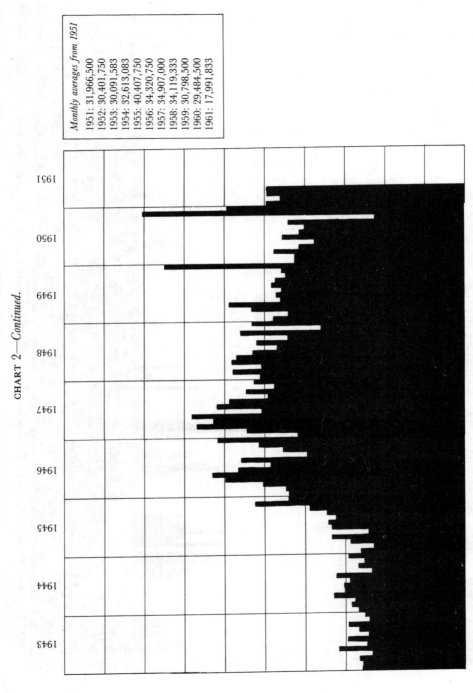

CHART 2—Continued.

Monthly averages from 1951

1951: 31,966,500
1952: 30,401,750
1953: 30,091,583
1954: 32,613,083
1955: 40,407,750
1956: 34,320,750
1957: 34,907,000
1958: 34,119,333
1959: 30,798,500
1960: 29,484,500
1961: 17,991,833

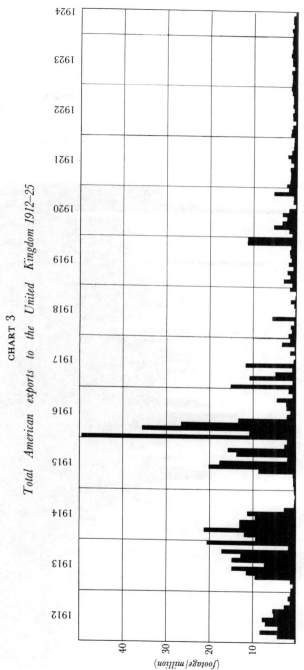

CHART 3

Total American exports to the United Kingdom 1912–25

Note: 1912 to mid-1917, total positive, negative and raw stock. Figures after mid-1917 are for exposed footage only.

(footage/million)

229

Index

Korea, 74
Latin America (See Central America, South America, Caribbean region, and specific countries)
Latvia, 135
Lithuania, 135
Luxembourg, 129
Malay States, 70–5
Mediterranean region, general, 46
Mexico, 48, 49, 54, 72, 81, 97, 140
Middle East, general, 5, 46, 145
New Zealand, 42–4, 55, 73, 81–2, 92, 138, 157, 166
Newfoundland, 157
North America, general, 47–8, 63, 91
Norway, 38, 46, 67, 72, 84, 128–9, 147–8, 160
Oceania, general, 50, 92
Orient, general, 31, 44–6, 48, 64, 78, 90
Palestine, 147
Panama, 40–1, 80–1
Paraguay, 55, 72–3
Persia, 145–7
Peru, 42, 72, 79
Philippines, 44–5, 68–9, 144
Poland, 5, 102, 134–6, 160
Portugal, 69, 72, 131–2, 159–160
Portuguese East Africa, 147
Puerto Rico, 41, 73–4, 77, 81, 140
Romania, 39, 133, 137, 157, 160, 166
Russia, 5, 40, 46, 54, 68–9, 87, 90–1, 94, 97–8, 102, 132–3
San Domingo, 74
Scandinavia, general, 53, 68, 70–1, 73, 84–5, 97, 102, 128–9, 149, 158, 163
Siam, 75–6, 144
Singapore (See Straits Settlements)
South Africa, 5, 45–6, 71, 73, 75, 146
South America, general, ix, 40–2, 46–8, 50, 54–5, 63, 69–72, 76–80, 86, 90, 92–3, 97–8, 103, 118, 122, 139, 161–2
Spain, 5, 39, 53, 68–9, 72, 74, 87, 90–1, 96, 121–2, 131–2, 160, 166
Straits Settlements, 33, 44, 64, 74–6, 157
Sweden, 67, 72, 85, 128–9, 157, 160, 166
Switzerland, 53, 73, 84, 87, 90, 97, 102, 129–30, 154–5, 157, 160
Syria, 33, 147, 166
Turkey, 43–4, 133, 145–6, 160
Union of Soviet Socialist Republics, 115–7, 157, 169
Uruguay, 42, 55, 72–3, 79
Venezuela, 80–1
West Indies, 70, 73
Yugoslavia, 133–4, 136–7, 157, 160

232

PERSONS
Abel, Richard, 168
Ador Louis, 98
Aitken, Roy, 83
Arbuckle, Fatty, 111
Armat, Thomas, 16
Aubert, Léon, 112
Bardou, Camille, 89
Barker, Will G., 20
Barnet, Boris, 116
Barrymore, John, 161
Beecroft, Chester, 103
Bernhardt, Sarah, 26
Berst, J. A., 4, 10, 57–8, 94, 96
Blaché, Herbert, 57
Blackton, J. Stuart, 77
Brady, William A., 94
Brezillon, Léon, 112
Brockliss, J. Frank, 36, 52
Brown, Clarence, 161
Brulator, Jules E., 94–6
Bunny, John, 37
Canty, George R., 117
Chaplin, Charlie, 28, 76, 81–3, 87, 95, 114
Cher, John, 51
Clair, René, 115, 165
Creel, George, 93, 95, 97–8
Cromelin, Paul H., 24, 77
Curtiz, Michael, 161
Darling, Joseph R., 66
De Mille, Cecil B., 87, 114
Delac, Charles, 121
Diamont-Berger, Henri, 89
Dieterle, William, 161
Dietrich, Marlene, 162
Dreyer, Carl, 115
Dulac, Germaine, 115
Dyer, Frank L., 6, 11
Edison, Thomas A., 8–9
Eisenstein, Sergei, 116
Fairbanks, Douglas, 28, 87, 90, 95
Feyder, Jacques, 161
Freund, Karl, 115
Friedman, Joseph, 109
Fröhlich, Gustav, 161
Gallone, Carmine, 115
Gance, Abel, 113, 115
Garbo, Greta, 161–2
Gaumont, Léon, 57, 61
Gilmore, William E., 3, 6, 8–9
Glucksmann, Jacobo, 139
Glucksmann, Max (See also Max Glucksmann company), 103
Golden, Nathan D., 117–18, 164

235

RCA, 154, 156
RKO, 156, 160, 162
R. W. Paul, 11, 19, 20
Raleigh & Roberts, 11, 19
Rank, 165
Reliance, 25
Remington Typewriter, 95
Republic, 25
Rex, 25, 38, 46
Roma, 55, 80
Rossi, 11, 19
Russian, 58
SA Films Sonori, 153
SCAGL, 58
Savoia, 39, 56
Scandinavian Film Agency, 103
Select, 81
Selig Polyscope, 10–12, 18, 29, 34, 38, 51, 55, 68, 80
Shochiku, 141
Siemens & Halske, 150–1, 154, 156
Sociedad General Cinematografica, 54, 80, 90
Société des Films Sonores Tobis, 154, 166
Société Franco Film, 154
Solax, 25, 38, 46
South American Feature Film Co., 33
South American Film Service Corp., 79
Sovkino, 115–16
Spenser's, 55
Standard Oil Co., 15
Star Films, 4, 6–7, 11–12, 17–19
Stinnes, 113
Svensk Filmindustri, 116, 129
Tanagra, 40
Telefunken, 150, 154
Tennen-Shoku Katsudo Shashin Co., 74
Terra, 116
Thalie, 58
Thanhouser, 25, 39, 52, 55, 58, 77, 80
Théophile Pathé, 11, 19
Thomson-Houston Electric Co., 13
Tobis, 148, 151, 154
Tobis-Klangfilm, 148–50, 152–6, 158
Tonbild Syndikat A-G (See Tobis)
Torino, 80, 133
Trans-Atlantic, 74, 90
Triangle, 80–1, 83, 85–6, 90
U.S. Comedies, 58
United Artists, 28, 141, 160, 165
Universal, 25–8, 55, 72, 74–7, 79, 82, 90, 94, 96, 106–11, 123, 141, 144, 149, 160
Universumfilm Aktiengesellschaft (UFA), 84, 107–13, 116–17, 119, 127, 129–30, 149–50, 155–6

236

Urban, 43, 45
Urban-Eclipse, 7, 11–13, 17, 19
VLSE, 94
Vim, 79
Vitagraph, 3–4, 11–12, 18, 28–9, 37–40, 43, 46, 52, 54–5, 74, 77, 80–1, 86, 90
Walturdaw [& Warwick], 11, 19–20
Warner Bros., 28, 149, 154, 156, 160, 162
Warwick (See also Walturdaw & Warwick), 11, 19, 45
Wengeroff, 118
West, 56
Western Electric, 154, 156
Westi, 113
Williams, Brown & Earle, 7, 11, 16, 19
Williamson & Co., 11, 20
World, 77, 81, 90, 98
Wrench, 20
Yoshizawa and Co., 45

FILM TITLES
A nous la liberté, 166
Allied Nations' Official War Review, 96
America's Answer, 98
Anna Boleyn, 105
Anna Christie, 161
The Battle of Elderbush Gulch, 38
The Birth of a Nation, 78–9, 81, 97
The Blue Angel, 162
Broadway, 160
Broadway Melody, 158
The Cabinet of Dr Caligari, 105, 112
Carmen, 78
The Cheat, 87
Civilization, 31, 78, 81
The Coming of Columbus, 38
The Coward, 86
Dante's Inferno, 26
Death Bay, 116
Deception, 105
Don Juan, 149
Die Dreigroschenoper, 162
The End of St Petersburg, 116
The Exploits of Elaine, 76, 88
The Fall of a Nation, 91
Fliers, 161
The Girl From Arizona, 18
The Great Gabbo, 161
The Hazards of Helen, 74
The Home Towners, 149
Intolerance, 79, 86, 97
The Iron Claw, 90
Ivanhoe, 36
The Jazz Singer, 149, 158
Judith of Bethulia, 53